LISTENING TO EDITH STEIN

Wisdom for a New Century

EDITH STEIN
Watercolor by Teresa Buczynska

LISTENING TO EDITH STEIN

Wisdom for a New Century

A Collection of Essays

Carmelite Studies 12

Edited by Kathleen Haney

ICS Publications
Institute of Carmelite Studies
Washington, D.C.

ICS Publications
2131 Lincoln Road NE
Washington, D.C. 20002-1199
www.icspublications.org

Book and cover design by Rose Design

Cover illustration of Edith Stein by Teresa Buczynska, © 2011;
Published with the kind permission of the artist and
Dom Edyty Stein (The Edith Stein Society), Wrocław, Poland.
www.edytastein.org.pl

Back cover: Edith Stein's passport photo (1938), taken for her
transfer to Echt, the Netherlands; courtesy of the Cologne Carmel
and Archivum Carmelitanum Edith Stein

Produced and printed in the United States of America

Library of Congress Cataloging-in-Publication Data

Names: Haney, Kathleen M., editor.
Title: Listening to Edith Stein : wisdom for a new century : a collection of essays / edited by Kathleen Haney.
Description: First [edition]. | Washington, D.C. : ICS Publications, 2018. | Series: Carmelite studies ; 12 Includes bibliographical references and index.
Identifiers: LCCN 2016040175 | ISBN 9781939272454 (alk. paper)
Subjects: LCSH: Stein, Edith, Saint, 1891-1942. | Christian philosophers—Germany. | Carmelite Nuns—Germany. | Christian martyrs—Germany.
Classification: LCC BX4705.S814 L57 2016 | DDC 271.97102 [B]—dc23
LC record available at https://lccn.loc.gov/2016040175

ISBN 978-1-939272-45-4

5 4 3 2 1

The Collected Works of Edith Stein in English

Critical editions translated from the original German
Published in English exclusively by ICS Publications

Contents

PART II

In Dialogue with Moderns and Postmoderns

Foreword

Two words readily come to mind when we consider the writings of Edith Stein: breadth and depth. Stein conveys a broad range of scholarly interests and knowledge, as well as a profound desire to plumb whatever subject matter she was investigating. This can be seen in a few ways. First of all, not only do her writings demonstrate her grasp of phenomenology and the work of her contemporary phenomenologists from Husserl to Heidegger, but Stein's works also display her knowledge of Plato, Aristotle, Augustine, Pseudo-Dionysius, Thomas Aquinas, Duns Scotus, Teresa of Ávila, and John of the Cross, among others. Stein did not simply bring together the work of various great philosophers and theologians; rather, she delved into their work after having first wrestled with given topics herself. As she writes, some thinkers who are "born phenomenologists" apply "their efforts to a direct investigation of the actually-given world of things." Such thinkers "arrive at an understanding of other minds and of the products of their intellectual labor only with the aid of what they have been able to ascertain by the exertion of their own intellect."[1] Such an approach accounts for the originality in Stein's work. She connects her thought to the work of other scholars and, because of this connection, anyone engaging in only a cursory reading can easily overlook Stein's originality and unique contributions to the world of philosophy and theology.

Secondly, Stein's writings also cover a broad range of topics: empathy, sentient causality, the individual and the community, the state, women's issues, commonalities and differences between Thomistic philosophy and phenomenology, ontology, the Trinity, and the tripartite structure of the human being, to name a few. Whatever the subject matter, her study is always in-depth, incorporating numerous insights and other related themes that she deems necessary for her investigation of a given topic. Stein is a seeker of truth, and her writings convey what she has uncovered in her search. Ultimately, she invites readers to do their own deep seeking; as she writes, "one cannot learn and teach philosophy, but only philosophizing."[2]

Unlike many other philosophers, Stein never had the opportunity to gather university students around her who, through direct interaction, could become familiar with and expound on her sometimes dense thought. While this was unfortunate, one advantage of this circumstance is that each generation of Stein scholars must grapple directly with her thought. In this volume, Kathleen Haney has brought together the work of numerous Stein scholars who have done just that and whose essays reflect both the breadth and depth of Stein's philosophizing and shed light on Stein's originality in approach and thought.

Ann Astell explores the concept of "place" in Stein's life from the time of her entrance into Carmel until her death in Auschwitz. Angela Ales Bello describes Stein's exposition of the spirit and the growth of spiritual life. Prudence Allen writes on Stein's passion apparent in her love of others, love of truth, and love of God. Sarah Borden

Sharkey examines Stein's analogy between emotional perception and other sense perceptions. Johanna Valiquette highlights Stein's awareness that in some way, all creation reflects the Trinity in a threefold manner. Kathleen Haney utilizes a poem written by Stein to begin an exploration of the influence of Pseudo-Dionysius on Stein's work and her semiotics of mystical theology. Michael Andrews looks into the relationship between prayer and knowledge that surfaces in Stein's essay on Pseudo-Dionysius, "Ways to Know God." John Sullivan explicates the many ways that the theme of renewal via the Spirit of God comes up in Stein's life. Walter Redmond examines Stein's approaches to the world above—absolute being, God—which are rooted in her search for reality. Based on Stein's essay "Martin Heidegger's Existential Philosophy," appended to *Finite and Eternal Being*, Mette Lebech explores Stein's interest in contesting Heidegger's work. Stein's alternative approach toward the use of phenomenology and the incorporation of other philosophical traditions results in a different and fuller understanding of the meaning of being. Opening up a relatively new avenue of study, Antonio Calcagno mines Stein's works for her treatment of death and dying and wrestles with some of her claims. Michael Paradiso-Michau explores how the two students of Husserl, Stein and Levinas, each treat the topic of ethical responsibility to the Other. Isobel Bowditch looks at the different approaches taken by Stein and Michel Henry in their rendering of an affirmative understanding of life. In a second contribution, Angela Ales Bello, noting John Paul II's inclusion of Edith Stein among a list of Christian philosophers in his encyclical *Fides et Ratio* (On the Relationship between Faith and Reason), expounds on Stein's work to bring Thomistic thought into conversation with secular philosophy while determining both the limits and connections between them. Finally, Kathleen Haney contributes a second essay that discusses themes shared by Stein and John Paul II regarding women and the importance of personhood.

As can be demonstrated by these essays, the breadth and depth of Stein's writings offer a wide terrain for scholarly exploration and often make it possible to bring her thought into dialogue with others in the history of philosophy as well as with her post-Kantian contemporaries. As Kathleen Haney correctly states in her introduction, Stein's work does not fit neatly into any single category, as some might have previously supposed. Stein has added her own voice to what she considered to be some of the fundamental questions of philosophy, theology, life, and faith—questions that have been taken up by great minds over the centuries. Because of the intricacy of her thought and the many interconnections she perceives, as well as her respect for other thinkers and for what she found to be true in their thought, the singularity of her contributions is not always readily apparent. By focusing on various aspects of Stein's multifaceted work, each author of this volume, aptly titled *Listening to Edith Stein: Wisdom for a New Century*, contributes to the important task of identifying Stein's distinctive voice in the human search for truth, a voice that beckons us to maintain a vital contact with the wisdom of the past, to pay close attention to the many academic and cultural achievements of the human spirit in the present, and to draw on our individual experience and talents so as to add our own contributions, no matter how great or small, to the human quest for truth.

Marian Maskulak, c.p.s., phd, s.t.d.
Theology and Religious Studies
St. John's University, Queens, N.Y.

Notes

1. Edith Stein, *Finite and Eternal Being: An Attempt at an Ascent to the Meaning of Being*, trans. Kurt Reinhardt, CWES, vol. 9 (Washington, D.C.: ICS Publications, 2002), xxx.

2. Edith Stein, *Einführung in die Philosophie*, ed. Claudia Marièle Wulf, Edith Stein Gesamtausgabe, vol. 8 (Freiburg: Herder, 2004), 6; hereafter abbreviated as ESGA.

Acknowledgments

This collection of essays began as the Fall 2006 issue of *Listening: Journal of Religion and Culture*, dedicated to "Edith Stein: Phenomenologist and Theologian." My dear friend and splendid Husserlian Marilyn Nissim-Sabat proposed that I edit the journal and later suggested expanding it into a book of essays on Stein. Her inspiration and openness are the reason behind this effort. So the present volume includes revisions of four of the essays originally written for *Listening*: "Edith Stein and Renewal" by Father John Sullivan, O.C.D.; "Edith Stein: Paradox and Prayer" by Michael F. Andrews; "The Spiritual Life and Its Degrees According to Edith Stein" by Angela Ales Bello; and "Edith Stein on the Structure of Being: Body, Soul, Spirit" by Johanna Valiquette.

Sister Prudence Allen's essay was posted in an electronic version in a *Festchrift* to honor the hundredth birthday of Father Eleutherius Winance, O.S.B., July 10, 2009. Father Winance taught phenomenology to many graduate students at Claremont Graduate University through the years. The posting is available at *http://www.laici.va /content/dam/laici/documenti/donna/filosofia/english/the -passion-of-edith-stein.pdf*. The paper was previously presented as a lecture at the Edith Stein Project Conference, University of Notre Dame, February 14, 2009.

An earlier draft of Sarah Borden Sharkey's essay was presented at Notre Dame's Center for Ethics and Culture

xvi LISTENING TO EDITH STEIN

conference on Formation and Renewal, October 4, 2003. Anthony Calcagno's "Being, Aevum, and Nothingness: Edith Stein on Death and Dying" is a revised version of an article that first appeared in *Continental Philosophy Review* 41, 2008, 59–72. We are grateful to *Continental Philosophy Review* for permission to include it in this volume.

"Images of the Unseen: Stein's Semiotics of Mystical Theology" was previously published in *Semiotics 2008: Specialization, Semiosis, Semiotics*, edited by John Deely and Leonard G. Sbrocchi (New York, Ottawa, Toronto: Legas, 2009); the paper was presented at the thirty-third Annual Meeting of the Semiotics Society of America, held October 16–19, 2009, in Houston, Texas. I am very grateful to my friend Lois Zamora, the originator of the New World Baroque construct, who helped me so much to clarify my thinking and to simplify my prose. I think she's even responsible for the title of the essay.

The other essays have been written for this volume.

I owe thanks to many people, first to the authors of these fine essays for allowing me to make a whole out of their many different studies. Their insights into Edith Stein's work demonstrate the range of her thought as well as its remarkable consistency and continuity. Marian Maskulak, C.P.S., is gratefully to be thanked for her careful and generous reading of the entire manuscript and her numerous suggestions for improvement. Father John Sullivan and Professor Walter Redmond provided encouragement throughout the lengthy processes of editing and readying the manuscript for publication. Thanks to Pat and Jim for being with me and helping during the many years I worked on this project. Virginia Galloway knows how much she contributed. Lastly, my gratitude to the editorial team at ICS Publications (the Institute of Carmelite Studies) for bringing their dedication and professional skills to this book on Edith Stein. Their commitment to seeing this book through to publication despite many challenges and delays ensures that Stein's thought and these reflections on it will be available to a wide readership.

Abbreviations

CWES   Collected Works of Edith Stein (ICS Publications)

EES   *Endliches und ewiges Sein—Versuch eines Aufstiegs zum Sinn des Seins* (The German version of *Finite and Eternal Being*)

EES, HA   *Mette Lebech's translation of the Heidegger Appendix from Endliches und ewiges Sein—Versuch eines Aufstiegs zum Sinn des Seins*

ESGA   Edith Stein Gesamtausgabe

ESW   Edith Steins Werke

JPPF   *Jahrbuch für Philosophie und phänomenologische Forschung*

MHE   "Martin Heideggers Existentialphilosophie," in *Welt und Person*, Edith Steins Werke, vol. 6, ed. Lucy Gelber and Romaeus Leuven (Louvain, Belgium: Nauwelaerts, 1962)

Introduction

Edith Stein, saint and scholar, made remarkable, original contributions to both philosophy and theology. She reconciled the subjectivity that modern philosophy emphasizes with the objectivity that premodern philosophy assumes. In so doing, she reintegrates the history of the philosophical tradition and examines some of the bridges between philosophy and theology. The essays in this volume magnify her vibrant voice so that the reader can hear her words clearly, whether she speaks about the triune nature of the Christian God or the impending dangers in the German state, or the relationship between faith and reason. Stein's biography is well known: her birth in Breslau, Poland, in 1891 to Jewish parents; her father's death when she was two years old; her loss of faith in her early adolescence; her phenomenological training with Edmund Husserl; her conversion to Catholicism in 1922; her entry into the Discalced Carmelite Order in 1933; and, as Sister Teresa Benedicta of the Cross, her death in Auschwitz in 1942. Other biographical details include a short stint as a nurse during World War I and years of teaching women and lecturing on feminist topics.

Given these extraordinarily varied cultural and intellectual commitments, the continuity of Stein's thought is noteworthy. Post-conversion and pre-conversion Edith Stein differ in authorial intention but not in interpretative principles, which remain constant throughout her work, binding it together. Of course, her post-conversion writings are informed by her acquired Catholic faith, but when she engages in speculations based on the revealed truths of Christianity, her speculative philosophy shows her phenomenological formation. Post-conversion here does not refer to a transformation or a disruption of her work so much as a subordination or ordering of her early themes according to the doctrines of the Church, when her interests are theological as well as philosophical. Unlike Martin Heidegger's famous *Kehre*, Stein makes no turn.

Stein's way enacts a passionate search for truth. She assures us that if we seek the truth, we shall find it. That all truths must be consistent with Christian faith justifies her belief in the harmony of truth. This sense of truth conjures up the deity's point of view. Faith, according to Stein, is a dark Light. Faith, or the contents of the doctrines of Christian Scriptures, cannot be fathomed. The relationship between reason and its supplement, the "dark light of faith," is dynamic; they mutually engage each other. Although Stein believed in the truth of the Christian faith, she also recognized that reason on its own is obliged to admit the possibility that Christian truth is in fact the truth. Although it may seem unlikely, the idea that Christian truth is true does not contradict itself. Stein knew that faith, much less the Christian faith, is not for everyone, so she suggests that the unbeliever entertain the doctrines of the Catholic Church as hypotheses. The hypothetical suspends truth claims; as phenomenal, the hypothetical requires an analysis of the transcendentally necessary conditions for its possibility. Not all that is possible exists, but nothing that is impossible exists. Stein's teacher, Edmund Husserl, advocated a similar movement in the phenomenological reduction or suspending of existence claims. One is free to open toward such thinking. We are always free to take on thought experiments, and, indeed, Stein maintains that intellectual honesty obligates the genuine philosopher to do so:

> And unbelievers must judge for themselves whether by accepting this additional knowledge they may perhaps gain a deeper and more comprehensive understanding of that which is. They will at any rate not shrink back from such an attempt if they are really as unbiased as, according to their own conviction, genuine philosophers ought to be.[1]

For the unbeliever, "what if" or "assuming" take the place of the "I trust" for the believer; nevertheless, the believer's theses and the unbeliever's hypotheses might be doctrinally equivalent.[2] Communication between faith and reason can occur with alacrity, as we see especially in Stein's later works. The unbeliever can engage in this thinking by adopting a scientific spirit of adventure. Stein envisions "a common effort, [a]dhering to the principle, 'Examine everything, and retain the best.' Christian philosophy is willing to learn from the Greeks and from the moderns and to appropriate for itself what can meet the test of its own system of measurement."[3]

Stein maintained a phenomenological orientation, even as she integrated ancient and medieval philosophy into her systematic metaphysics. The intellectual milieu of her time largely restricted the scope of philosophy to Descartes and post-Cartesian thinkers, but Stein also acquainted herself with the great philosophers of the past. We shall see her rigorous adherence to revealed truth when it was relevant to her analyses as well as her rejection of both naïve realism and subjective idealism in favor of acknowledging the interactions between subjects and objects. Her thought provides a system to complement the philosophy of substance with a philosophy of relations and proposes an alternative direction for phenomenology from that of Martin Heidegger and the postmoderns who follow him. The result of Stein's synthesis is a contemporary philosophy that truly moves beyond modern philosophy, which, after all, distinguished itself by altogether rejecting the past. Whether one believes that the Renaissance was a rebirth of knowledge or of ignorance, modern philosophy's emphasis on the new must be supplemented by attention to the philosophy of the past if we seek to stand on the shoulders of giants as we look for truth. Stein's philosophy integrates much of, in Matthew Arnold's phrase, "the best that has been known and thought in the world," according to her own synthetic genius. This is a source of the freshness and originality of Stein's thought.

The following essays contextualize Stein's work by locating her thought in relation to the views of early philosophers as well as to various contemporary perspectives. They invite readers to expand beyond specialized training into the terrain that Stein makes available. Her merger of the entire philosophic tradition produces a system that displays the bounty of influence, rather than any anxiety about it. Although the authors focus on different facets of Stein's work and offer divergent interpretations, they concur in showing how she challenges the remnants of modern philosophy as well as its development into postmodernism. Although not all the contributors are as sympathetic as the editor to reading Stein as a phenomenologist who provides rich and satisfying extensions of Husserl's philosophy, all acknowledge her distinctive contribution that St. John Paul II recognized as a model for the "feminine genius."

There can be no question that Stein's theology is more indebted to St. Thomas Aquinas, St. Augustine, and the church fathers than to Husserl. Readers might also note the influence of John Henry Newman, Dionysius the Areopagite, Max Scheler, and Hedwig Conrad-Martius. Philosophically, she bears the stamp of Plato, but she also studied René Descartes, Immanuel Kant, and Martin Heidegger. Her historical perspective provides foundation for an imaginative synthesis of the various strands that it includes. Even today, more than seventy years after her death, few philosophers write with her scope and range.

Stein dialogues with past thinkers; she is a synthesizer on the order of St. Augustine and St. Thomas Aquinas. And she, too, submits the thought of the day to the truths of the Catholic Church. In her work, classical and medieval philosophy and theology speak to each other anew; even mysticism has its say. She disciplined her spirit so that she lacks the impulse to criticize and reject; rather, she is open to truth wherever it is to be found.

Robert Sokolowski wrote that phenomenology represents "a restoration of the convictions that animated ancient and medieval philosophy. Like premodern philosophy, phenomenology understands reason as ordered to truth."[4] In this matter, Sokolowski coincides with Stein's interpretation of phenomenology, neither discarding modernity nor rebelling against the perennial tradition in philosophy. For him, too, phenomenology is "a recovery of the true philosophical life, in a manner appropriate to our philosophical situation."[5] Pre-Kantian philosophy must face the doctrines of our time if the contemporary notions of naturalism, materialism, secularism, skepticism, and nihilism are to be challenged.

The essays that follow show us how Stein interrogates the presuppositions of modern philosophy. Even in her earliest work, *On the Problem of Empathy*, she boldly disregarded the Cartesian mind/body split that haunted the moderns; her experience as a person, related to other persons, cannot corroborate such a divide. Stein wrote on psychology, politics, feminism, feelings, evolution, physics, angels, prayer, transcendental realism, temporality, and death; she famously worked out a theology of the cross. This collection of essays highlights some of these achievements, which map new dimensions for contemporary philosophy beyond Nietzsche, Heidegger, and the legions of their postmodern cohorts. As these essays show, Stein's incorporation of some of the dominant features of modernity, especially the significance of the knower for knowing, allows us to redress some modern losses, by opening up a space for both subjectivity and objectivity.

The theme of the person persists throughout Stein's work. She began her studies at Breslau in psychology because, even in her teens, she was already concerned with the question of the human person. She moved to the University of Göttingen (Germany) to study philosophy with Husserl, after she had become convinced that the field of psychology was too narrow to deal properly with what it means to be a person. Later, she followed Husserl to Freiburg (Germany) and eventually became his first assistant. In that capacity, she edited *Ideas II*, Husserl's early treatment of the personal world, including topics such as bodily nature and psychic subjectivity. Husserl's phenomenology provided the methodological formation to take on the questions that led her to university training; nevertheless, the late American Stein scholar Mary Catharine Baseheart noted that "(E)ven in her dissertation, Stein exhibited, young as she was, a marked independence in appropriating Husserl's ideas in her own way and for her own purposes."[6] Stein's version of philosophy demanded requisite experiential validation; she consistently proceeds from close phenomenological analyses based on intuition of the presence given in experience. Even so, she remained committed to a position of transcendental realism, loyal to the epistemological necessity that the subject see for itself when reflecting on experiences of objects.

Many of the essays in this collection recognize Stein's formation. When the aged Husserl was unable to attend the ceremony surrounding her final vows because of his failing health, he expressed his regret and his respect for her and her work. She was, he said, his "best pupil."[7] Note that he did not provide such a commendation to Heidegger, his disappointing second assistant. Mette Lebech and Antonio Calcagno in their essays each point out differences between the two thinkers whom Husserl chose to help him continue his work. The inevitable suggestion arises: Stein's work might serve as an alternative to Heidegger's and indicate new directions for phenomenological theory and praxis. With this prospect in mind, we now turn in detail to the specific topics of the essays.

The essays in this volume roughly divide according to themes and influences that Stein shares with the ancients and Scholastics and those that she shares with the moderns and postmodern philosophers. That this division is rough speaks to the thesis of the collection. When Stein speaks to the premoderns, she has already incorporated traditional philosophy and theology into her phenomenological approach so that her original contributions have to do with retrieval and revival in order to enrich and extend this tradition. She addresses the later thinkers with an infusion of traditional thought, especially Catholic theology and philosophy. As an example of how rough these partitions are, Walter Redmond's essay on Stein's proof for the existence of God approaches apologetics from the perspective of transcendental philosophy. It is included with the moderns since it is to this audience that Stein directs her efforts, since, except for Max Scheler, modern philosophy, until the recent theological turn in phenomenology, discounted the significance of the question. Her lifelong goal, as Redmond points out, is a synthesis of Scholastic and phenomenological thought.

Part One: In Dialogue with the Premoderns

Ann Astell, in her opening essay, "Carmel in Cologne, Echt, and Auschwitz: Edith Stein's Last Journeys and the Meaning of Place in Exile," turns reflection outward, overcoming mind/body division in the unity of the nature of the person, in body, soul, and spirit. The author specifically addresses phenomenological themes of place and position but from a perspective that is sympathetic with experiences reported particularly by Carmelite mystics. Their spirituality figures into her discussion of physical location in the world. Astell disrupts the notions of place and position so that exteriority and interiority image each other. In so doing, she enriches our appreciation of Stein's lived experiences as well as our understanding of place. Stein grew up in a Jewish family wherein she located familiar family life. Later, she left that world for the cloister of Carmel.

When the Nazis forced her to leave Carmel, she "laboriously contains it within herself," as Astell writes. This abbreviated biography of Stein shows hermitage in the interior castle where she dwells with the truth that she seeks, never forgetting her concern and love for her family and friends. Astell describes how Sister Teresa Benedicta of the Cross was at home in Carmel with its Jewish founder and its reformer, as well as the Jewish star in its symbology. Stein found her place in Carmel, which she identified with the life of the soul, in its garden and in its desert; thus, Carmel lived in her.

Angela Bello's essay provides a companion piece to Astell's description of the journey to the interior castle. An erudite explicator of Stein's phenomenological philosophy and of her theology, Bello analyzes spirit in the subjective, intentional consciousness that classical phenomenology takes as its point of departure. She describes the journey of the spirit ever more deeply into itself in order to discover the triune God. The core (*Kern*) of the person, in the God-given soul of the soul, is the profoundest point of the castle with its many rooms through which St. Teresa of Jesus leads us. All growth in the spirit is movement toward the core of a person. It is in the core that one encounters God directly. Bello's essay joins Carmelite mysticism with the existential themes of self-knowledge and freedom to be found in Stein's phenomenological theology. We see here a revival of traditional mysticism within the framework of the contemporary emphasis on the subject who transcends mere subjectivity in a space for union with the divine.

Sister Prudence Allen's contribution familiarizes readers with details of Stein's intellectual biography, as well as the milieu in which Stein wrote. More importantly perhaps, she points out the organic unity of Stein's thoughts and actions. Allen illustrates her exposition of Stein's theory of the passions with Stein's unification of her passion for truth with her love for journeying with her friends to seek it. She quotes Sister Teresa Benedicta: "The soul cannot live without receiving. . . . In these experiences the soul appropriates to itself what it needs in order to become what it is destined to be."[8] Thus, we read in this essay that "the canonization of Edith Stein/Sister Teresa Benedicta of the Cross implies that she became . . . the unique pure form of her own particular identity as that specific woman philosopher who lived in Germany between 1891 and 1942." Again in her discussion of Sister Teresa Benedicta's work on St. John of the Cross, *The Science of the Cross*, Allen shows how Sister Teresa Benedicta's passion for Christ led to her passion for the cross, even to her own cross and martyrdom. Allen quotes from a letter written by Sister Teresa Benedicta to a Dominican friend, Sister Agnella:

> What can we do? Try with all our might to be empty: the senses mortified; the memory as free as possible from all images of this world and, through hope, directed toward heaven; the understanding stripped of natural seeking and ruminating, directed to God in the straightforward gaze of faith; the will (as I have already said) *surrendered to God in love*.[9]

Exhibiting her exceptional scholarship in the history of the question of woman, Allen's essay also provides glimpses of Stein's emotional life and her integrity. Later on, we shall see that this integrity prevented her from conflating the sciences of philosophy and theology.

In her essay, Sarah Borden Sharkey, though a Scholastic rather than a phenomenologist by training, takes up the theme of emotions. She sympathetically explains and supports Stein's analysis of the emotions as immediate means of experiencing value. In contrast to Aquinas, Stein includes three reigning capabilities of the free human being. The human person is capable of freedom and self-making by irreducible and interdependent forces of the soul: reason, will, and the emotions. None of these is self-sufficient or autonomous; each is imbued with the others. This position is not to be confused with a relativistic one that would homogenize the value of all values, as a naïve ethics of feeling might. Rather, Borden Sharkey shows that for Stein, although the values that the emotions perceive are based in subjective experience, they also move beyond the personal to a shared intersubjective world that manifests the values instilled by its Creator.

Johanna Valiquette analyzes the structure of all being as it is to be found in Stein's phenomenological and Scholastic synthesis, *Finite and Eternal Being*. She introduces us to Stein's picture of the structures of similarity in the tripartite image of all created beings. Stein does not understand Genesis to mean that only men and women were created in the image of the Creator. The fundamental structure of all creation, endlessly embodied in body-soul-spirit, mirrors its Creator. We can recognize spirit in all things as that which goes out of itself, while remaining within itself. For Stein, the spiritual is not only known but it is also felt as value. The highest value, love, can bind us together; each kingdom of ends can unfurl a unique core that contributes to an epiphany for all humanity. Valiquette evokes for us Stein's intuition of the unity of the diversity of all creation in the love that binds it together.

Not only was Stein's metaphysics influenced by the philosophers of the Middle Ages, but also her hermeneutics (theory of interpretation) owes a great deal to Dionysius the Areopagite in particular. Although he was only rediscovered in the last century, Stein and others considered Dionysius to be among the most important theologians of the sixth through the fifteenth centuries.

"Images of the Unseen: Stein's Semiotics of Mystical Theology" applies Stein's account of the Areopagite's teachings to the question that has become so heatedly disputed in our times: can we talk about God without violating the Holy One's sacred dignity and Otherness? Stein, contrary to Heidegger who believes that philosophy must be atheism, demonstrates how God reveals Himself to the prophets and to their audience. Phenomenal experience can motivate allegorical systems that evoke the ineffable. God, the primary theologian, speaks to some who long to hear. The prophet conveys that which he has been given. The Word is truly God, who "gives his theologians the words and images that enable them to speak of him to others."[10] The symbol need not be restricted to correspondence of x to y as in Peirce's semiotics; x might point to a z beyond the horizon of y. The excess of the given that links Stein's thought with Jean-Luc Marion reflects Dionysius's reverence for the transcendence of God and the need for revelation.

Michael Andrews leads us along the via negativa to a deeper understanding of prayer. His essay on faith and phenomenon points us to the paradox of prayer according to Stein, that prayer constitutes a dialogical relation between the creature and his Creator. God authors prayer; God calls to prayer; God manifests himself to an I in space and time. According to Andrews, Stein's thought recognizes that the I's response to God's initiative reveals God in his absence as well as his presence. Stein's study of Dionysius the Areopagite led to the Old Testament God of Job, the God who made the leviathan. God cannot be domesticated by prayer; God cannot be cognitively grasped. God is present in his absence, as the Wholly Other who calls to us, as thinkers within the theological turn in contemporary phenomenology are prone to say.

Part Two turns our attention to Stein's commentary on the moderns and her usefulness for a genuine postmodernism.

Part Two: In Dialogue with Moderns and Postmoderns

In "Edith Stein and Renewal," Father John Sullivan, O.C.D., chair of the Institute of Carmelite Studies whose ICS Publications publishes the official English translations of Stein's work, shows rare appreciation for her character and personality as well as for her thought. He begins with a quotation taken from a letter that Stein wrote to her sister in the dire and dismal days of the First World War. "The new spirit already exists and will prevail," she said. Where those around her could see only carnage, destruction, sorrow, and death, Stein experienced hope for a better tomorrow. With her characteristic consistency of thought, this hope would become her belief that God works all for good, even in the destruction of the pre-war world and the pain that Germany experienced and would inflict. Sullivan shows how this hope moves us closer to social and political justice in the church and in humankind's self-realization. *Angst* does not lead us to an authentic life, as Heidegger thought, since being toward death, as we see in later essays, moves us away from truth about the origin and *telos* of human life. Hope leads to authenticity since it energizes acts that embody the subject's values. Hope can imagine that the epochs in philosophy can be unified in a history that includes them all.

Stein's philosophy can address our contemporaries, regardless of religious affiliation or lack of one. As we see in other essays also, she can easily be brought into dialogue with Scholastics and postmoderns, with anyone who seeks to follow truth to its source. Walter Redmond's essay—based primarily on Stein's *Potency and Act*, which he translated—works out her proofs for the existence of God, emphasizing their sources in St. Augustine and St. Thomas Aquinas. He shows that Stein imports Aristotelian doctrine without adapting it wholesale. Important for the theme of this collection of essays, Redmond also directs our attention to her demonstration of God's existence from the necessities of consciousness. Stein refuses to duplicate earlier thought. Husserl's absolute consciousness cannot finally be absolute. The absolute consciousness of self-experience suggests that the absolute of consciousness depends upon a more Absolute consciousness. In this brilliant essay, Redmond integrates Stein's Greek and Scholastic influences with the Husserlian phenomenology that provided Stein with her philosophical formation.

"Empathy and the Face: Edith Stein and Emmanuel Levinas," by Michael R. Paradiso-Michau, compares Stein's thought with that of another thinker who was deeply concerned with the value of the person, though not himself a philosopher of personalism. Stein and Levinas both studied Husserl closely. Their dissertations on empathy and intuition, respectively, expertly discussed major themes in Husserlian and post-Husserlian phenomenology. Their writings parted ways on the topic of the genesis of a phenomenology of ethical responsibility. This chapter shows how Levinas's phenomenology can be brought to bear on Stein's thought so that we can better envision her radical phenomenological ethics of love, which trumps duty by subsuming it.

Mette Lebech's work, "Edith Stein and Martin Heidegger: On the Meaning of Being," investigates Stein's text "Martin Heidegger's Existential Philosophy," an appendix to her magnum opus, *Finite and Eternal Being: An Attempt at an Ascent to the Meaning of Being*. This discussion of Stein's critique includes significant ontological (and, by inference perhaps, ideological) differences between Stein and Heidegger on the question of being and leads us to another, more faithful rendition of the question of *Being and Time* than Heidegger provided.

According to Lebech, Stein wrote about Heidegger because she was aware of the influence that he had on the phenomenological movement and recognized that Heidegger's work subverted Husserl's aim for phenomenology. Stein proposed alternatives to Heidegger's methodological and ontological revisions. She could not agree that *Dasein* exhausted the meaning of being, nor did she share Heidegger's penchant for rethinking the tradition at the expense of the history of thought. Interestingly for the debate concerning a theological turn for phenomenology, Heidegger's belief that philosophy must be atheism was antithetical to Stein. For her, phenomenology not only continued the great task of philosophy but also provided the means for recovering the losses that philosophy had undergone due to its dispersal into empiricism and rationalism and their twentieth-century developments. Lebech concludes that the meaning of authenticity requires a responsiveness to value, justified by a rational eidetics and lived with an existential loyalty. Being is not nothing. Being comes in various forms: finite and eternal; personal and nonpersonal. Heidegger's mistake leads to the impoverishment of phenomenological philosophy by limiting the search for truth.

Like Lebech's essay, Antonio Calcagno's "Being, *Aevum*, and Nothingness: Edith Stein on Death and Dying," shows Stein's thought to be an advance over that of her colleague. Although Stein shared many concerns with her contemporaries in the continental tradition, Calcagno urges us to distinguish her solutions to problems from theirs. How is Stein's description of death different from Heidegger's? Calcagno refuses Heidegger's conception of *Dasein* as being-toward-death in favor of Stein's vital personalism. In contrast, Calcagno delivers Stein's alternative view that death is not simply an utmost possibility of being but also that it introduces being beyond being. He shows the stark contrast between Heidegger's fundamental ontology and the being toward life in Stein's tripartite metaphysics, a phenomenological approach to death and dying that finds the nature of human temporality to pertain beyond the death of the body.

"Life and the Other World: Edith Stein and Michel Henry" considers Stein's work in light of recent developments in French phenomenology, with Michel Henry as spokesman. Playing on his well-known discovery of the Word outside the world, Isobel Bowditch examines Henry's auto-affection, arguing that it excludes the possibility of shared experience or communal life. The profundity of Henry's radical subjectivity might lead him to constitute an outside that is life, albeit not personal life. Stein's life-long explorations of empathy build a case against the possibility of raw individualism as such. Although the I of Stein's inquiry is conscious of itself, this I lives in a physical and social world. Stein's vitalist motifs detail revelatory realms of intersubjective and utterly private experiences.

In the essay "Edith Stein: Between Husserl and Thomas Aquinas," Angela Bello thoroughly considers the import of Stein's Husserlian formation when she discovers the great Scholastic's thought. One of the similarities that Angela Bello points out is that truth is the *telos* that drives both thinkers. Aquinas and Husserl also share a reverence for reason that many late moderns, Nietzsche first among them, disdain. This allegiance directed them into genuine philosophy. They are both philosophers of essence; both study theory of knowledge; they reflect on the offices of faith and reason. Bello suggests that Husserl's position arises from his conversion to Protestant Lutheranism, which adheres to a strict separation of faith and reason, while Aquinas and Stein seek for their harmony. Bello deftly illumines Stein's thought through her development, following Maritain, of her own Catholic philosophy. As Angela Bello writes, "Philosophy can allow itself to be illumined by faith in order to proceed further."[11] Philosophy can discover that it shares one truth with theology and mysticism.

The last essay analyzes the thought of the two writers who were foundational for New Feminism, Edith Stein and St. John Paul II. Their thought transcends Genesis by moving beyond its structures of domination, given as punishment for sin. Their nuanced understanding of feminism stresses the integral complementarity of woman and man rather than positions of inferiority and superiority that make some persons into objects to be used. Persons each have their own unique value as well as their value as women and men. St. John Paul II shares Edith Stein's conviction that love is the common vocation of both men and women.

These essays amply show the contributions that St. Teresa Benedicta has made to contemporary philosophy and theology. She synthesizes the Western tradition in order to develop the idea of the human person who can be in relationship to the Truth as well as to others. Edith Stein is a Catholic philosopher and theologian who enriches the legacy handed down to her by the Scholastics and the phenomenologists. What she has to say can lead us to see the treasure of the history of philosophy enhanced by philosophical theology. Readers will find much worth listening to in these essays.

Notes

1. Edith Stein, *Finite and Eternal Being: An Attempt at an Ascent to the Meaning of Being*, trans. Kurt Reinhardt, CWES, vol. 9 (Washington, D.C.: ICS Publications, 2000), 29.

2. Ibid., 28.

3. Ibid.

4. Robert Sokolowski, *Introduction to Phenomenology* (Cambridge, England: Cambridge University Press, 2000), 202.

5. Ibid., 203.

6. Mary Catharine Baseheart, *Person in the World* (Dordrecht, The Netherlands: Kluwer, 1997), 22.

7. Adelgundis Jaegerschmid, O.S.B., "Conversations with Edmund Husserl, 1931–1938," *The New Yearbook for Phenomenology and Phenomenological Philosophy* 1 (2001): 331–50.

8. Stein, *Finite and Eternal Being*, 373.

9. Stein to Sister Agnella Stadtmüller, O.P., March 30, 1940, Letter 311, *Self-Portrait in Letters, 1916–1942*, trans. Josephine Koeppel, O.C.D., CWES, vol. 5 (Washington, D.C.: ICS Publications, 1993), 318; hereafter cited as *Letters*.

10. Edith Stein, *Knowledge and Faith*, trans. Walter Redmond, CWES, vol. 8 (Washington, D.C.: ICS Publications, 2000), 117.

11. Essay 14 in this volume, 327.

PART I

In Dialogue with the Premoderns

1

CARMEL IN COLOGNE, ECHT, AND AUSCHWITZ:

Edith Stein's Last Journeys and the Meaning of Place in Exile

ANN ASTELL

In the topography of the thought of René Girard, the desert holds special significance. It is, first of all, the place of expulsion for the scapegoat, the deadly frontier to which the unclean victim is cast out as a curative for the violent contagion that has afflicted the community. Quoting Georges Glotz, Girard notes that the word "'elimination' . . . must be taken in its etymological sense—of expulsion beyond the frontiers," the physical borders or territorial limits of a society.[1] The desert has another meaning for Girard. In his discussion of heroic *askesis*, Girard recalls "the life of privation led by the hermit monks in the desert,"[2] whose ardent renunciation of worldly desires for the sake of their desire for God enables God to fulfill that very desire. "The mystic turns from the world," Girard writes, "in order that God may turn toward him and give him the gift of his grace."[3]

In the first case, the scapegoat is driven out into the wilderness. In the second, the ascetic, perhaps literally clad in the goatskin of penitents, actively seeks out the desert as a place of intimate encounter with God. These two experiences, passive and active, of the desert can, through a phenomenological reduction, point to what the desert is: that place where the one who is alone (literally, "all one"), who has been deserted or who has deserted, discovers that he is never alone, that his very being is relational. "The real structures," as Girard puts it elsewhere, "are intersubjective. They cannot be localized anywhere."[4]

The question of the intersubjective arises early in the writings of Edith Stein (1891–1942), appearing in her 1916–17 doctoral dissertation, *On the Problem of Empathy*, which she wrote under the direction of Edmund Husserl. Her discussions there about the location(s) of the "I" help to explain how her acute sense of place heightens to a point of paradoxically disoriented orientation, a new "zero point," in her later, specifically religious writings. Here, I first discuss Stein's published work on Carmel as a place. I draw upon Stein's personal letters to sketch the historical circumstances that brought the theme of place strongly into her consciousness during the years from 1933, when she first entered the Carmelite cloister in Cologne, to 1938, when she was transferred to the Carmel in Echt, the Netherlands, to 1942, when she was taken from Echt to Auschwitz to die in the concentration camp. I then read these personal writings as an extension of her philosophical reflections in her dissertation. Finally, I turn to her theo-aesthetic, final work, *The Science of the Cross*, a study of Carmelite spirituality, which was published posthumously. It conjoins the topics of identity and place in a way, I argue, that radically underscores the intersubjectivity at the heart of all personhood.

For Stein, Carmel is at once the desert and the garden. In her 1935 essay, "On the History and Spirit of Carmel," she retells the story of the prophet Elijah, the legendary founder of the Carmelite Order. In the book of Kings, the prophet appears suddenly, without any previous introduction, to announce to the wicked King Ahab a period of drought: "'As the Lord the God of Israel lives, before whom I stand, there shall be neither dew nor rain these years, except by my word'" (1 Kgs 17:1). The biblical narrative of Elijah, as Stein emphasizes, sets the desert world of Ahab's idolatrous worship, parched by drought, against the desert world of the hermit Elijah, who "stand[s] before the face of the living God" and thus epitomizes the vocation of the Carmelites, who "watch in prayer."[5] The desert world of Elijah is undeniably the domain of persecuted scapegoats. King Ahab and his wife, Queen Jezebel, have killed the prophets of the Lord; those who have survived this genocide have hidden, like Elijah, in caves in the wilderness (1 Kgs 18:13). Under a death sentence, Elijah dresses in animal hide. "The hide of a dead animal," Stein writes, "reminds us that the human body is also subject to death."[6] What Stein stresses, though, is not this persecution and passive hiding, but rather the prophet's active renunciation of Ahab's world and single-minded desire for God, whose presence he seeks in the desert:

He stood before God's face because this was the eternal treasure for whose sake he gave up all earthly goods. He had no house; he lived wherever the Lord directed him from moment to moment: in loneliness beside the brook of Carith, in the little house of the poor widow of Zarephath of Sidon, or in the caves of Mount Carmel.[7]

Elijah's voluntary dislocation of himself—his flight from the world, his stripping away of earthly goods, his life outside all natural human relationships—powerfully alters the world itself, turning the wilderness into a garden, where Elijah is miraculously sustained with food and drink, where he encounters the Lord himself "in soft rustling after a thunderstorm"[8] and gains a spiritual, paternal fruitfulness in his spiritual son and heir, the prophet Elisha, Elijah's nonrivalrous double.

Stein's essay endeavors to show that the legendary founding of the Carmelite Order by the prophet Elijah is significant: "We who live in Carmel and who daily call upon our Holy Father Elijah in prayer know that for us he is not a shadowy figure out of the dim past. His spirit is active among us in a vital tradition and determines how we live."[9]

Stein's commentary on the living presence of Elijah among twentieth-century Carmelites gains added importance when read alongside her personal history and correspondence. A Jew who never disavowed her Judaism but rather saw it as fulfilled in Christ, Stein found herself especially at home in a Catholic religious order that claimed a Hebrew prophet as its founder. Like Elijah,

Stein's coming to Carmel resulted from a double movement of estrangement, exclusion, and persecution, on the
one hand, and of active longing on the other.

Because the postdoctoral habilitation was at that time
not generally granted to women, her application at the
University of Göttingen (Germany) was denied in 1919,
even though she graduated *summa cum laude*, was generally regarded as one of the most brilliant of Husserl's students, and had worked closely with him as his assistant
on volume two of his *Ideen*.[10] Her decision in 1921–22
to become a Catholic was incomprehensible to many
of her close friends and family members. She obtained
teaching posts in the college run by Dominican sisters
in Speyer, Germany (1923–32), and later at the German
Institute for Scientific Pedagogy in Münster, Germany
(1932–33), all the while struggling (as she wrote) "to justify [her] scholarly existence" through continued publications, despite her "ten-year exclusion from the continuity
of academic work."[11] With this work, she kept alive the
hope for an eventual habilitation and professorship (perhaps at the University of Freiburg through the mediation of Martin Heidegger and Martin Honecker).[12] This
hope met its last disappointment in 1931 because of "the
economic crisis."[13] In 1932 she wrote to her good friend
Hedwig Conrad-Martius that she had "lost connection
with [her life's work] on all sides" and regarded herself as
"generally incompetent for this world."[14] "But," she concluded, "as long as the indications are that the Lord wants
me in this position, I may not desert."[15] In the spring of
1933, shortly after Hitler seized power, she was barred

from giving public lectures and from teaching "because of [her] Jewish descent."[16] In October of that same year, she entered the Carmel at Cologne. "The *umsurtz* [military coup] was for me a sign from heaven," she writes to her Jewish friend Fritz Kaufmann (1891–1959) "that I might now go the way that I had long considered as mine."[17]

Discussions of place and position abound in the letters between 1919 and 1933, as Stein struggled to fulfill her scholarly and womanly calling; however, here I focus on the meaning of Carmel for her. Entering Carmel meant, first of all, a change in her exterior environment that certainly affected her soul, no matter how much she had already been living a convent-style life while still in the world.[18] To Elly Dursey, a former student of hers who was considering a move, Stein wrote on November 25, 1936, "Every change in the external circumstances is already apt to disturb one's inner peace. Therefore, one should never seek [such a change] unless God provides it."[19] In another letter, Stein confesses herself to be "a very awkward child in the novitiate," who requires the "great love and patience" of her superiors and fellow sisters.[20] "It will be a good while," she writes, "before I become a nun who is useful in any way."[21] The life behind convent walls can be one of deep peace, she confesses to Conrad-Martius, adding, "but then one has to have a calling for it. And for those who have their place outside, there is also a way outside."[22] Commenting on the adjustment of another woman to the life in Carmel, Stein provides a self-portrait: "Perhaps only someone who has personally experienced what it means to wait for years and to have the pressure of living in an environment totally differing in its value system from one's own can appreciate what the days here meant for her. She completely blossomed here."[23]

Carmel became a "garden" for Stein, albeit one like the biblical cave and mountainous ravines of Elijah: "The walls of our monasteries enclose a narrow space," she observes. "To erect the structure of holiness in it, one must dig deep and build high, one must descend into the depths of the dark night of one's own nothingness in order to be raised high into the sunlight of divine love and compassion."[24] As a plant grows in the space allotted to it so, too, Stein imagines her spiritual development to be conditioned by the exterior surroundings of Carmel, its physical structure and temporal schedule.[25] This *umwelt* (surrounding world) is maternal, in the sense that it (in the words of Joseph Grange) "gives identity an opportunity to become."[26]

The cloister of Carmel, an enclosed garden, centers on God, who alone suffices: As Stein explains, "We . . . fulfill our Rule when we hold the image of the Lord continually before our eyes in order to make ourselves like Him. . . . He is present to us in the most Blessed Sacrament. . . . To stand before the face of God continues to be the real content of our lives."[27] The Carmelite faces the face of God, but at her back is the world that opposes God; in her heart is the whole world that needs and seeks God.

In this sense, the Carmelite, as Stein knew, never leaves the world behind. Stein's letters from the Carmels in Cologne and Echt are full of concern for the fate of family members and friends exposed to the Nazi persecution. "Please pray for my brothers and sisters," she begs in a letter dated October 10, 1936: "My mother's last great sorrow was that my brother Arno (who had always worked as her associate) had decided to sell the business, intending to go to America. His wife and two of their children are already there."[28] Letter after letter contains some reference to the worsening situation. To Paula Stolzenbach, for example, she writes: "I would like to commend my relatives to you. The situation gets more and more difficult for them."[29]

Stein did not yet imagine herself to be in a dangerous situation. Her 1935 essay on the history of Carmel includes pointed references to the sixteen nuns of Compiégne, France, beheaded during the French Reign of Terror.[30] She alludes to the martyrdom on July 24, 1936, of three Discalced Carmelite nuns in a letter dated May 7, 1937: "So far we still live in deep peace, entirely unmolested within our cloister walls. But the fate of our Spanish sisters tells us, all the same, what we must be prepared for."[31] In October 1938, she describes herself as "a very poor and powerless Esther" who, like the biblical queen, "was taken from among her people precisely that she might represent them before the king" in prayer, petition, and self-offering.[32] In another letter, dated December 9, 1938, she reveals that she had already offered herself as a *holocaustum* in 1933,[33] when she entered Carmel and chose the name Teresa Benedicta a Cruce (literally, Blessed by the Cross): "By the cross I understood the destiny of God's people which, even at that time, began to announce itself."[34]

As "the atmosphere . . . [grew] steadily darker"[35] in the winter of 1938, the prioress of the Carmel at Cologne arranged for Stein's transfer to the Carmel at Echt, the Netherlands. Stein arrived there on New Year's Eve. Her letters of the early months of 1939 describe her new home as a haven of warm welcome and protection, where she is "again in Carmel, surrounded by cordial maternal and sisterly love."[36] In Echt, she can continue her life of prayer, study, and charitable intercession. Stein highlights the continuities between the Carmels in Cologne and Echt, observing that "this house [in Echt] was founded by Carmelites from Cologne, when they were exiled in 1875."[37] Stein reports that these persecuted exiles, with whom she surely identified herself, "are buried here," in a cemetery "within the enclosure," where she is able "to greet [them]."[38] Many of the Carmelites living in Echt are "German Sisters," Stein writes, "several of them from Bavaria."[39] In another letter from Echt, Stein points out that "[t]he altar in our choir and many other [items] were brought along from Cologne," and praises "the true spirit of Carmel here."[40] She describes the Carmel in Echt as a home away from home, an extension of the monastery that she painfully left behind her in Cologne.

Echt is a place of tolerance, but also of vulnerability. Stein's earliest letters from Echt refer to an ultimate shelter, not within physical walls or national boundaries but in "God's will . . . the most secure port of peace."[41] Grateful for the refuge afforded her in Echt, Stein writes in April 1939, "At the same time I always have a lively awareness that we do not have a lasting city here."[42] Stein uses geographical locations—Bethlehem, Nazareth, the desert—to structure her brief biography of Carmelite Sister Marie-Aimée of Jesus (1839–74), composed in 1939. "In the desert solitude," Stein writes, "the instrument was forged, hardened in the fire of suffering."[43] A place that is precisely a no-place, a place within and yet outside the world, the "'desert' of Carmel" eludes her description.[44] As Stein observes in a letter dated November 20, 1941, "the story of the souls *in* Carmel" remains "a secret history, hidden deep in the Divine Heart: And what we believe we understand about our own soul is, after all, only a fleeting reflection of what will remain God's secret until the day all will be made manifest."[45]

Declared stateless, all non-Aryan Germans in the Netherlands were ordered "to report for emigration by December 15" (1941).[46] The last months of her life in Echt were marked by efforts to secure permission for Edith Stein and her sister Rosa to be transferred to a Carmel elsewhere—in Switzerland or Spain.[47] Those efforts failed. Deported in the company of 987 internees, Edith and Rosa Stein died together with 766 Jews from Drancy, France, on August 9, 1942, in the gas chamber at Auschwitz.[48]

Carmel as a place, a cloister, remained permeable to the atmosphere surrounding it. Its physical sanctuary could be entered, violated. The terrible historical situation in which Stein lived her life in Carmel might be analyzed as a background experience to Stein's specifically religious experience, a background to her facing of God and to the discovery in God of her inmost self, but what sort of background? The philosophical understanding of Stein, as articulated in her doctoral dissertation, *On the Problem of Empathy*, militates against a simple juxtaposition of her person against a historical or geographical background, even as it demands that those backgrounds be taken into account. As the preceding pages have endeavored to show, the background experiences of Stein—her past experiences, her solicitude for loved ones, her fear of an ever-impending danger to them and to herself—continually codetermined her present experience within Carmel, as they came to mind, filled her letters, and colored her prayer. Understood "in a pregnant sense,"[49] the categories of "inside" and "outside" apply neither to Stein's feelings nor to Carmel itself as she came to understand it. Driven into Carmel, she found that she had always already been at home there. Taken forcibly from it, she never really left it, because she had found her way to its innermost chamber in her soul.[50]

Notes

1. René Girard, *Violence and the Sacred*, trans. Patrick Gregory (Baltimore: The Johns Hopkins University Press, 1977), 298–99.

2. René Girard, *Deceit, Desire, and the Novel: Self and Other in Literary Structure*, trans. Yvonne Freccero (Baltimore: The Johns Hopkins University Press, 1985), 156.

3. Ibid., 155.

4. Ibid., 2.

5. Edith Stein, *The Hidden Life: Essays, Meditations, Spiritual Texts*, trans. Waltraut Stein, CWES, vol. 4 (Washington, D.C.: ICS Publications, 1992), 1–3.

6. Ibid., 2.

7. Ibid.

8. Ibid.

9. Ibid.

10. See Stein to Fritz Kaufmann, November 8, 1919, letter 31, in Stein, *Self-Portrait in Letters, 1916–1942*, trans. Josephine Koeppel, O.C.D., CWES, vol. 5 (Washington, D.C.: ICS Publications, 1993), 35–36; hereafter cited as *Letters*. *In 1931 she renewed her effort to gain habilitation, this time at the University of Freiburg (Germany). See Stein to Fritz Kaufmann, June 14, 1931, Letter 93a, in Letters*, 91.

11. Stein to Sister Adelgundis Jaegerschmid, June 9, 1932, letter 116, in *Letters*, 114.

12. Stein to Fritz Kaufmann, June 14, 1931, Letter 93a, in *Letters*, 91. See 2n7.

13. Stein to Mother Callista Brenzing, December 23, 1931, letter 108, in *Letters*, 107. See also Stein to Martin Honecker, July 8, 1932, letter 119, in *Letters*, 116.

14. Stein to Hedwig Conrad-Martius, November 13, 1932, letter 126, in *Letters*, 125.

15. Ibid.

16. Stein to Elly Dursy, May 7, 1933, letter 141, in *Letters*, 141.

17. Stein to Fritz Kaufmann, October 17, 1933, letter 158a, in *Letters*, 161. Kaufmann was a fellow student of Husserl's with Stein in Göttingen, and they maintained a long-term correspondence.

18. Stein to Mother Petra Brüning, O.S.U., February 12, 1933, letter 133, in *Letters*, 132: "It means so much to me that you can sense in me an identification with the 'corpus monasticum' [the religious life] and that you see [wearing] a habit as unessential. That is already a little bit of a cloister-home."

19. Stein to Elly Dursy, November 25, 1936, letter 230, in *Letters*, 242.

20. Stein to Mother Petra Brüning, O.S.U., October 18, 1933, letter 159, in *Letters*, 162.

21. Ibid.

22. Stein to Hedwig Conrad-Martius, October 31, 1933, letter 160, in *Letters*, 164.

23. Stein to Sister Adelgundis Jaegerschmid, O.S.B., January 28, 1937, letter 235, in *Letters*, 247.

24. Stein, "On the History and Spirit of Carmel," in *The Hidden Life*, 6.

25. On the "cave metaphor" as a "fixed point, a center, from which it is possible to found a world," see Kerstin W. Shands, *Embracing Space: Spatial Metaphors in Feminist Discourse*, Contributions in Women's Studies, vol. 176 (Westport, Conn.: Greenwood Press, 1999), 123.

26. Joseph Grange, "Place, Body, and Situation," in *Dwelling Place and Environment: Towards a Phenomenology of Person and World*, ed. David Seamon and Robert Mugerauer (Dordrecht, The Netherlands: Martinus Nijhoff, 1985), 1–84, at 78.

27. Ibid., 4–5.

28. Stein to Hedwig Conrad-Martius, October 10, 1936, letter 228, in *Letters*, 239.

29. Stein to Paula Stolzenbach, July 21, 1938, letter 271, in *Letters*, 282.

30. Stein, "On the History and Spirit of Carmel," in *The Hidden Life*, 6.

31. Stein to Sister Callista Kopf, May 7, 1937, letter 238, in *Letters*, 250.

32. Stein to Mother Petra Brüning, October 31, 1938, letter 281, in *Letters*, 291.

33. Stein uses the term *holocaustum* with reference to herself.

34. Stein to Mother Petra Brüning, December 9, 1938, letter 287, in *Letters*, 295.

35. Ibid., 296.

36. Stein to Anni Greven, January 14, 1939, letter 292, in *Letters*, 300.

37. Stein to Baroness Uta von Bodman, January 22, 1939, letter 293, in *Letters*, 301.

38. Ibid.

39. Ibid.

40. Stein to Anni Greven, April 12, 1939, letter 298, in *Letters*, 306.

41. Stein to Mother Petra Brüning, O.S.U., February 17, 1939, letter 294, in *Letters*, 303.

42. Stein to Mother Petra Brüning, O.S.U., April 16, 1939, letter 300, in *Letters*, 309.

43. Stein, "A Chosen Vessel of Divine Wisdom: Sister Marie-Aimée de Jésus of the Carmel of the Avenue de Saxe in Paris, 1839–1874," in *The Hidden Life*, 84.

44. Ibid., 80.

45. Stein to Mother Johanna van Weersth, O.C.D., November 20, 1941, letter 329, in *Letters*, 340.

46. Stein to Hilde Vérène Borsinger, December 31, 1941, letter 331, in *Letters*, 342.

47. See ibid.; Stein to Mother Johanna van Weersth, O.C.D., February 2, 1942, letter 333, in *Letters*, 344; Stein to Hilde Vérène Borsinger, April 9, 1942, letter 337, in *Letters*, 347–48; Stein to August Pérignon, July 29, 1942, letter 339, in *Letters*, 350; Stein to Mother Ambrosia Antonia Engelmann, O.C.D., August 6, 1942, letter 342, in *Letters*, 353.

48. See Sylvie Courtine-Denamy, *Three Women in Dark Times: Edith Stein, Hannah Arendt, Simone Weil*, trans. G. M. Goshgarian (Ithaca, N.Y.: Cornell University Press, 2000), 174.

49. Edith Stein, *On the Problem of Empathy*, trans. Waltraut Stein, 3rd rev. ed., CWES, vol. 3 (Washington, D.C.: ICS Publications, 1989), 100.

50. This marks the end of part one of three parts of the study (and the paper I presented at the Colloquium on Violence and Religion, International Association of Scholars of Mimetic Theory [St. Louis, 2015]).

2

The Spiritual Life and Its Degrees According to Edith Stein

ANGELA ALES BELLO

TRANSLATED BY ANTONIO CALCAGNO

An analysis of spirit[1] must be conducted in a twofold manner: in its subjective and its ontological aspects. The being of humans enables us to establish whether spirit exists and what the nature and the gradations of the life of the spirit might be. We can understand these questions by referring to a plurality of spiritual realities, including the life of the spirit itself. Edith Stein makes these two aspects evident, and it is opportune to follow her analysis, which moves from subjectivity to being. Her analysis permits us to see how human beings are structured in their complexity and how to localize them within the context of reality that surrounds and transcends them. In fact, it is clear that every investigation begins because human beings ask themselves questions about the meaning of things. It is necessary, then, to pose the problem concerning the way one is to proceed theoretically; that is, ought one to move from the analysis of the subject and, if so, how? Modern thought accords privilege to the subjective method as it tries to establish whether the goal of an investigation is the subject itself or whether the subject is only a point of departure for a more ample inquiry.

The Human Subject as the Initial Point of Philosophizing

> The first fact given is the most simple and it is that about which we are most immediately certain, namely, our being. It is the nucleus that forms the examination of the doubt of Augustine, [René] Descartes and [Edmund] Husserl. "I think, therefore I am" is not an inference, but a simple certainty. Thinking, feeling, willing, or whatever I may be spiritually experiencing, I am and I am conscious of this being. This certainty of being precedes all other types of knowing. This does not mean that all other types of knowing, as is the case with a fundamental principle, must be derived from it as a logical consequence. Neither is this starting point to be understood as a measure of all other types of knowing nor as the initial point that does not allow us to retrocede to a more original awareness. The certainty of being is a non-reflexive certainty that precedes all rational types of knowing.[2]

Philosophical inquiry has always been characterized by the search for the starting point, the port from which one departs to explore the sea of reality. In the above-cited passage, Edith Stein declares herself to be in tune with those philosophers who have begun their investigations from the first certainty, namely, that of existence proper. They did this not to absolutize their investigations by closing themselves off in them, but because they were pushed by the knowledge that philosophy, as an operation of the human being that seeks to orient itself in the world, begins with the subject and must first consider the capacities that allow one to carry out such an operation. Stein refers to Augustine, René Descartes, and Edmund Husserl; hence, she names not only modern thinkers but also a philosopher and theologian who starts a mode of thinking that will characterize ten centuries of Western culture.

The scope of this essay does not allow for examining the differences between the above-mentioned philosophers and Stein's views of their respective positions. The important thing to note is that the anthropological theme was foundational from the very start of her philosophical project. Specifically, we recall her choice to work on the problem of empathy, that particular mode of gathering together human beings, carried out in her doctoral dissertation.[3] Concerning the above-mentioned philosophers, Stein's path in a chronological sense was regressive. She was formed under the instruction of Husserl, who from his start as a student of Franz Brentano explored human subjectivity by first interesting himself in the psychological dimension and then by trying to locate "a new territory of being," as he describes it, represented by the knowledge of the operations we accomplish within consciousness, including cognitive, volitional, and affective acts. Such acts are to be understood as lived experiences, which give us the keys that allow us to enter into ourselves and simultaneously to go out of ourselves.

We cannot speak of Edith Stein without referring to Edmund Husserl, the teacher who remains always present in her work even until the end, even when she encounters medieval thought: Husserl and Augustine, as we saw in the passage cited, but also Husserl and St. Thomas Aquinas, as we shall see in what follows. The book from which the above-cited passage was taken is, in fact, dedicated to the study of Aristotle's concepts of potency and act, understood through Aquinas's use of them. Is it possible to bring together thinkers so seemingly different and far away from one another? Isn't this eclecticism? Not at all: The novelty of Stein's theoretical approach consists in the depths of each thinker's thought, which she goes to not only to seek agreements between them but also and, more important, to seek any clarifications that their works can give concerning the nature of reality.

By proceeding in such a way, Stein discovers that many of the analyses that Husserl and Aquinas carried out can be used to understand the human being in his or her complexity, including one's inner world. Here one must consistently take into account the significance of Augustine, yet it was in 1931, after translating Aquinas's *Quaestiones disputatae de veritate* (Disputed Questions on Truth), that Stein formalized her plan to "attempt to go from Scholastic thought to phenomenology and vice-versa," as she wrote in a letter to her friend and godmother, Hedwig Conrad-Martius.

The Force of the Spirit

Before turning to the question of spirit, I would like to
first examine Stein's *Potency and Act* since it represents
the final destination of her theoretical investigations.
Though they will be made more specific in *Finite and
Eternal Being*,[4] and provided with additional support, the
later work deepens and amplifies her earlier themes. In
every case, Stein's examination of the spiritual dimension
returns to her strictly phenomenological period and is
already documented in her doctoral dissertation dedicated
to the topic of empathy.

One could say that Husserl merits being credited with
bringing to the fore, especially with his reflections on the
ever-growing field of psychology, not only the theme of
the psyche but also that of the spirit. Stein transcribed the
second volume of *Ideas* wherein he presents these reflections. She always remained faithful to the conclusions
that Husserl reached in this work, accepting the tripartite division of human beings into body, psyche, and spirit
and opposing the reductive analyses of the then-prevalent
materialistic or psychologistic positivism. This tripartite
division is not new in Western thought. It can even be
found in St. Paul, and who knows if Husserl's reading of
Pauline texts did not influence him in his conversion to
the Lutheran Church at the age of twenty-eight? What
is new about both thinkers is the way in which they went
about justifying this tripartite division.

The discovery of the conscious dimension of lived
experiences characterizes Husserlian phenomenology.
Experiences present themselves to us as phenomena that

are difficult to analyze because they are so present that they escape us in their transparency. Perceiving, remembering, imagining, and feeling are all constitutive of our modes of being, so much so that we take them for granted without stopping to ponder that these lived experiences are messages that stem from the complexity of our human structure. Sensations derive from our perceptions, and these sensations lead to our corporeity. Similarly, our emotional responses tell us that we are constituted by a psychic dimension that is qualitatively different from that of our bodily one, but when we execute intellectual or willed acts we cannot assimilate them to or confuse them with the preceding ones. These acts speak forth a life of the spirit.

Already in her early *Philosophy of Psychology and the Humanities*, Stein is dedicated to leading us back from our lived acts, of which we are conscious, to the larger realities that underlie them. Consciousness does not always indicate a reflective stance, but demonstrates an implicit knowledge of living its acts. Lived experiences, examined in their essential structure, constitute a pure sphere that is structurally present in all human beings, specifically that of the pure I, the concrete I that lives its vital states, that is animated by the life force and characterized by the psyche. It transcends lived experiences insofar as it is different from its lived experiences. Stein writes: "We shall designate this real ego, its properties and states, as the sentient. We now see that consciousness and sentience are distinguished from one another in their basic essences: consciousness as realm of 'conscious' pure experiencing, and sentience as a sector of transcendent reality manifesting itself in experiences and experiential content."[5]

The I is also spiritual with a spiritual life force present within it. We enter into the domain that Stein terms the "domain of the spirit," thanks to the recognition of the presence of acts that we knowingly execute. Motivated acts executed by the I preclude other acts, which it does not execute. Such acts are not that which happen or pure spontaneities, as is the case in psychic life. The domain of the spirit is the domain of free acts characterized by a fiat, which implies both a decision and the taking of a certain position. One enters into the sphere of willing and acting, a sphere that is far removed from any determinism, a sphere where one can act or let go, and this is where ethical life and moral choice are engaged.

The analysis given has distinguished, for methodological reasons, the psychic dimension from the spiritual one. We must remark, though, that Stein always underlines the profound unity of the human being as we see in her treatment of being embodied, despite her stratified description of the body's various constitutive elements. A short passage might help us to understand this relationship.

> The life of sentience appears to us, in our investigations, as a result of the cooperation of powers of various kinds. We distinguish a sensory lifepower, which converts itself into the reception of sensory data (into different capacities for the reception of sensory data, that is) as well as into sensory impulses and their activities. Besides that, sensory lifepower serves for the conservation of mental

lifepower, from which the mental activities are fed. But mental lifepower doesn't represent a mere conversion of sensory lifepower; rather, it harbors within itself a new power source which, nevertheless, can attain deployment only with the assistance of sensory lifepower and at its expense. . . . Before, the psyche seemed to be embedded in material nature and rooted within it; but now we see the psyche fitted into the mental world, . . . It appears that with this we are led to distinct power sources from which the mindpower of an individual psyche receives its substance: to "objective mind" (the world of values that we took under consideration at the start of our investigations, if we may call it that), and to "subjective mind," that is, to the mindpower of other individuals and to the divine mind.[6]

The Life of the Spirit: Phenomenological and Scholastic

Having made these distinctions between sentient and spiritual life, which she never renounces after her conversion to Roman Catholicism, Stein turns to the study of Aquinas's works and to a wider reading of other major figures in medieval philosophy. Stein never simply followed authority; she closely examined the possibilities offered by past thinkers, including Greek thinkers such as Plato and Aristotle, in order to penetrate more deeply into questions of anthropology, cosmology, and theology in her search for the ultimate meaning of reality. Stein feels that she was fortunate to have been formed in phenomenology because she became used to researching the essence of what it is to be human by examining lived experiences and the essential recognition of bodily, psychic, and spiritual reality.

In chapter five of *Potency and Act*, Stein examines the significance of the spirit, by moving from phenomenology to Scholastic thinking and vice versa. Interestingly, she finds the possibility of an accord between the two perspectives. On every page, in every assertion, we can observe a confluence between the two positions, though Stein elaborates each position in her unique way. The beginning of her treatment reads: "We may begin by using the polarity of subject and object that we are calling 'intentionality' to describe *what being that is spiritual in the subjective sense is. Spiritual life* or *living*, the highest form of spiritual being, means being stretched between these two poles and aiming at an object."[7] This phenomenological definition, which leads back to Scholastic thought, is deepened by an investigation of the spiritual life in its intentionality.

Intentionality for modern thought is an act, and Stein adds that she understood it—drawing from Husserl—to be so in her earlier writings. She also adds that she discovered in the Scholastic use of the word a triple meaning: "act" as the intrinsic principle of form, "act of being," and "act of active being" that is actuality and activity. Modern thinking has emphasized activity, thereby giving actuality a secondary place. This is the case because modernity has fixed its attention primarily on finite, temporally limited spirits. Stein believes that the field of inquiry must be amplified to include other spirits, including pure spirits,

the angels, and the Holy Spirit. Aquinas helps her expli-
cate the trajectory she had sketched in *Philosophy of Psychology and the Humanities*. More precisely, in order to
understand the human spirit it is necessary to proceed
with a closer examination of the other modalities of the
spirit. Here, she decisively enters an ontological domain,
yet it is possible to discover metaphysical structure even
for finite being.

The subject is the bearer of spiritual life. Stein understands the subject as the one from whom spiritual life
extends. She understands substance as that which stays
by itself; it is independent. Here she uncovers the deep
sense of the term "person" by bringing Husserl and Aquinas together to examine their agreement. They both speak
of spiritual being but, while Husserl achieves this result
by investigating the essence of spiritual acts and by not
engaging the question of substance, Aquinas considers
questions of spiritual substance. Stein admits that in order
to understand the depths of human being it is necessary
to recognize that the person is a spiritual substance. On
the basis of this definition, Stein proceeds to compare the
divine person, angels, and human beings. She uses analogy
to establish commonality between God and finite beings.
"God alone possesses personhood as self-sufficiency in
the restricted sense of *aseitas* [being from oneself]. But
there is a genuine analogy between the infinite person
and created spiritual subjects that justifies our speaking of
them, too, as persons."[8]

Continuing along with analogical thinking makes it
possible to proceed with a description of the spiritual life

in its essential characteristics and its ontological development. Clearly, the analysis of the human subject allows one to identify grades of spirit by examining potency and act. The potency[9] of the soul, which Stein examined first, is the intellect. It indicates an essential characteristic of the spirit:

> If we consider the pure spirit and the soul only insofar as it is spirit, the understanding or intellect denotes an essential property of spirit: *being illumined* [*durchleuchtet*] (that is, being visible to oneself [*für sich selbst sichtbar*] and being open [*geöffnet*] (turning the attention to something else by grasping it). In God both are infinite. This is why His understanding is eternally actual and perfect knowledge of Himself and of all else knowable. Finite spirits are not everything they are in enduringly changeless actuality. Their being is parceled out to them, confined to a limited measure. Their being illumined and open is also limited. The *mode* of their being [*Seinsmodus*] denotes first the *degree* of the actuality of their being as well as of the being of their knowing [*Erkennendsein*] and second the *range* of what they can in *general* turn to by knowing and of what they can turn to in the highest measure of their actuality.[10]

The condition of being illumined and being open is not a continuous condition for human beings. There are latent states, for example, sleep, that do not violate the continuity of spiritual being. Sleep does not constitute an interruption of the spiritual life but marks a return to a state of potentiality that one also finds in children, but with an essential difference that characterizes the development of the human being. One can see the stirring of something new "is increasingly happening that presumably was not happening before. So spiritual existence, we should say, does not necessarily begin when it first becomes verifiable for us. The onset of verifiability points to a change in the be-ing itself, a transition to a higher type of spiritualness, to intellectuality; it marks a heightening of the actuality of life and consciousness and at the same time an expansion in the range of openness."[11]

The passage from potency to act also results in the passage to knowledge as habit. This notion, taken from Aquinas but also used by Husserl,[12] indicates the realization of an act. To understand more deeply that which happens in one's interior life, Stein re-establishes another notion, and this time it is Husserlian. From the subjective perspective, that is, from the active side, habit is a superior grade of spiritual being. From the perspective of the process itself, every actualization of knowledge constitutes an object that remains in my spiritual world, respecting the meaning Husserl understood as belonging to the relation between the lived experience, for example, perception, and the content of the lived experience, the perceived object.[13] Stein employs the content of the Husserlian analysis to demonstrate that it is possible to dig deeper into the Thomistic position concerning the operations executed by the subject. The phenomenological method has the advantage of showing with great acuity the meaning of acts proper to the subject. Stein also asserts that Aquinas, from the perspective of the nature of the subject, demonstrates the validity of the metaphysical structure. In such a manner the advantages of the two positions are united without conflating the differences between them.

Husserl himself implicitly used the concepts of potency and act as Stein does as she leads them back to their philosophical sources. For example, Stein follows the theme of recollection, which Husserl described as a presentification (something that comes to mind by imagining, recalling, or anticipating an object that does not directly confront it). The possibility for recollection is the passage from the potential for forming habits to actuality. Even those phenomena of consciousness that Husserl so finely examined from the perspective of the acts that grasp them, including memory, recollection, association, and reproduction, all lead back to a passage from potency to act. Likewise, Husserl explains gaps in consciousness through an analysis of the flow of lived experience. Inner-time consciousness allows one to understand the fact that consciousness of a living duration remains valid even if there are spans of consciousness that are not filled. In this way, Husserl accounts for the continuity of spiritual life, avoiding a crisis that could provide a space for a reductionistic, materialistic description of the human being.

A reawakening of the content of consciousness, freely undertaken, brings us to the second grade of the spirit, that is, the will. Intellect and will constitute the two essential attributes of subjective spirit. Husserl, in *Ideas II*,[14] speaks about a circularity between them that the agent intellect attests to so that the potency toward certain types of doing/making directs movement to knowledge. Because every doing/making implies the will, the active intellect is either a volitional potency or an intellectual one; moreover, the intellect is not only an agent but also a potentiality that is to be understood as the potency toward the knowledge of objects that maintains until it reaches its final end. The volitional element is, then, intrinsic to the intellect and this permits us to say that the act of knowledge is creative and re-creative, productive of an objective spirit that characterizes a world independent of the subject or subjects that it supports. This account justifies the presence of spiritual objects in the human world. But these products are based on a spiritual sense already present in things that speak to us and, in such a way, push us to intervene, thereby introducing new realities endowed with meaning. According to Stein, spirit pervades all reality insofar as all reality, even material reality, is characterized by meanings.

Human doing/making, which is the concrete and continual condition that characterizes us, does not only refer to an external world but also refers to us as well as to other spiritual subjects. Husserl's and Stein's positions are often deemed to be intellectualist because they seem to give importance to theorizing. In fact, they recognize the operative dimension of the human being as circulating between active theorizing and practice without absolutizing either of these two moments. If the intellect and the will are the characteristic potencies of the spirit, they do not live by themselves alone but exercise themselves upon other interior realities. The territory of the soul is vast. Not only do the intellect and the will dwell in it but also the mind. Employing a spatial image, we started from the act in the description of this territory, but this description is not complete; it is necessary to dig deeper.

As a superb phenomenologist, Stein does not forget the peculiar realm she investigated in her *Philosophy of Psychology and the Humanities*, namely, that of the psyche. In fact, she observes that contact with the external world does not happen immediately at the intellectual level; and we can add that it happens, in the first place, at the perceptual level, an interior reaction is produced, characterized as psychic, that of pleasure and displeasure, followed by a certain attraction or repulsion of assent or refusal. In human beings such comportment is expressed successively in the greatest degree in the spiritual sentiments of love and hate. We are always accompanied by an affective tonality that we are conscious of, and such tonalities are not of an intellectual order. Here one cannot speak of an explicit self-consciousness, but of feelings that accompany us in every moment of our waking lives.

From this initial contact and from this first sensing, our volitional comportment and our intentional doing/ making are born in our encounter with things and human subjects. This is what Stein defines as mind. Every person manifests inclinations, dispositions, and diverse reactions, and each person expresses these differently. If it were possible to reconstruct a map of the human being's complex interiority and to distinguish the operations and acts that characterize the spiritual sphere and the mind in their essentiality, it would be difficult to say which lived experiences are activated by single subjects as subjectivity is truly something that is unique and nonrepeatable. We must ask from where such nonrepeatability derives.

Husserl maintained that the person was a unified being, though complex and stratified. He insisted on the theme of individuality, such that existence allows "absolute individuation to penetrate the personal I." Also, he maintained "that originary and absolute individuation resides in the I itself."[15] Stein attributed such individuation to the personality core (*Kern*) that she had already examined in her early works, *On the Problem of Empathy* and *Philosophy of Psychology and the Humanities*. In them, she had clearly distinguished the core of personality from the life of the spirit as "something new and particular not already included in it."[16]

In *Potency and Act*, Stein again takes up the question of the core with respect to the density of the human being. Stein distinguishes that which is found to be at the periphery and that which is to be delineated in one's profundity. Digging deeply allows one to discover the core, which tells us what the person is. The person, thanks to the core, is "like a center located in the world in order to receive it in the intellect's form or in a mode such that it is struck by it, or in such a way that by conquering it, penetrates it."[17] The core distinguishes itself by its simplicity—it is not composed of parts—it is a potential with respect to the actualization of the spiritual life in which it externalizes itself in an adequate way in order to fulfill itself as act. Certainly, the core can remain obscure, but even in this case it has its actuality because it is always active and real, even if it is imperfectly realized. Since the core is the distinctive element of the human being and since it actualizes itself fully in the spiritual life, one can hypothesize that while such an actualization is constantly threatened in the earthly life, in the afterlife the core of the human person is able to realize itself "as an actuality that is constantly and massively achievable of those things that are there in themselves, in such a way that nothing is more obscure and unconscious behind the actual spiritual life and in such a way that the alternating between potential and actuality is not suppressed for the core of the person and the core itself is freed from temporality and placed in eternity."[18]

Virtue and Sanctity

Given this background, we move now to an analysis of the otherworldly dimension, and we open a series of considerations that will permit us to comprehend the relationship between time and eternity. This argument in particular revolves around the connection that one can establish between character and sanctity. The analyses concerning the core provide the key to understanding human destiny. The arguments, and this is peculiar to Stein, deal with a rigorous philosophical reflection on the ultimate backdrop of truth, which is religious revelation. This philosophical reflection not only serves to clarify such truths, thereby completing an operation that could be defined as theological in scope, but it also serves to demonstrate the process that renders them rational without performing qualitative leaps that sometimes impede establishing a connection between the different realms.

Different sources illuminate the same reality; the philosophical search and revealed truth encounter one another without difficulty in the clarification of what it is to be human. In such a way, religious philosophy comes to some kind of completion; it comprises in its path of rigorous research elements that arise from another source, but with respect to them an intrinsic connection, not merely juxtaposition, shows itself.

The core of the person, according to Stein, prescribes that which it ought to be; personal freedom is, however, a salvo. In fact, becoming oneself can be realized or interrupted; nothing is determined. "It is possible that the core does not unfold [*Entfaltung*] fully [*rein*] in its development [*Entwicklung*]."[19] Every person feels as though he or she ought to exist, but he or she may not always realize his or her possibilities because of a series of inhibitions; Stein even calls these privations and gives an example by recalling the difference between diffidence and not always being trusting. What distinguishes these two comportments is that the former consists of believing that someone is capable of any sort of evil without any real basis for this assertion, whereas the latter could be determined by prudence that is born from the knowledge of human limits. Human beings have aspects that are both positive and negative. Their core is always positive. Stein writes: "by the person's 'core' we should obviously understand only the positive side. If during his earthly existence a person by virtue of his freedom has overcome the obstacles as far as he could, then in the *status termini* or in the purification after death everything that hindered him, all privation, fades away and the core enters eternity without dross."[20] We have a process of purification in which inhibitions are eliminated and a way of being is produced that is superior to all that was actualized in the earthly life. Either one is saved entirely or one is lost. If one says that there is more or less beatitude, this does not mean that only one part of the core enters eternity. The core is unitary; the doctrine of purification confirms this. Its simplicity is always relative because we can distinguish its essence from its existence, which can never be said of God; moreover, its unity will be full only in the end state. Notwithstanding external changes of infancy and old age, notwithstanding even radical transformations, the core maintains its permanence. Every single human being knows that he/she exists despite changes of the body. Additionally, this permanence must not simply be considered as memory, which is also important, but as a more profound ontological permanence. We recognize how deeply we live in the profundity of the self when we focus on the core as it is given at the moment of birth. It cannot develop, understood in a transformational sense, even if the human being is able to mature fully within the course of life. In this way, we can understand why we must enter heaven as a child.

The connection between the ethical moment and the question of salvation is deepened further by our author through a reflection on the theme of guilt and forgiveness. Stein decisively tackles the theme of sin, connecting it ontologically to nonbeing. In the case of serious sin, one willfully opposes absolute being, which results in an emptying of the person. We must note the impossibility of producing our own annihilation because this can only happen through the intervention of the Absolute Being; hence, spiritual being survives even in sin. The negation present in sin is never a total negation of being because it also contains in itself the affirmation of one's being, and this always permits the possibility of conversion.

Absolute negation is purely diabolical insofar as it is definitive and cannot be renounced. For human beings there is always the core of the person that exercises its activity and that can have a positive influence. With sin, negation has entered the human being: if one believes in God, one will suffer anxiety because of this negation; if one does not believe in God, the negation will enter the human being as the negation of the absolute being. Stein describes atheism with much precision as the flight into the theoretical negation of the existence of God that leads to anguish before nothingness.

What makes conversion possible? It consists in a theoretical clarification that suppresses the negation of the absolute being and in an affirmation of being itself that also includes affectivity. In the distancing from negation, a directing of oneself toward substitutes, and an increase in being, an elevation to a higher grade of being that is called grace results. "The negation of the negation in freely turning toward and the heightening in being together yield justification."[21]

In the case of venial sin, an internal contrast between believing in God and the transgression presents itself, but this only happens through an openness that permits self-correction. That which is at play in the distinction between venial sin and mortal sin is the affective and intellectual comportment vis-à-vis God, which also determines one's condition in the end. Reconciliation discovers reparation for practical errors and the elimination of internal conflict.

Our author acutely describes the state of sanctity and that of damnation, although she does not use these terms. As always, Stein focuses great attention on that which is positive: the possibility of conversion, liberation from sin, repentance. If all this is realized, then it becomes possible for the human being to access the state of "being born of the spirit," that is, to live life in grace. This state is obtained by having an open disposition and acceptance; it simply requires not comporting oneself in a defensive manner. Stein may be referring to her experience of conversion and to her call, which was not willed or sought. She underwent or bore that experience, to which she was never radically opposed. For this reason, I do not believe that one can speak of Stein as an atheist in her younger years. Certainly, one can describe her as distancing herself from God and the religious dimension, but not with a knowing hostility or one that was knowingly practiced.

We have seen how the spiritual dimension was involved in the moral life and that of religion: intellect, will, openness, and being were all disposed toward the absolute being. There can be an ethics without religion, but it is a strong characteristic of the spirit, namely, that of openness toward others and toward the Other, that strictly correlates the ethical and spiritual dimensions. If religious openness is lacking, if it becomes interrupted by flight, the human spirit must make an appeal to its forces and there is always the risk of it being spoiled, finding itself in a state of emptiness, impotence, and nothingness. The great theme that Stein concentrates on at all levels is that of power, the power of sensation, spiritual power, all present as constitutive of the human being, but given the weakness of finite human beings, a further force is necessary, namely, grace. A state of sanctity is attainable through it.

Spirit and Body Toward Sanctity

Until now, the bodily dimension appeared to be excluded from our reflections as if our investigations could be undertaken purely at the psycho-spiritual level, but the connection between the body and the psyche is profound, and Stein never underestimated corporeity. In fact, she always maintained that the body was constitutive of the human being. She admits that there is a possible sort of independence of the life of the soul that actualizes itself in ascetic practice, but the practice cannot be an end in itself; it is only through the help of grace that it can become a pathway to salvation. Here one must recognize that one does not eliminate radically the life of the body, but only those aspects of corporeity that are negative because they disturb the life of the soul. The living body is the bearer of positive values that can be exalted, including beauty and health. One need not sacrifice all of these, for in the work of redemption "one need not deny the idea that even here grace makes use of totally different ways."[22]

At this point our author confronts the question of ecstasies by initiating her investigation of mystical experience. Stein observes that it involves the triumph of the life of the spirit, which seizes even the body through a total rapture. Mysticism is an effect of grace, which moves from the internal to the external, yielding its fruits even if the soul is opposed. In every case, as was said already, one must be deeply disposed because God fully respects human freedom.

Stein hypothesizes that not only can the living body be illuminated by the life of the soul but also that sanctity can move directly from the living body to the soul. Grace can also save the living body and therefore could justify the thaumaturgic function of the body. It is for this reason that a saintly person is also a miracle-worker. In fact, a saintly person takes care to transform into his/her image everything that he/she comes into contact with, and it is in this sense that one can speak of miracles. This is the case because corrupt substances are led back to their original natures through the effect of grace. "There is no law by which when each time that a holy body touches another body that the latter must be transformed. But in every case where there is similar contact one can verify the effects."[23] All this can happen because "[a] holy living body does not oppress the soul. It is the prepared abode that makes possible for them a life that is holy and free."[24]

Following this line of argument surrounding the body, the function of the sacraments, which are capable of producing sanctity, could be justified. In particular, the Eucharist, upon which Stein often meditates,[25] has a salvific value insofar as it is the nourishment that can save the living body. "She/he who receives the Body of the Lord will see his or her own living body sanctified."[26] The significance of the sacrament is not to produce a miraculous healing; rather, it serves to place the living body in its proper place, to establish the psycho-physical equilibrium of the human being as the spiritual that is visible through the body. This is the profound reason why the Word became flesh. The whole human being is involved; the spirit does not operate without being connected with the psyche and the body. If the sacrament of the Eucharist can be employed to understand the functioning of the body, the sacrament of penance and reconciliation operates above all on the psychic level. "The word of the Lord that absolves one of sin is capable of allowing a force that acts against psychic pressures to penetrate the soul."[27]

The Night of the Spirit: The Mystical Path

Ethicality, sanctity, and mysticism constitute three moments that possess their own characteristics, even if they can be connected with the function of salvation. Mysticism reveals its peculiarity in exceptional conditions of contact with the divine in the course of earthly existence. In fact, mysticism entails the presence of God in the soul. This can enable us to ask what role the spirit plays in relation to this union. On the pathway toward mystical experience there exists a double attitude of the spirit: passivity and activity cross into one another, freedom and trust are racing with one another in order to get ahead, and such moments, which seem so opposed to one another, are finally synthesized in an extraordinary way.

Commenting on the works of St. Teresa of Ávila and St. John of the Cross, Stein retraces the journeys of their souls. We recall that for her the spirit, with its peculiar force, is that which characterizes the human being in its specific activities. On a preliminary note, it must be remarked that a difference exists between religious experience and mystical experience, and the difference lies in the contact that establishes itself with the divine.

We can observe that in lived religiosity it is precisely the openness of the spirit that consents to contact with the divine, a contact that is sought and willed and is consequently the fruit of human freedom. Stein always points out the importance of divine action through grace that is enlarged gradually. In an encounter between the human being and God, a mutual exchange, the divine always occupies a fundamental place. The human being responds to the divine call with an act of faith.

The term "faith" can mean many things. It can indicate various modalities of trust such as certainty, conviction about a certain state of affairs, which is a purely human knowledge. In the case of religious experience, faith "distinguishes itself . . . from conviction and its modifications by the fact that its correlate is not a state of affairs, but is a primary object and, consequently, it itself is not a founded act." This is so because it does not resolve itself in a theoretical act "but that which I understand penetrates me; while I understand it, it seizes me in my personal center and holds me to itself."[28]

The grasping of the center or the core is such that the more it is seized the more I become attached to and understand it. The act of faith is also an act of understanding, love, and action, and because of this it requires both trust and collaboration. Stein explains all of this in her description of the spiritual path outlined by St. John of the Cross. In the first stage the spirit enriches itself through its contact with God and conforms its will to the divine will, but one can go beyond this, which is where mystical experience begins.

At a central point, the soul subtracts from every spiritual exercise and immerses itself in obscurity and emptiness. It is as if there were a battle between the human spirit, with all of its capacity, and a determined abandoning of faith that takes place in an arid, nauseating, and afflicted place. This is the purely spiritual cross. The soul is despoiled of everything; it seems to be overwhelmed and is unable to react. Even here one sees a small fragment of autonomy. "If one accepts it [and Stein is referring here to the cross], then one can experience a gentle yoke and a light burden."[29]

It is "the death by the cross in the living body, in the senses and in the spirit," as St. John says, that leads us finally to a union with God. Here faith terminates its function; mystical contemplation is communicated to the soul. There is no longer an accepting or a turning away but, by being touched by God, by experiencing God, this contact becomes that union that the image of mystical marriage tries to convey. As St. Teresa contends, it truly is an experience: If touching and experiencing indicate a passivity of the soul, the powers of the soul as indicated by Augustine, including intellect, will, and memory, even if they are not active, are always in part aware of what is happening and to such a degree that they can refer to what is happening, as is often the case with those who have lived through such experiences.

As a cognitive part of the human being, the spirit truly receives the presence of God who is both triune and one, as St. Teresa records. The spirit is present in the most profound recesses of the human being, in the personal core and in the encounter with the three divine persons. In the seventh dwelling place: "This happens within an intellectual vision in which the three persons bow to the spirit. For a miracle of knowledge that is granted to it, the soul sees with the most absolute certainty that the three persons are one essence, one power, a unique wisdom, and one sole divinity."[30] The spirit knows, the soul sees. It is precisely St. Teresa who proposes the distinction between the soul and its powers, among which one finds those of the spirit. It is from her experience that the confirmation of the stratification and complexity of the human being come.

As a phenomenologist, Edith Stein lets herself be led, but also verifies: If the soul is rooted in the core from which it draws its nourishment, then it is in the profoundest point, in the core, that one encounters God directly. The image of the castle with its series of dwelling places that lead to the innermost center, as St. Teresa describes, presents the structure of the human created with space within for God.

Notes

1. Sometimes in various translations and traditions "spirit" (*Geist oder geistlich*) might be translated as "mind" [translator Calcagno's note].

2. Edith Stein, *Potency and Act*, trans. Walter Redmond, CWES, vol. 11 (Washington, D.C.: ICS Publications, 2009), 9–10.

3. Edith Stein, *On the Problem of Empathy*, trans. Waltraut Stein, CWES, vol. 3 (Washington, D.C.: ICS Publications, 1989).

4. Edith Stein, *Finite and Eternal Being: An Attempt at an Ascent of the Meaning of Being*, trans. Kurt Reinhardt, CWES, vol. 9 (Washington, D.C.: ICS Publications, 2002).

5. Edith Stein, *Philosophy of Psychology and the Humanities*, trans. Mary Catharine Baseheart and Marianne Sawicki, CWES, vol. 7 (Washington, D.C.: ICS Publications, 2000), 23–24. The English translators have used "sentience" instead of "the psychic" to designate what Stein designates as *psychische*. The English translation reduces the psyche to a quasi-sensing or sensate reality, whereas the German implies some reflectivity, especially when it comes to understanding natural processes of cause and effect [translator Calcagno's note].

6. Ibid., 115–16. Again, please note that *Geist* or *geistlich* can be translated as either "mind" or "spirit." Sawicki and Baseheart use "mind," but I prefer "spirit" as it can refer to the life of the mind and the will, both human and divine, which is more in tune with Stein's whole project. "Mind" is the Anglo-American rendition of *Geist* and connotes today the analytic mind/brain distinction, which Stein was unfamiliar with [translator Calcagno's note].

7. Stein, *Potency and Act*, 121.

8. Ibid., 128.

9. Note: *Potenza* in Italian, as it does in Latin, means both "power" and "potential," and Stein uses the Latinate term *Potenz, which means both "power" and "potentiality"* [*translator Calcagno's note*].

10. Stein, *Potency and Act*, 154.

11. Ibid., 156.

12. Edmund Husserl, *Ideas Pertaining to a Pure Phenomenology and to a Phenomenological Philosophy*, vol. 2, trans. R. Rojcewicz and A. Schuwer (Dordrecht, The Netherlands: Kluwer, 1989), sec. 3, ch. 2, sec. 61, p. 289.

13. Ibid., 285.

14. Ibid.

15. Ibid., 315.

16. Stein, *Philosophy of Psychology*, 95.

17. Stein, *Potency and Act*, 190.

18. Ibid., 201.

19. Ibid., 209.

20. Ibid., 210.

21. Ibid., 217.

22. Stein, "Die ontische Struktur der Person und ihre erkenntnistheoretische Problematik," in *Welt und Person*, Edith Steins Werke, vol. 6, ed. L. Gelber and P. R. Leuven (Freiburg: Herder, 1962), 178; hereafter Edith Steins Werke will be cited as ESW.

23. Ibid., 180.

24. Ibid.

25. See in particular Stein, "Das Pädagogische Bedeutung der eucharistischen Wahrheiten," in *Der Aufbau der menschlichen Person*, ed. L. Gelber and M. Linssen, ESW, vol. 16 (Freiburg: Herder, 1994), pt. ix, sec.II, pp. 196–200.

26. Stein, "Die ontische Struktur der Person und ihre erkenntnistheoretische Problematik," in *Welt und Person*, ESW, vol. 6, 180.

27. Ibid., 184.

28. Ibid., 188.

29. Stein, *Science of the Cross*, trans. Josephine Koeppel, CWES, vol. 6 (Washington, D.C.: ICS Publications, 2002), 121.

30. Stein, "Die Seelenburg," in *Welt und Person*, ESW, vol. 6, 58.

3

THE PASSION OF EDITH STEIN — REVISITED

PRUDENCE ALLEN, R.S.M., PH.D.

Edith Stein/Sister Teresa Benedicta of the Cross (1891–1942) approached the themes of love and friendship through various meanings of passion in her life: first, the natural passion of love; second, the love of truth and philosophy; and third, the love of God by participating in the passion of Christ.[1] This essay draws upon several previously published articles and includes new material from the third volume of *The Concept of Woman: The Search for Communion of Persons, 1500–2000*.[2] For clarity, Edith Stein will be identified when drawing upon her work as a laywoman, and Sister Benedicta when drawing upon her work as a Carmelite nun.

The Natural Passion of Love

Stein turned to the study of St. Thomas Aquinas well before her conversion to Catholicism on January 1, 1922.[3] In her words from *Finite and Eternal Being*, Sister Benedicta directly states her debt to Aquinas's description of the passions: "And has not St. Thomas given us a carefully worked out *theory of affectivity* with sharply defined concepts and classifications, higher and lower orders?"[4]

Aquinas states in the *Summa Theologiae* that "passion is a movement of the irrational soul, when we *think* of good or evil."[5] This movement is not simply an occurrence without direction. Instead, it is a movement toward or away from what he calls "a sensible good or evil." What this means is that the passion springs up in response to something perceived with the senses, something imagined, or something experienced as either good or evil for the person.[6] Aquinas understands the passions themselves to be morally neutral in that they simply move through a human being in response to the objects experienced in the world.[7]

Aquinas laid the foundation for the philosophical analysis of natural passions in Part I–II of the *Summa Theologiae* where he describes the six concupiscible passions of love and hatred, desire and aversion, and pleasure and pain as having as their object a sensible (or imagined) good or evil that causes pleasure or pain; and the five irascible passions of hope and despair, fear and daring, and anger as having as their object a sensible (or imagined) good or evil that is arduous.[8]

Stein, who had studied psychology before turning to philosophy, displayed a keen interest in how passions, emotions, feelings, or affectivity operate in the human person. In her major philosophical work, *Finite and Eternal Being*, Sister Benedicta suggests that feeling should be joined with thinking and willing as a three-part understanding of the human person in analogy with the Holy

Trinity. Adopting the insight of Theodor Haecker she states:

> The genuine three-part division of the spiritual life is that in *thinking, feeling, willing*. Modern psychology has discovered it without anticipating that with this lies the basis to a new and more corresponding *analogia Trinitatis*. The emphasis on feeling as an equal domain near thinking and willing is, thus, important to him because he sees here the proper home of love.[9]

Many different kinds of love may be distinguished, such as the natural passion of love that springs up from within the human person and spiritual love or charity that is infused into the person from the action of the Holy Spirit. In her doctoral dissertation, *On the Problem of Empathy*, under the direction of Edmund Husserl, Stein begins with the natural passion of love and offers a rich description of the passions, introducing four different classifications often used by psychologists to measure a particular passion: reach, duration, intensity, and depth. The reach of a passion is described as follows:

> We can say that every feeling has a certain mood component that causes the feeling to be spread throughout the "I" from the feeling's place of origin and fill it up. Starting from a peripheral level, a slight resentment can fill me "entirely," but it can also happen upon a deep joy that prevents it from pushing further forward to the center. Now, in turn, this joy progresses victoriously from the center and fills out all the layers above it.[10]

Duration, another dimension of passions, is characterized as: "They not only fill up the 'I' in its depth and width,
but also in the 'length' of experienced time they remain in
it."[11] Intensity of feeling, separate from reach and duration, provides a third distinction. The most intense passions tend to set the will in motion almost automatically,
unless we develop the capacity to think about them before
choosing and acting.

The fourth dimension of a passion is its depth in our
personality. This dimension particularly opens up for us
the objective intention of a passion as it reveals our hierarchy of values. The intentionality of consciousness, the fact
that it is directed outward toward particular real objects at
the same time as it is experienced inwardly is a key claim
of phenomenology as practiced by Husserl and his doctoral student Stein.[12] She offers an example of the hierarchy of values revealed through experiencing the passions
of anger and of love:

> Anger over the loss of a piece of jewelry comes from a
> more superficial level or does not penetrate as deeply
> as losing the same object as the souvenir of a loved
> one. Furthermore, pain over the loss of this person
> himself would be even deeper. This discloses essential
> relationships among the hierarchy of felt values, the
> depth classification of value feelings, and the level of
> classification of the person exposed in these feelings.
> Accordingly, every time we advance in the value realm,
> we also make acquisitions in the realm of our own
> personality.[13]

In another example from her *Life*, Stein describes how she loves different forms of music:

> I loved the classical operas as much as I did the great tragedies. The first I heard was *The Magic Flute*. We bought the piano score and soon knew it by heart. So, too, with *Fidelio* which always remained my favorite. I also heard Wagner and during a performance found it impossible wholly to evade its magic. Still I repudiated this music, with the sole exception of *Die Meistersinger*. I had a predilection for Bach. This world of purity and strict regularity attracted me most intimately. Later when I came to know Gregorian chant, I felt completely at home for the first time; and then I understood what had moved me so much in Bach.[14]

Aquinas argues that love has a natural complementary passion of hate or hatred toward the loss of something or someone who is loved;[15] thus, ironically, love is a kind of cause of hate. If we juxtapose some events in the relation between Stein and her mother, we can perhaps grasp this dynamic more clearly. In her memoir, *Life in a Jewish Family*, Stein recounts many a tender moment between mother and daughter and remarks that her long evening study sessions were often accompanied by her mother bringing her refreshments and always kissing her good night. She shared these maternal signs of love for her family. Regarding Stein's effusive expressions of love, Professor Gertrud Koebner said: "She never let anything interfere with her love for her sisters and brothers and their children. It's impossible to imagine a more devoted nurse or babysitter than she. When she looked at the infants born during those years back home in Breslau, her face wore a smile from another world."[16]

When Stein wanted to leave the university during World War I to serve as a nurse, she relates:

> I had heavy opposition to face from my mother. I did not even tell her that it was a lazaretto [i.e., for those with contagious diseases]. She was well aware that no suggestion of hers that my life would be endangered could ever induce me to change my plans. So as an ultimate deterrent, she told me all the soldiers arrived from the front with clothes overrun by lice and that I could not possibly escape infestation. Naturally that was a scourge I dreaded, but if the people in the trenches all had to suffer from it why should I be better off than they?
>
> When this tactic failed, my mother declared with all the energy she could muster: "You will not go with my permission."
>
> My reply was every bit as determined. "Then I must go without your permission."
>
> My sisters were downright shocked at my harsh retort. . . . Now, however, granite was striking granite. My mother said no more and was very silent and depressed for several days, a mood which always affected the entire household.[17]

It is well known that at a later date, after Stein entered the Carmelite monastery, her mother remained silent toward her for years, hating the decision her daughter had made.

In *Finite and Eternal Being*, Sister Benedicta describes how a person must engage with his or her natural passions in order to act according to the proper hierarchy of values; she reflects on how natural attraction and aversion or love and hate arise in the soul and what the person should do in relation to a particular passion:

> Of course, one indeed regards love and hate as elemental powers which fall upon the soul without it being able to resist them. Already from their inclination and disinclination men used to say that they "could do nothing about them." And in fact: the soul "responds" to the "impression" which it receives from a man—often, at once, with the first movement; otherwise, with longer acquaintance—involuntarily with preference or dislike, perhaps also with indifference; it feels drawn or repelled; and, it can concern [itself] there in an absolutely meaningful coming-to-grips of its own being [*Seins*] with the foreign; a feeling-itself-drawn to what promises its enrichment and challenge, a detour for someone for whom it signifies a danger.[18]

Sister Benedicta's approach, both Thomistic and phenomenological, to the passions of love and hate continues when she argues that it is extremely important to advert to a passion and make a decision about it:

> On the other hand, here serious deceptions are possible: externals can cover the true being [*Sein*] of man and with this, also the significance which belongs to him for others. These natural impulses are, therefore, not

something one simply may ignore; it is, however, also not "rational" to abandon them; they are a verification with the help of the intellect and an influence accessible through the will and are needed.[19]

The human person is able to make a decision for or against a particular passion, while at the same time adverting to it as real. In the third step, Stein describes how this can happen with respect to the passions of aversion or hate:

> And, against all games, the inclination and disinclination stand upright by the command of the Lord: You shouldst serve with charity others as yourself. This holds without conditions and deductions. . . . The saint who resolves on it in confidence to heroically love his enemy, has experienced that he has the freedom to love. A natural aversion is perhaps still maintained for a time; however, it is powerless and not able to influence behavior which is guided by supernatural love. . . . Love is, indeed his ultimate sense of devotion of his own being [*Seins*] and becoming-one with the beloved.[20]

In her doctoral dissertation, *On the Problem of Empathy*, Stein made some other important distinctions between a primordial experience and a secondary experience of the same passion. She gives an example of this distinction when discussing joy:

> I actively bring to mind a former joy, for example, of a passed examination. I transfer myself into it, i.e., I turn to the joyful event and depict it to myself in all its joyfulness. Suddenly I notice that I, this primordial,

remembering "I," am full of joy. I remember the joyful event and take primordial joy in the remembered event. However, the memory joy and the memory "I" have vanished or, at most, persist beside the primordial joy and the primordial "I." Naturally, this primordial joy over past events can also occur directly. . . . Finally, I may be primordially joyful over the past joy, making the difference between these two acts especially prominent.[21]

This distinction between two different experiences of joy, primordial and secondary, soon becomes the foundation for her original analysis of empathy. Stein lays the foundation for her more complex analysis of interpersonal relations and love of friendship.

Now let us take the parallel to empathy. My friend comes to me beaming with joy and tells me he has passed his examination. I comprehend his joy empathically; transferring myself into it, I comprehend the joyfulness of the event and am now primordially joyful over it myself. I can also be joyful without first comprehending the joy of the other. Should the examination candidate step into the tense, impatient family circle and impart the joyful news, in the first place, they will be primordially joyful over his news. Only when they have been "joyful long enough" themselves, will they be joyful over their joy or, perhaps as the third possibility, be joyful over his joy. But his joy is neither given to us as primordial joy over the event nor as primordial joy over his joy. Rather it is given as this non-primordial act of empathy that we have already described more precisely.[22]

In the following passage Edith introduces the theory that in friendship and love a human passion can be a shared experience even in a primordial way:

> Should empathy persist beside primordial joy over the joyful event (beside the comprehension of the joy of the other), and, moreover, should the other really be conscious of the event as joyful (possibly it is also joyful for me, for example, if this passed examination is the condition of a trip together so that I am happy for him as the means to it), we can designate this primordial act as joy-with-him or, more generally, as fellow feeling. . . . The joy of the most intimate participant will generally be more intense and enduring than the other's joy. But it is also possible for the other's joy to be more intense. They may be naturally capable of more intense feelings than he; they may be "altruistic" and "value for others" eo ipso mean more to them than "values for themselves"; finally, this even may have lost some of its value through circumstances unknown to the others. On the other hand, in the ideal case (where there is no deception) empathic joy expressly claims to be the same in every respect as comprehended joy, to have the same content and only a different mode of being given.[23]

With this theoretical introduction of Stein's phenomenological analysis of the human passions, I now turn more directly to her passion for truth and the way in which human friendships supported and strengthened her love for truth.

The Love of Truth

In *Fides et Ratio* (On the Relationship between Faith and Reason), Pope John Paul II identifies the desire for truth as a fundamental passion in human nature: "Born and nurtured when the human being first asked questions about the reason for things and their purpose, philosophy shows in different modes and forms that the desire for truth is part of human nature itself."[24] Stein, in her essay "Husserl and Aquinas: A Comparison," describes this drive within the philosopher as part of the potentiality of human nature:

> the spirit of genuine philosophy alive in every true philosopher, in anyone who cannot resist an inner need to search out the logos [logos, mind, reason] of this world, its ratio (as Thomas translated the word). The born philosopher brings this spirit with him into the world— as potency, in Thomistic terminology. The potency becomes actualized when he meets a mature philosopher, a "teacher." This is the way true philosophers reach out to one another over the bounds of space and time.[25]

In *Fides et Ratio* John Paul II also proposes Stein and Aquinas as models of how to integrate faith and reason in the elaboration of pathways to the truth. Stein herself reflected on this question when she noted a material and formal dependence of philosophy on faith and the place of supernatural reason in philosophy.[26] One of her axioms is summarized as "Philosophy aspires after truth to the greatest possible extent and with the greatest possible certainty."[27]

As a young woman Stein was driven by an intellectual desire for truth, a love for truth, and an intellectual
delight and joy in discovering truth. Her passion for
truth is captured by several authors in many recent works:
Joyce Avrech Berkman, Angela Ales Bello, Terry Wright,
Rhonda Chervin, and Josephine Koeppel, O.C.D.[28]
An important characteristic of Stein's philosophical
passion for truth is her collaboration with others in the
search for objective truth. Stein describes how she forged
a friendship with three girlfriends to study psychology,
medicine, and philosophy. "Without a moment's hesita-
tion . . . we plunged into Kant's *Critique of Pure Reason*.
I no longer recall how far into it we got. With death-de-
fying fervor, during one semester, we plowed through all
of Meumann's *Experimental Psychology*."[29] Their shared
intellectual excitement flowed over into her private life as
well. She continues her account:

> I had just finished my first semester (at the university)
> and had brought along Spinoza's *Ethics* to read during
> that vacation. I was never found without the small book.
> If we went into the woods, I carried it in the pocket of
> my rainproof cape; and while the others lolled around
> under the trees, I would search out a deer lookout,
> climb up to it, and then become absorbed, alternately,
> in deductions about the sole substance, and then in the
> view of sky, mountains, and woods.[30]

These complementary ways of expressing her love
for truth include both dialogue with friends and times
of solitary contemplation. Added to this is a vigorous

disposition to work hard on writing. She provides us with a remarkable description of this process as she worked on her doctoral dissertation in 1916.

> Now I resolutely put aside everything derived from other sources and began, entirely at rock bottom, to make an objective examination of the problem of empathy according to phenomenological methods. Oh, what a difference compared to my former efforts! Of course, each morning I seated myself at my desk with some trepidation. I was like a tiny dot in limitless space. Would anything come to me out of this great expanse— anything which I could grasp? I lay as far back as I could in my chair, and strenuously focused my mind on what at the moment I deemed the most vital question. After a while, it seemed as though light began to dawn. Then I was able, at least, to formulate a question and to find ways to attack it. And as soon as one point became clear, new questions arose in various directions (Husserl used to call these "new horizons"). . . . [P]age after page was filled. The writing would bring a rosy glow to my face, and an unfamiliar feeling of happiness surged through me. . . . I was amazed at all the knowledge I now had about things of which I had been totally unaware a few hours earlier.[31]

Later on in her life, Sister Benedicta lost this early enthusiasm for her philosophical writing, but she still worked because that was her gift to others. In a letter written in 1934 to the provincial of the Dominican fathers in Cologne, she writes:

In recent years, it has cost me a great deal to become ever more aware that I lack the necessary equipment to undertake the tremendous intellectual tasks imposed on us by our times, which I am convinced I see very clearly.

Even more painful is the insight that it is too late to make up these deficiencies. I would be very happy not to have to do any more writing. But as long as my superiors are of the opinion that through my knowledge I may be able and obligated to be of use to others, I shall have to accept the fact that the shortcomings, so well known to me, will also become apparent to others.[32]

One of the most striking aspects of her love for truth was her engagement in dialogues of friendship to help correct her errors and participate in a community of Catholic scholars once she had converted to the faith (requesting baptism, as is so often reported after reading the life of Teresa of Ávila with the words: "This is the Truth!").[33] Her love of truth led her to her great love of friendship; and her love of friendship led her to an evergreater love of truth. Aquinas identified four essential characteristics of friendship: it is based on benevolence, is mutual, is founded on communication, and is a form of charity.[34] These characteristics flourished among Stein and her philosopher friends: Roman Ingarden, Jacques and Raïssa Maritain , and Hedwig Conrad-Martius. Each of these examples will be described in turn.

We saw above how in undergraduate university Stein studied philosophy and psychology together with her friends. In graduate school, among her many friends was Roman Ingarden (1873–1970), who later introduced her work to the young Karol Wojtyla. Ingarden himself described his intimate intellectual friendship with Stein:

> [W]e conversed together every day [1916–17] on many subjects, but especially on various details of her personal activities as an assistant [to Husserl]. . . . When eventually I went for several months to my own country, a lively correspondence took place between us. [When] I came back to Freiburg [1917–18] . . . [h]ardly a day passed during that period in which we did not meet and talk together. Having passed my doctor's degree examination I returned to Cracow, and from that time till the outbreak of war in 1939 we met only twice; . . . but during the whole of that period we continually wrote letters to each other. After the end of the war I was told that she had been killed.[35]

Alasdair MacIntyre, in *Edith Stein: A Philosophical Prologue, 1913–1922*, often refers to the relationship between these two intellectual friends.[36] From the more than 150 letters exchanged in their correspondence between 1917 and 1918, Stein shares her work of preparing the manuscript of "the Master" Husserl's Part II of *Ideas* for publication. She also speaks with Ingarden about her frustration that her relationship with Husserl is not one of genuine collaboration, even though she is offering introductory classes in phenomenology: "[O]nly habilitation [prerequisite for appointment as professor] is out of reach for me (though Elly [Husserl's daughter Elisabeth] pleaded my case in that regard), for that is opposed 'on principle.'"[37]

In a letter she thanks Ingarden for his critique of her
doctoral dissertation and adds that she needs to clarify the concept of psyche, which in turn is dependent
upon the clarification of the concept of intellect. Stein
adds: "I must learn to go into greater depth. In any case,
I believe that is the weak spot of my talent. Basically, I
work more with my poor understanding than with intuitive gifts; perhaps that is why I am especially suited to
be the Master's assistant."[38] During this period she was
working for Husserl on his concept of the person, as she
often shared with Ingarden. At the same time, however,
she tells her friend: "At present I am occupying myself
somewhat with physics and mathematics (in the interest
of natural philosophy)."[39] Stein tried to mediate for Ingarden with Husserl, and she writes about her failure. As
MacIntyre recounts: "In a letter to Roman Ingarden in
June (1918) she tells how she had visited Husserl in the
hope of discussing Ingarden's work with him, but 'on the
doorstep I met the little Heidegger, the three of us took
a long walk—very nice—and talked about the philosophy of religion.'"[40]

The second friendship that Stein loved was with
Jacques and Raïssa Maritain. Although this relationship
did not have the intimacy of her student friendships, it
offered a new experience of love of professional friendship
among scholars. Jacques Maritain (1882–1973), invited
Stein, when she was a professor at the College Marianum
in Münster, at the height of her research and lectures on
the concept of woman, to attend some intellectual retreats
with others interested in Aquinas. Maritain describes

the dynamics of the study circles and annual retreats at Meudon [France], one of which Stein attended:

> [T]hose who attended them formed a most varied ensemble. There were young persons and old persons, male students and female students, and professors— laymen (in the majority), priests and religious— professional philosophers, doctors, poets, musicians, men engaged in practical life, those who were learned and those who were uneducated—Catholics (in the majority), but also unbelievers, Jews, Orthodox, Protestants. . . . The unity came either from a *profound love*, or from a more or less great interest in Thomist thought. It came also from *the climate of friendship* and of liberty in which all were received.
>
> They did not go to class. . . . They were received into the hearth of a family, they were the guests of Raïssa Maritain. Such meetings and such a work in common are inconceivable without a feminine atmosphere. . . .
>
> Without her [Raïssa]—and without her little sister [Vera]—there would have been no Thomist circles, any more than there would have been a Meudon (any more than there would have been a Jacques Maritain).[41]

In one letter of 1932, Stein writes to Jacques Maritain: "My heartfelt thanks for your kindness in sending me your important new work [*The Degrees of Knowledge*]. To study it will be a great gain for me. . . . I recall with great pleasure the wonderful day in Juvisy and the hours spent in your home. With grateful and most cordial greetings to your dear wife (Raïssa). . . ."[42] Jacques Maritain later wrote about his own experience of meeting Stein in earlier years: "How can one describe the purity, the light which shone from Edith Stein at the time of her conversion, the total generosity which one felt in her and which was to bear fruit in martyrdom?"[43]

In 1933, Stein wrote a second letter to Jacques and Raïssa Maritain, in which she thanked them for another gift:

> You have given me great joy with your beautiful book [no indication of which book]. . . . I, too, cherish a grateful memory of the beautiful hours in Juvisy and Meudon. All during the past month I have been greatly consoled by the thought of having such *good friends united to us by the bond of faith*. I no longer have my position with the Pedagogical Institute and "All things work together for the good of those who *love* God."[44]

Shortly after Hitler came into power, all those with Jewish heritage were denied the opportunity to teach; and so Stein then requested entrance into the Carmelite monastery in Cologne. She seemed to have experienced a foretaste of the deeper reality of Christian friendship that builds communion on earth that will become eternal in heaven. St. Augustine, St. Thomas Aquinas, Aelred of Rivaux, and the Maritains all described Christian friendship as the foundation for eternal relations among human beings.[45]

In the third example, Stein developed a great love for her friend Hedwig Conrad-Martius (1888–1966), who had published several books and major articles on ontology and metaphysics, establishing herself as "the 'first lady' of German philosophy."[46] Their correspondence began around 1918 with a formal salutation of "Dear Frau Dr. Conrad" and signed "Best regards, Edith Stein"; and it developed by 1938 into the more intimate salutation of "Dear Hatti" and signed "In the love of Christ, your Benedicta."[47] Conrad-Martius, completed her doctoral dissertation[48] and finally secured a teaching position in philosophy at the University of Munich in 1949, which she held for more than fifteen years.[49] Martius and Stein shared a love of metaphysics, phenomenology (Husserl in particular), and the profound bond of Conrad-Martius being her "beloved baptismal sponsor" when Stein was received into the Catholic Church in 1922.[50]

In some of their letters they clarified points of agreement and disagreement in their respective thoughts about the relation of ontology to metaphysics and about the proper range of metaphysical inquiry. For example, in 1932 Stein states: "But I have another idea about metaphysics: as a grasp of the whole of reality through an inclusion of revealed truth, and therefore grounded on philosophy *and* theology."[51] In 1933, she describes more of her methodology and the cross-fertilization of their two philosophical minds: "[T]he paper on *Potency and Act* that I wrote in the summer of 1931 . . . is in no way in a condition ready for publication and I believe I've advanced in many points this winter, but at least you would see in it the attempt to come from a scholasticism to phenomenology, and vice versa. (You might also be moved . . . to make available to me as soon as possible your work on matter and mind and the one on substance and soul.)"[52]

In the same letter Stein admits to her godmother her insecurity as a scholar and asks for her intercessory prayers:

> Yes, if you will undertake to mediate for your godchild the meaning of her life's task, I shall be very glad to send you this monstrous opus [on Catholic pedagogy], obviously so you may criticize it severely; a *radical* critique for I have often asked myself whether, in fact, I am not overreaching my own capabilities in the philosophical work I have undertaken. I believe this doubt haunts me ever since Lipps . . . criticized my long article in the fifth *Jahrbuch* so radically: and at that same time Frau Reinach attempted to show me that the shortcomings in my work . . . lay in the fact of my having far deeper shortcomings.[53]

The beautiful example of intellectual friendship that this letter reveals puts a face-to-face dialogue on the metaphysical retrieval that Stein will develop. Even with suffering from the sting of previous critiques, she asks her friend to give her a radical critique as well. Before long they exchanged complete copies of each other's collected works.[54]

The significance of this dynamic of critique and honest evaluation of philosophical work between the two women philosophers in the first part of the twentieth century anticipates an important development in the church in the middle of the century. In 1964 Pope Paul VI, in chapter three of *Ecclesiam Suam*, declared: "To this internal drive of charity which seeks expression in the external gift of charity, we will apply the word 'dialogue.'"[55] Just four years later the young Karol Wojtyla, in *The Acting Person*, describes critical dialogue as "the one that may be applied to the formation and the strengthening of inter-human solidarity through the attitude of opposition . . . The principle of dialogue seems to be best suited to select and bring out what in controversial situations is right and true, and to eliminate any partial, preconceived, or subjective views and attitudes."[56] Pope John Paul II developed this notion further in *Ut Unum Sint*:

> If prayer is the "soul" . . . of the yearning for unity, it is the basis and support for *everything the council defines as "dialogue."* This definition is certainly not unrelated to today's *personalist way of thinking.* The capacity for "dialogue" is rooted in the nature of the person and his dignity. As seen by philosophy, this approach is linked to the Christian truth concerning man as expressed by the Council: man is in fact "the only creature on earth which God willed for itself"; thus he cannot "fully find himself except through a sincere gift of himself." Dialogue is an indispensable step along the path *towards human self-realization*, the self-realization both of *each individual* and of *every human community.* Although the concept of "dialogue" might appear to give priority to the cognitive dimension. It involves the human subject in his or her entirety; dialogue between communities involves in a particular way the subjectivity of each.

This truth about dialogue, so profoundly expressed by Pope Paul VI in his encyclical *Ecclesiam Suam*, was also taken up by the Second Vatican Council in its teaching and ecumenical activity. Dialogue is not simply an exchange of ideas. In some ways it is always an "exchange of gifts."[57]

Stein anticipated in her Christian friendship with Conrad-Martius the authentic attitude of interpersonal engagement encouraged by Pope John Paul II in *Vita Consecrata*:

> The experience of recent years widely confirms that *"dialogue is the new name of charity,"* especially within the Church. Dialogue helps us to see the true implications of problems and allows them to be addressed with greater hope of success. *The consecrated life*, by the very fact that it promotes the value of fraternal life, *provides a privileged experience of dialogue.*[58]

It was very fortunate that Conrad-Martius had all of Stein's works, for upon entering religious life she took nothing with her. By the end of 1934 she now writes as Sister Benedicta to her old friend: "I am very grateful that you occupy yourself with *Akt und Potenz* [Act and Potency]. I had just intended to ask you for that book in this letter. Mother Subprioress is very eager for me to prepare it for publication. . . . I would appreciate very much knowing whether you consider it worth publishing."[59] Then five months later, "For the past few days our Father Provincial was here with us and he has given me the task of preparing *Akt und Potenz* for publication. . . . [T]he discussion of your *Metaphysische Gespräche* [Metaphysical Discourses] cannot remain as it is. . . . Now I would have to use Seinsstufen [Degrees of Being] and the book on plants as a basis. I would be most grateful if you could send me both as soon as possible."[60]

By summer 1935, Sister Benedicta is deep into the revision process and shares with Conrad-Martius: "I was stuck in the first part of my manuscript and, to get on with it, I urgently needed to consult other sources, particularly Aristotle and Thomas . . . [and] the article on substance and soul that you wrote for *Recherches*, and I need it badly. . . . Probably very little of my manuscript will remain, for I now find it completely inadequate."[61] Sister Benedicta clarifies for Conrad-Martius the new direction that she is taking in her thought in another letter a few months later: "I seem to be more Platonic and more Augustinian than you, perhaps precisely because I proceed from Aristotle–Thomas. What I say about substance resulted from a tough wrestling to understand the Aristotelian *ousia* [substance.] Essentially I owe the whole breakthrough from the first draft to the second to my work with Aristotle."[62]

In an additional paragraph with significance for the history of the concept of woman, Sister Benedicta invites Conrad-Martius to share her intellectual friendship with Gertrud von le Fort: "I believe you would be pleased to read Gertrud von le Fort's book *Die ewige Frau* [The Eternal Woman]. . . . It has three sections: The Eternal Woman, Woman in Time, The Timeless Woman. The final section is [on] the mother. And you would make Gertrud von le Fort very happy were you to send her the plant book; *you will notice yourself how much the two belong together.* After all, at my very first meeting with Gertrud von le Fort I found a strong affinity with you. It would be wonderful if the two of you got in touch."[63] In this attempt to join the two scholars, one a metaphysician and the other a poet, Sister Benedicta, perhaps unknowingly, begins to prepare the way for her departure from their lives.

From this time on, their correspondence begins to share the dark clouds that were gathering in Germany, that is, nephews going to America and the suffering and death of her mother. Yet Sister Benedicta continues her writing on what will become *Finite and Eternal Being*: "Now I have been able to resume work on the endless opus. For several weeks I have been plaguing myself with an appendix on [Martin] Heidegger's *Philosophy of Being*. And, because I had to plow through all his works to do so, I could not even read your reprints."[64] In another letter of 1936, after sharing her news of the possible publication of her "small attempt" at ontology, she supported her friend: "Your ontology is eminently ahead of mine, even if it is not written; it stands behind everything you have said and written in the past years." She asks Conrad-Martius for her review of Heidegger's *Being and Time*; and "[b]esides that I would like *very* much to have an introductory presentation on the latest on atomic theory, if you have anything on that."[65] This request is likely a response to the excitement in the 1930s upon the meetings of the International Congress for the Unity of Science in Copenhagen in 1934 and 1936. At the center of this excitement was the challenge for positivism of the developing restated claims of Niels Bohr for theories of complementarity for the relations between different explanatory theories of kinetic-dynamic complementarity and wave-particle complementarity.[66]

By 1938 her manuscript *Finite and Eternal Being* was being bounced around different publishers who apparently feared publishing it because of the situation in Germany and Austria with respect to her Jewish heritage. In 1940 Sister Benedicta sent her last very guarded letter, with no salutation, but asked if Conrad-Martius could send her a new book so that she could write something again, "since the printing of the book came to a standstill."[67]

Love of God through Participation in the Passion of Christ

The passion of Christ is related to the gift of martyrdom as a suffering for the faith, in obedience to a call from God the Father, for the redemption of others. It also included a notion of passing over or alteration due to an action of another with a specific goal of sharing in the redemptive sufferings of Christ.[68] James Collins notes that Stein was discussing this mystery as early as a lecture in 1931:

> In company with [Erich] Przywara and other leaders of German Catholic intellectual life she participated in the many conferences which were indicative of a deep-rooted and articulate religious quickening. Her lectures delivered before university audiences as well as at popular meetings of Catholic associations sought to impart to others the fruit of her meditation upon the Mystery of Faith and the mystery of being. In one such address

given at Bendorf-on-Rhein she affirmed her belief that all our educational and cultural endeavor must be directed to forming ourselves on the model of the Person of Jesus Christ. To become an *alter Christus* is the norm of our conduct, the final goal of earthly existence.[69]

In *Finite and Eternal Being*, Sister Benedicta describes how the soul acts as the three-dimensional meeting space for the dual nature of the essence of a particular person:

> The soul is the "space in the center of the body-soul-spiritual totality. As *sentient soul it abides in the body*, in all its members and parts, receiving impulses and influences from it and working upon it formatively and with a view to its preservation. As *spiritual soul it rises above itself*, gaining insight into a world that lies beyond its own self—a world of things, persons, and events—communicating with this world and receiving its influences. . . . [I]n the soul the personal I is in its very home. . . . Here, in this inwardness of the soul everything that enters from these worlds is weighed and judged, and here there takes place the appropriation of that which becomes the most personal property and a constituent part of the self—that which, figuratively speaking, "becomes flesh and blood."
>
> . . . The soul cannot live without receiving. . . . [T]he recipient is an existent with an essence of nature of its own (i.e., an *ousia*), an existent which has its own specific mode of receiving and which incorporates into its own being that which has been received. What discloses and reveals itself in these experiences is

the very essence or nature of the soul, with all the qualities and powers that are rooted in the essence. In these experiences the soul appropriates to itself what it needs in order to become what it is destined to be.[70]

When considering the human being in general, Sister Benedicta argues, according to the Reinhardt translation, that "[n]ot the essential form but only the pure form of the essence of which things '*partake*' by their essential form is what is 'communicable' to a multitude of individual things."[71] In the Gooch translation, the same passage reads: "'Participating' in a multiplicity of individual things is not the form of a nature, but a pure form or essence with which things '*participate*' through their form of a nature."[72] Either by participation or partaking, the pure form of human being is communicated to the essential form of an individual thing of its kind:

> [T]he being human of this particular human being is actual and actuating in this person. This person shares it with no other human being. It is not, prior to the person's own being, but steps into existence together with the person. It determines *what* this particular human being is at any particular time, and this changing is what expresses a more or less extensive approximation to the end, i.e., to the *pure form*.[73]

The pure form is outside of time and space, but as a real end it provides the goal for the actualization of an individual woman or man. In Sister Benedicta's words: "The human being who attains to his or her end does not thereby become a *pure form* but rather a perfect image or copy of the pure form. And whether the person attains to the end or not, the person bears within the self the 'seed' of the end."[74] From this we can say that the canonization of Edith Stein/Teresa Benedicta of the Cross implies that she became a perfect copy of the pure form of human being and of the unique pure form of her particular identity as that specific woman philosopher who lived in Germany between 1891 and 1942.

In 1936, Sister Benedicta was asked to write a book about the mystical way of St. John of the Cross, the sixteenth-century cofounder with St. Teresa of Ávila of the Carmelite reform. She titled the work *The Science of the Cross*; and in it she directly linked the passion of Christ with the dark night of the soul: "To engage in battle with one's desires or to take up one's Cross means actively to enter into the Dark Night."[75]

In her final years, some of the ways that Sister Benedicta lived her spiritual passion of love for the passion of Christ may be seen in her correspondence and in others' witness to her actions. In 1938 she wrote to Mother Petra Brüning of the Ursuline order, from Cologne Carmel, describing her vocation, the suffering of her family members, and the facts of her current situation:

December 9, 1938

Dear Reverend Mother,

Many thanks for your loving letter of November 23. I must tell you that I already brought my religious name with me into the house as a postulant. I received it exactly as I requested it. By the cross I understood the destiny of God's people which, even at that time, began to announce itself. I thought that those who recognized it as the cross of Christ had to take it upon themselves in the name of all. Certainly, today I know more of what it means to be wedded to the Lord in the sign of the Cross. Of course, one can never comprehend it, for it is a mystery. . . .

Our Reverend Mother has asked our sisters in Echt (Holland) to receive me. Today their loving acceptance arrived. If it is possible to get all the necessary papers together in time, we would like to make the transfer even before December 31st. These are the facts.

And now I would like to wish you a very grace-filled Christmas feast. As the atmosphere around us grows steadily darker, all the more must we open our hearts for light from above. Most cordial thanks once more for all the *love* you have shown me in these five years in the Order. Since your way sometimes leads to Holland, I may even have the hope of seeing you again. I commend myself to your prayers for the next weeks and months.

In caritate Regis qui venturus est (in the *love* of the King who is to come), your grateful,

Sister Teresa Benedicta a Cruce[76]

In another letter written in 1940 to Sister Agnella Stadtmüller, O.P., the goal of St. John of the Cross's mystical way of prayer is stated clearly and simply:

"*Pure love*" for our holy Father John of the Cross means *loving God for his own sake*, with a heart that is free from all attachments to anything created: to itself and to other creatures, but also to all consolations and the like which God can grant the soul, to all particular forms of devotion, etc.; with a heart that wants nothing more than that God's will be done, that allows itself to be led by God without any resistance.[77]

Sister Benedicta continues by describing to her Dominican friend both the value and the method of this self-passion, or dying to self:

Should we strive for *perfect love*, you ask? Absolutely. For this we were created. [Perfect love] will be our eternal life, and here we have to seek to come as close to it as possible. Jesus became incarnate in order to be our way. What can we do? Try with all our might to be empty: the senses mortified; the memory as free as possible from all images of this world and, through hope, directed toward heaven; the understanding stripped of natural seeking and ruminating, directed to God in the straightforward gaze of faith; the will (as I have already said) *surrendered to God in love*.

This can be said very simply, but the work of an entire life would not attain the goal were God not to do the most essential. In the meantime we may be confident that he will not fail to give grace if we faithfully do the little we can do.[78]

She concludes that if a person willingly engages in the battle of the active night of the senses, or accepts the suffering of the passive night of the senses, then the person "exchanges sensual for spiritual joy and remains permanently united to God."[79]

On August 7, 1942, the transport in which Sister Benedicta and her sister Rosa were traveling to their death at Auschwitz stopped at the train station of Schifferstadt, not far from the town of Speyer where Stein had lived and taught for so many years at the Dominican school. Apparently the prisoners were allowed some access to the outside air as the train waited on a side rail. Stein identified herself to the station master, Valentine Fouquet; and she sent greetings to the Schwind family, who resided nearby, and to the sisters of St. Magdalena's convent. She then added the comment, "We are heading east."

Later that same day, having been transferred to a cattle train, she reportedly stopped briefly in her old hometown of Breslau and was reportedly sighted by the postal worker Johannes Weiners, who was working in the railroad depot in Breslau (now in Poland). Weiners noticed the nun appearing at the entrance of the railway car as the door was slid open by a guard. After their initial conversation, Sister Benedicta looked around to see where she was; then she said: "This is my beloved hometown. I will never see it again." She added: "We are riding to our death." Johannes Weiners asked her: "Do your companion prisoners believe that also?" She answered: "It's better that they do not know it."

The account continues with a description of the postal workers arguing among themselves whether they should do anything for those in the railway car. When some of them asked her if they could bring them any food or drink, she answered: "No, thank you, we accept nothing."[80] These gentle words of refusal, of gratitude, and of detachment are the final words recorded from her. If Sister Benedicta spoke these words as a way to protect the railroad workers from retribution, then the act of charity through self-denial would have freed the postal workers from their difficult situation. Other accounts of people who observed Sister Benedicta during the transport to her death record that she gave special attention to the needs of the children and of their mothers during this traumatic time.[81]

At her canonization, Pope John Paul II described her as "a Catholic during Nazi persecution, [who] remained faithful to the crucified Lord Jesus Christ, and as a Jew, to her people in loving faithfulness."[82] Pope John Paul II declared St. Teresa Benedicta of the Cross/Edith Stein, a martyr of the faith. To conclude: the following poem written by Sister Benedicta provides a holy echo of the chamber in which she gave her life of Bridal Love to her Bridegroom, Jesus Christ:

> The inmost chamber of the human soul
> Is favourite dwelling to the Trinity,
> His heavenly throne right here on earth.
>
> To free this heav'nly realm from hostile hand,
> God's Son descended as the Son of Man.
> He gave His blood as ransom.
>
> Within the heart of Jesus pierced with lances,
> The realm of heaven and earth become united.
> And here we find the spring of life itself.

This is the heart of Trinity divine,
The center also of all human hearts.
Source of our life from God.

It draws us close with its mysterious might,
It keeps us safe within the Father's lap
And floods us with the Holy Spirit.[83]

Notes

1. Father Eleutherius Winance, O.S.B., was my professor of phenomenology at Claremont Graduate School, second semester of 1963–64; and he was instrumental in my being received into the Catholic Church at St. Andrew's Priory, Gaudete Sunday, December 13, 1964. It is with great joy that I dedicate the publication of this essay to him in honor of his one-hundredth birthday, July 10, 2009. This paper was presented at the Edith Stein Project Conference, University of Notre Dame, February 14, 2009. Since it draws upon phenomenology and witnesses to the value of intellectual and spiritual friendship among philosophers, it seems particularly appropriate for inclusion in a publication in honor of Father Winance, who fostered these precious values among his graduate students at Claremont. I graduated (Christine Hope Allen) with a PhD in philosophy in 1967 and have taught in this field ever since at Concordia University–Sir George Williams University, Montreal, from 1969 to 1996, and St. John Vianney Theological Seminary, Denver, from 1998 to 2012).

2. Material for this article is extracted and revised from Prudence Allen, "Sex and Gender Differentiation in Hildegard of Bingen and Edith Stein," *Communio* 20 (Summer 1993): 389–414; "The Passion of Saint Edith Stein," *Fides Quarens Intellectum* 1, no. 2 (Winter 2001): 201–50; Elizabeth A. Mitchell, *Edith Stein: Seeker of Truth* (Denver: Endow, 2008); and *The Concept of Woman*, vol. 3, The Search for Communion of Persons *1500–2015*, Pt. 1, Metaphysics (Grand Rapids, Mich.: Eerdmans, 2016), chap. 5.

3. Jude Dougherty states in "Edith Stein: The Convert in Search of Illumination," in *Western Creed, Western Identity* (Washington, D.C.:

Catholic University of America Press, 2000), that "long before her baptism she began to study Saint Thomas" (204). Noting that after her baptism Stein began a systematic study and translation of Aquinas, Ralph McInerny asks in his essay "Edith Stein and Thomism," in *Edith Stein Symposium: Teresian Culture,* ed. John Sullivan, O.C.D., Carmelite Studies, vol. 4 (1987): 74–87, "Why of all the great doctors of the Church does she turn first to St. Thomas Aquinas? There seems little doubt that she does so because the Church has put him forth as the preeminent master of Catholic intellectuals. Her response is one of docility" (80).

4. Edith Stein, *Endliches und Ewiges Sein: Versuch eines Aufstiegs zum Sinn des Seins,* 2nd ed. (ESW, vol. 6) (Freiburg: Herder, 1962); translated by Augustine Spiegelman Gooch as *Finite and Eternal Being: Attempt at an Ascent to the Meaning of Being* (PhD diss., University of Dallas, 1981), 636. All the passages in my paper were taken from the Gooch translation unless otherwise indicated with the words (Reinhardt translation). Square brackets are used occasionally to indicate Gooch's references to the original German. Kurt F. Reinhardt produced a later translation: *Finite and Eternal Being: An Attempt at an Ascent to the Meaning of Being,* CWES, vol. 9 (Washington, D.C.: ICS Publications, 2002). When this translation is used, it will be particularly identified.

5. Thomas Aquinas, *Summa Theologiae* (Westminster, Md.: Christian Classics, 1948), I–II, q. 22 (my emphasis).

6. For a detailed account of this aspect of passion, see Howard Gil Weil, *The Dynamic Aspect of Emotions in the Philosophy of St. Thomas Aquinas* (Rome: Pontificia Studiorium Universitas, A.S. Thoma Aq. en urbe, 1966).

7. The Catechism of the Catholic Church repeats this view of Aquinas: "In themselves passions are neither good nor evil. They are morally qualified only to the extent that they effectively engage reason and will" (1767); and "Strong feelings are not decisive for the morality of the holiness of persons; they are simply the inexhaustible reservoir of images and affections in which the moral life is expressed. Passions are morally good when they contribute to a good action, evil in the opposite case. Emotions and feelings can be taken up into the *virtues* or perverted by the *vices*" (1768).

8. See Aquinas, *Summa Theologiae* I–II, qq. 22–48.

9. Stein, *Finite and Eternal Being*, 636. The reference to Theodor Haecker is to *Schöpfer und Schöpfung* (Leipzig, Poland: Hegner 1934).

10. Stein, *On the Problem of Empathy*, trans. Waltraut Stein, CWES, vol. 3 (Washington, D.C.: ICS Publications, 1989), 104.

11. Ibid.

12. See Robert Sokolowski, *Introduction to Phenomenology* (Cambridge, England: University Press, 2000), 8–16. See also Max Scheler, *Formalism in Ethics and Non-Formal Ethics of Values* (Evanston, Ill.: Northwestern University Press, 1973), 1–11.

13. Stein, *On the Problem of Empathy*, 101.

14. Stein, *Life in a Jewish Family* (1891–1916), trans. Josephine Koeppel, O.C.D., CWES, vol. 1 (Washington, D.C.: ICS Publications, 1986), 172.

15. Aquinas, *Summa Theologiae* I–II, q. 29, a. 2.

16. Edith Stein Archive, Cologne Carmel, cited in Mitchell, *Edith Stein, Seeker of Truth*. See also the detailed description by Susanne M. Batzdorff, *Aunt Edith: The Jewish Heritage of a Catholic Saint* (Springfield, Ill.: Templegate, 1998), esp. chap. 10, 119–29.

17. Stein, *Life in a Jewish Family*, 319.

18. Stein, *Finite and Eternal Being*, 631.

19. Ibid.

20. Ibid., 632a.

21. Stein, *On the Problem of Empathy*, 14.

22. Ibid., 13.

23. Ibid., 14–15.

24. John Paul II, *Fides et ratio*, 3.

25. Stein, "Husserl and Aquinas: A Comparison, Version I," in *Knowledge and Faith*, trans. Walter Redmond, CWES, vol. 8 (Washington, D.C.: ICS Publications, 2000), 7–8. For a more complete analysis of Stein's work on Aquinas and Husserl, see Sister Mary Catharine Baseheart, S.C.N., *The Encounter of Husserl's Phenomenology and the Philosophy of St. Thomas in Selected Writings of Edith Stein* (PhD diss., University of Notre Dame, 1960). See also John Nota, "Edith Stein and Martin Heidegger," in Sullivan, ed., *Edith Stein Symposium: Teresian Culture*, 50–73.

26. Stein, "Husserl and Aquinas: A Comparison," 17–20.

27. Ibid., 17. See also Mary Catharine Baseheart, S.C.N., who states: "The most striking characteristic of her [Stein's] investigations has been mentioned above: her passionate pursuit of truth." *Person in the World: Introduction to the Philosophy of Edith Stein* (Dordrecht, The Netherlands/Boston/London: Kluwer Academic Publishers, 1997), x.

28. See Joyce Avrech Berkman, "The Intellectual Passion of Edith Stein: A Biographical Profile," in *Contemplating Edith Stein* (Notre Dame, Ind.: University of Notre Dame Press, 2006), 15–47; Angela Ales Bello, *Edith Stein: La passione per la verità* (Padova, Italy: Edizioni Messaggero Padova, 1999); Terry Wright, "Artistic Truth and the True Self in Edith Stein," *American Catholic Philosophical Quarterly* 82, no. 1 (Winter 2008): 127–42; Rhonda Chervin, "Edith Stein: Lover of Truth," in *Blessed by the Cross: Five Portraits of Edith Stein*, ed. James Sullivan (New Rochelle, N.Y.: Catholics United for the Faith, 1990), 17–20; Maria Ruiz Scaperlanda, "My Desire for Truth Was Itself a Prayer," in *Edith Stein: St. Teresa Benedicta of the Cross* (Huntington, Ind.: Our Sunday Visitor Inc., 2001), 59–60; and Josephine Koeppel, O.C.D., "Truth in Final Glory," in *Edith Stein: Philosopher and Mystic* (Collegeville, Minn.: Liturgical Press, 1990): 155–61.

29. Stein, *Life in a Jewish Family*, 122.

30. Ibid., 132.

31. Ibid., 376–77.

32. Stein to Father Laurentius Siemer, November 4, 1934, letter 184, in *Self-Portrait in Letters: 1916–1942*, trans. Josephine Koeppel, O.C.D., CWES, vol. 5 (Washington, D.C.: ICS Publications, 1993), 189; hereafter cited as *Letters*.

33. Joyce Berkman mentions also that Stein had carefully studied St. Ignatius's *Spiritual Exercises*, making a thirty-day retreat ending with her conversion. See Berkman, "The Intellectual Passion of Edith Stein," 36n73.

34. Aquinas, *Summa Theologiae* II–II, q. 23.

35. Roman Ingarden, "Edith Stein on Her Activity as an Assistant of Edmund Husserl: Extracts from the Letters of Edith Stein with a Commentary and Introductory Remarks," *Philosophy and Phenomenological Research* 23, no. 2 (December 1962): 155–75.

36. Alasdair MacIntyre, *Edith Stein: A Philosophical Prologue, 1913–1922* (Lanham/Oxford: Rowman and Littlefield Publishers, Inc., 2006), 74, 90. For example, between 1913 and 1916, "On her visit to Heidelberg, . . . she also deepened her friendship with Roman Ingarden . . . [who] was two years younger than Stein"; and from 1916 to 1922 after the war, "Roman Ingarden, on whom Stein had relied heavily for intellectual support, returned to a newly independent Poland."

37. Stein to Roman Ingarden, January 5, 1917, letter 3; January 28, 1917, letter 5; February 3, 1917, letter 6; February 9, 1917, letter 7; February 20, 1917, letter 8, in *Letters*, 3–4, 6–11. See also a letter from Stein to Sister Adelgundis Jaegerschmid, O.S.B., in which Stein describes her failed attempt to engage Heidegger in helping her (January 26, 1931, letter 85, in *Letters*, 83–84).

38. Stein to Roman Ingarden, April 27, 1917, letter 13, in *Letters*, 15.

39. Stein to Roman Ingarden, May 31, 1917, letter 14, in *Letters*, 17. See also Stein to Roman Ingarden, February 19, 1918, letter 19; February 28, 1918, letter 20, in *Letters*, 21–23.

40. MacIntyre, *Edith Stein*, 164. He cites a twice removed series of sources for this letter.

41. See Jacques Maritain, "Thomist Study Circles and Their Annual Retreats (1919–1939)," *Notebooks*, trans. Joseph W. Evans (Albany, N.Y.: Magi Books, Inc., 1984), 133–85, here 134–35, for his personal journals on the purposes and persons present at various meetings. Emphasis added.

42. Stein to Jacques Maritain, November 6, 1932, letter 125, in *Letters*, 124–25. Sarah Borden Sharkey notes that Stein does try to integrate some of Jacques Maritain's themes in her work *Finite and Eternal Being*, by employing Maritain's distinctions about Christian philosophy, in *Edith Stein* (London/New York: Continuum, 2003), 95.

43. Freda Mary Oben, *Edith Stein: Scholar, Feminist, Saint* (New York: Alba House, 1988), 19n25, which refers back to Jacques Maritain and forward to John M. Oesterreicher, *Walls Are Crumbling* (New York: Devin-Adair Co., 1950), vii.

44. Stein to Jacques and Raïssa Maritain, June 21, 1933, letter 145, in *Letters*, 146–47. In 1953 Jacques Maritain wrote another essay in which he referred to primordial forms of things that could be accessed through

the preconscious of an artist. There are interesting connections between Maritain's theme and Sister Teresa Benedicta's theme of pure forms. See Jacques Maritain, "The Preconscious Life of the Intellect," in *Creative Intuition in Art and Poetry* (New York: Meridian Books, 1955), esp. 69 (emphasis added).

45. See Prudence Allen, R.S.M., "Friendship, Gender, and Vocation," *Josephinum: Journal of Theology* 15, no. 1 (Winter/Spring 2008): 102–39.

46. James G. Hart, "Hedwig Conrad-Martius's Ontological Phenomenology" (PhD diss., University of Chicago Divinity School, 1972), 1. In addition to her doctoral dissertation, *Die erkenntnistheoretischen Grundlagen des Postivismus*, on the subject of the ground of the theory of knowledge of positivisms under Husserl at Göttingen in 1912, she published the following: *Our Anthology und Erscheinungslehre der realen Aussenwelt* (Halle, Germany: Niemeyer, 1916); *Metaphysische Gespraeche* (Halle, Germany: Niemeyer, 1921); *Realontologie* (Halle: Neimeyer, 1923); *Bios und Psyche* (Hamburg: Classen & Goverts, 1949); *Abstammungslehre* (Munich: Koesel, 1950); *Naturwissenschaftlich-metaphysische Perspectiven* (Heidelberg: F. H. Kerle, 1949); *Die Zeit* (Munich: Koesel, 1957); *Utopien der Menschenzuechtung, Der Sozialdarwinismus und seine Folgen* (Munich: Koesel, 1955); *Das Sein* (Munich: Koesel, 1957); *Der Raum* (Munich: Koesel, 1958); *Die Geistseele des Menschen* (Munich: Koesel, 1960); *Ser Selbstaufbau der Natur* (Munich: Koesel, 1961); and *Schriften our Philosophie*, I (1963), II (1964), and III (1965) (Munich: Koesel). See Hart, "Hedwig Conrad-Martius's Ontological Phenomenology," 639–41.

47. Stein to Hedwig Conrad-Martius, May 25, 1918, letter 23; and January 17, 1938, letter 257, in *Letters*, 26, 270.

48. See Hart, "Hedwig Conrad-Martius's Ontological Phenomenology," where he states that "[t]he work is referred to as 'die Preisschrift' because it won a prize at Göttingen. The university had offered a prize for the best essay on positivism. Husserl was willing to accept the work for a doctorate at Göttingen. However, because Göttingen did not recognize the 'real gymnasium' diploma of Conrad-Martius she took her degree at Munich under Alexander Pfänder—who acknowledged it immediately as a doctoral thesis," 12n1.

49. Ibid., 6.

50. See Oben, *Edith Stein*, 16–20.

51. Stein to Hedwig Conrad-Martius, November 13, 1932, letter 126, in *Letters*, 126.

52. Stein to Hedwig Conrad-Martius, February 24, 1933, letter 135, in *Letters*, 134.

53. Ibid., 135 (Stein's emphasis).

54. Stein to Hedwig Conrad-Martius, March 23, 1933, letter 138, in *Letters*, 137–38.

55. Pope Paul VI, *Ecclesiam suam* 64.

56. Karol Wojtyla, *The Acting Person* (Dordrecht, The Netherlands: D. Reidel, 1969), 344. The Polish edition was published in 1969.

57. John Paul II, *Ut unum sint* 28, referring to *Gaudium et spes* 24, and *Lumen Gentium* 13.

58. John Paul II, Post-Synodal Apostolic Exhortation *Vita Consecrata* 74. This principle is stated in the inverse in Congregation for Institutes of Consecrated Life, Fraternal Life in Community (1994): "Without dialogue and attentive listening, community members run the risk of living juxtaposed or parallel lives, a far cry from the ideal of fraternity," 32.

59. Stein to Hedwig Conrad-Martius, December 15, 1934, letter 189, in *Letters*, 194.

60. Stein to Hedwig Conrad-Martius, May 21, 1935, letter 201, in *Letters*, 206–7.

61. Stein to Hedwig Conrad-Martius, July 9, 1935, letter 205, in *Letters*, 212.

62. Stein to Hedwig Conrad-Martius, November 17, 1935, letter 213, in *Letters*, 220 (my emphasis). For an article on the relation between the early work of Stein on woman's *ethos* and Aristotle, see Jane Kelley Rodeheffer, "On Spiritual Maternity: Edith Stein, Aristotle, and the Nature of Woman," *Annual ACPA Proceedings* 72 (1999): 285–303.

63. Stein to Hedwig Conrad-Martius, November 17, 1935, letter 213, in *Letters*, 220. As a good friend, Sister Teresa Benedicta gave Conrad-Martius explicit directions on how to find the book and how to get in touch with Gertrude von le Fort.

64. Stein to Hedwig Conrad-Martius, August 20, 1936, letter 224, in *Letters*, 233–34. See also John Nota, "Edith Stein and Martin Heidegger," in Sullivan, ed., *Edith Stein Symposium: Teresian Culture*, 50–73.

65. Stein to Hedwig Conrad-Martius, October 10, 1936, letter 228, in *Letters,* 240. Niels Bohr's discovery of the principle of complementarity of classical and quantum physics with respect to understanding how to measure light as a wave or a particle would have been part of this new atomic theory that Sister Teresa Benedicta was seeking to understand. It is also significant that Dietrich von Hildebrand shortly after used the phrase "metaphysical complementarity" of a man and a woman in marriage, in his 1929 lecture *Die Ehe* (On Marriage).

66. See *The Philosophical Writings of Niels Bohr: Causality and Complementarity,* ed. Jan Faye and Henry J. Folse (Woodbridge, Conn.: Ox Bow Press, 1998). See especially the editor's introduction for a discussion of the complex relations between complementarity theories of logical positivism, realism, and metaphysics. See also the actual texts of his lectures on these themes between 1932 and 1938 in Cambridge, Copenhagen, and Warsaw, and publications in scientific journals during the same time frame up to and including 1962.

67. Stein to Hedwig Conrad-Martius, November 5, 1940, letter 315, in *Letters,* 326. See also Stein to Hedwig Conrad-Martius, January 17, 1938, letter 257, in *Letters,* 270–71.

68. See "Passion," in *The New Catholic Encyclopedia* (Washington, D.C.: Catholic University of America Press, 1967).

69. James Collins, "Edith Stein and the Advance of Phenomenology," *Thought: Fordham University Quarterly* 17, no. 67 (December 1942): 708.

70. Stein, *Finite and Eternal Being,* 373–74. Stein also speaks of an individual form. See Sarah Borden Sharkey, "Edith Stein and Thomas Aquinas on Being and Essence," *American Catholic Philosophical Association Quarterly* 82, no. 1 (Winter 2008): 87–104, for an excellent discussion of individual form.

71. Stein, *Finite and Eternal Being,* 486 (Reinhardt translation).

72. Stein, *Finite and Eternal Being,* [213], 319; and [445], 690 (Gooch translation).

73. Stein, *Finite and Eternal Being,* 226 (Reinhardt translation). (Stein's emphasis).

74. Ibid., 230.

75. Stein, *The Science of the Cross: A Study of St. John of the Cross* (Chicago: Henry Regnery Company, 1960), 32.

76. Stein to Mother Petra Brüning, O.S.U., December 9, 1938, letter 287, in *Letters,* 295–96 (emphasis added).

77. Stein to Sister Agnella Stadtmüller, O.P., March 30, 1940, letter 311, in *Letters,* 318 (emphasis added).

78. Ibid. (emphasis added).

79. Stein, *Cross,* 71.

80. Koeppel, in Stein, *Life in a Jewish Family,* 434.

81. For several detailed accounts of other witnesses, see Teresia Renata Posselt, O.C.D., *Edith Stein: The Life of a Philosopher and Carmelite* (Washington, D.C.: ICS Publications, 2005); in particular "The Way of the Cross," chap. 21: 211–22; and "The Last News," chap. 22: 223–31.

82. From the official program of the *Canonizzazione della beata Teresa Benedetta Della Croce/Edit Stein,* Piazza San Pietro, October 11, 1998, p. 32.

83. Stein, *Selected Writings* (Springfield, Ill.: Templegate, 1990), 49.

4

VALUE, EMOTIONS, AND EDITH STEIN

SARAH BORDEN SHARKEY

Fyodor Dostoyevsky's character Ivan Karamazov says to his brother, Alyosha, "It's not a matter of intellect or logic, it's loving with one's inside, with one's guts." Alyosha, the monk-in-training, agrees with his brother that "everyone should love life above everything in the world." Ivan then asks, "Love life more than the meaning of it?"[1] Ivan asks if we should love life, whether it has any value or meaning. For Ivan, loving life is quite distinct from understanding the world; our affective states have little to do with intelligently grasping reality.

This is not the traditional Christian story regarding emotions. Throughout the *Confessions*, Augustine condemns his "unholy loves," not because he is loving unholy things but because he is loving holy things in an unholy way. His wrong loves distorted his ability to recognize the differing ways in which things are holy and good; thus, Augustine calls us to a right *ordo amoris*, to rightly ordered loves, and this not only puts us in right relation with God but also puts us in right relation (including a right understanding) with our brothers, our sisters, and all creation.

This Christian story about the centrality of our loves and the need for a right *ordo amoris* has been revived and developed by several of the early twentieth-century phenomenologists, most famously Max Scheler, Dietrich von Hildebrand, and Edith Stein. In the following, I will focus on Stein's theory of emotions and look especially at her first two essays published in Edmund Husserl's 1922 *Jahrbuch* and translated as *Philosophy of Psychology and the Humanities*. In these texts, Stein describes the person and our affective experiences in a way that offers a defense for the claims (1) that our emotional responses are central to our character, and (2) that right emotional responses are necessary for true objectivity. Stein is convinced that values are not relative and that the quality of value perception, which occurs in our emotions, can be evaluated. In Stein's account, although we do have differing emotional responses and value judgments, it is not clear that, at least in all cases, we should.[2]

I will not be able in this essay to present fully Stein's defense for any of these claims, but I would like, first, to look at one piece of Stein's account of emotions, her analogy between emotions or emotional perception and other kinds of perception such as seeing or hearing. Second, I would like to consider two significant points of apparent disanalogy and, finally, to offer reasons for accepting the analogy despite the points of difference between emotional perception and other kinds of perception.[3]

Short Introduction to Phenomenology

Following the phenomenological tradition, Stein takes the analysis of consciousness and conscious experience as the appropriate starting point for philosophical investigation. One begins first with the subject and asks *how* we are related to the world;[4] however, there are a number of different ways in which we experience things. All thematic experience is intentional; that is, I see this *as* a podium, you *as* a human being, etc. We do not merely have sensations; we understand them as having structure and organization.

Not all of our awareness is so thematic: I can be tacitly aware of something that I might not yet have thematized. For example, I could be in a store with a friend, hurriedly trying to find a Father's Day card before the post office closes for the day. After leaving, my friend might ask, "Did you hear that great song that was playing?" Although it could take a moment or two, I might be able to remember. I might not have explicitly noticed the song at the time but, after the fact, can call it to mind. The condition of being able to remember and call to explicit awareness the song that I had already been aware of, albeit in a tacit way, indicates something that is not initially thematic to me.[5] We similarly have experiences of tacitly being aware of something but refusing to acknowledge and make thematic that of which we are aware. We might think of someone with a deep fear or phobia of spiders who suspects that there are spiders in the corner but, because of a need to accomplish some task, refuses to acknowledge or make that thematic. The person does not look nor ask whether spiders are present but just doggedly keeps working. Surely the condition of such studied avoidance is that one is not utterly ignorant; thus, it seems that experience can include both the thematic and the tacit.[6]

Stein further divides our awareness into various fields. We have aural, visual, and olfactory fields, for example, to which one can more or less attend. Stein understands thematic experience as "turning an eye toward" or making thematic that which is tacitly present in the various fields. One can be tacitly aware of one's tactile field while explicitly or thematically being aware of one's visual field; however, if one has a field, there is always at least some minimal awareness of that field.

Emotions as Affective Responses to Value

Stein uses this general model to develop an analogy between our perception of physical objects and our emotional perception of value.[7] (This analogy originates in Max Scheler's work; I will, however, follow Stein's rather than Scheler's account of the analogy.)[8] In order to perceive any visual object, one must have eyes to see and well-functioning cones and rods. A blind man cannot see a painting, nor can a deaf woman hear an orchestra. Similarly, Stein argues that an emotionally dead person cannot perceive value.[9] Further, just as one cannot hear sounds if one's ears are not stimulated, so one cannot perceive values if one's emotions are not stimulated. If a particular gorgeous landscape, for example, leaves me cold, then I have missed its beauty. Crucial to perceiving a value are certain feelings. (Stein distinguishes a number of types of feelings, including both emotions and moods. These are not identical and not all feelings indicate value perception.) We might say that just as perceiving a color is to see it, so, too, is perceiving a value to feel it. Values are, she claims, part of objects in a way analogous to other aspects or qualities of a thing. In order to perceive that part of the object, one must have an appropriate receptor. Just as the perception of color requires good eyesight, so the perception of value requires a well-developed heart and affective life.[10]

In addition, all perception requires sufficient energy and will to attend to the information given. When we are exhausted, we attend to fewer phenomena; we might be less quick to notice a mistake in a manuscript or a child running out in front of our car. Similarly, we might tune out altogether an entire sensory field, utterly ignoring the noisy house around us in order to read a book. We might be more or less attentive to our emotional states. We might misunderstand our emotions, confusing, for example, apprehensive excitement for fear. Stein is especially attentive to the confusion between an intense feeling of some emotion and an intense emotion. (We might think of an exhausted parent who certainly does not have a great anger when his child spills her milk, but who might nonetheless feel relatively minor anger and frustration quite intensely.)[11] We can fail to be attentive to our emotional lives and make such mistakes, or we might simply tune out our emotions and redirect our attention to other fields.

Stein claims that just as coming to understand the colors, sizes, shapes, sounds, and smells of the world requires that we have the ability to perceive each of these aspects of things as well as the energy and will to do so, so does perceiving value require that we have a differentiated and well-developed affective life, as well as the energy and will to attend to that field of information.

The notion of a value-free world is, Stein thinks, a misconception. One can only claim that objects are neutral or valueless by failing to attend to them. If one ignored a whole sense—for example, smell—one might think that the world is indeed scentless, but this hardly shows us much about the world, although it does say a tremendous amount about the perceiver. Analogously, to claim that the world is value-neutral is to ignore that by which we grasp the value of objects in the world.[12]

The Apparent Disanalogies, or Why We Might Hesitate about Stein's Comparison between Perceiving Color and Perceiving Value

There are various reasons that one might object to Stein's analogy. Certainly, her distinction between our emotions and the feeling of our emotions raises a number of questions. Perhaps the most challenging part is that we have more significant and more heated debates about our values and emotional responses than about colors and visual perceptions. Given Stein's analogy, one would expect no more mistakes or differences of opinion regarding the value aspects of things than one would regarding the visual or olfactory aspects of things. Certainly we acknowledge that some people are more attuned to certain aspects of the world—for example, a chef to different tastes and a perfume maker to smells—but there is not substantial disagreement about whether basil adds a different taste to a dish than dill. (Perhaps we might fight about whether one likes basil rather than dill in a dish, but not whether its addition makes some kind of difference.) Although many of us pay relatively little attention to various spices, few doubt that one can become an expert regarding tastes and spices. In the area of value, though, there is not merely inattention to value—those, for example, who fail to attend to the different value of various forms and degrees of betrayal—but also substantial disagreement about what kind of value to allot to different actions and objects.

These differences are precisely what have led many to deny that values are in any sense objective. It is not hard to find examples of substantial disagreement regarding what kind of value various objects have. For example, in contemporary debates regarding abortion and euthanasia, there is substantial disagreement about the value of an embryo or a life filled with intense and persistent physical pain. On both sides of the debates, there are people who have come to their judgments regarding the value of the life in question based on strong and seemingly genuine emotional responses. Disagreements such as this are rare regarding sights and smells but dominate our debates regarding value.

There is a second point of apparent disanalogy. Although one can point to numerous people who have visual, olfactory, and aural disabilities, most human beings have relatively healthy eyes, noses, and ears. We would be hard-pressed to find any sense for which 50 percent or more of the population is impaired in any significant way. In contrast, the heart is famously deceitful above all things. Whereas for most people, most physical senses function relatively well, in the realm of emotions most of us are quite disordered all too regularly. The great nineteenth-century masters of suspicion (Karl Marx, Friedrich Nietzsche, and Sigmund Freud) as well as contemporary psychoanalysis, feminist critiques, and critical theory have all been instrumental in uncovering a variety of ways in which our emotions and feelings, while claiming to be directed toward certain, usually noble, things, are actually motivated by less worthy causes. Even if the suspicion can be overstated on an occasion or two, it is not hard to accept that all of our hearts have had, at least occasional, serious bouts of emotional disorders— of *Schadenfreude* parading as a compassionate interest in others or indulgent self-interest and self-justification masking as a desire to share advice generously.

If our emotions are, like our eyes or ears, receptors for genuine (in this case) values, why are they disanalogous with our other senses in such striking and problematic ways? Despite these objections, I think that Stein is correct in claiming that right affective responses, far from hindering objectivity, are instead a condition of objectivity and that her analogy with perception can be preserved.

Emotion as a Basic Way of Engaging the World

Stein begins with descriptions of our experience and reads the structures of being from our lived experience of the world. Emotional attunement (thus, value constitution) is a fundamental way in which we engage the world. Feeling values is, Stein says, "the 'most natural' behavior for the person."[13] We are at home in the world of value. Consider, for example, the simple act of walking across a room. We take no concern for whether we smash down the carpet but immediately avoid stepping on the dog; that is, we make distinctions regarding the value of each and thus the proper treatment of each.[14] Consider the way in which each of us approaches a door. We have some orientation toward it: that it is an opportunity to be anticipated, something to be feared, or merely the contented feeling of something to which we are quite accustomed.[15]

The claim is not that we all agree about the value of the world or the various things in our world but that we are, in fact, always already (*immer schon*) emotionally attuned to the world and understand it in terms of value.[16] Because of our constant and continuous emotional and evaluative engagement with the world, we should be cautious about overstating the differences between various value judgments. There are certainly issues and objects that inspire quite varied emotional responses, but there is also a whole horizon of agreement. That animate and inanimate things should be treated differently, that the wrecking of automobiles is different from the wrecking of human beings, that skill and cleverness are better than bungling ineptness (even if the latter can be endearing in its own way) are all things on which we agree. Certainly, there are debates about what kinds of behavior count as wrecking a human life; who, precisely, counts as a human being; and what kinds of skills are most desirable, but these debates presume a great deal of agreement and take place on the general field of that agreement.

Addressing Differences of Opinion

The disagreements must be addressed. Even granting that there is more agreement—and even substantially more agreement—than disagreement, there still seems to be more controversy about values than about the color red. We have public debates about the precise value (and the proper treatment) of animals; we do not have analogous debates about the precise nature of some smell.

We can find at least two characteristics of emotions that might make these disagreements more understandable. First, in all perception, the subject must be developed in certain ways in order to perceive the object in question. A young infant might sense various colors, but she cannot see very clearly or focus on particular objects during the first few weeks after she is born. She gradually gains control over the eye muscles that are necessary to focus on objects. Similarly, children learn to distinguish, out of many different noises, particular words. All faculties of perception must develop to some degree before the person can perceive properly.

Such development can be refined, and noticing subtle nuances and distinctions requires further development and maturity. An artist, for example, learns a craft by, among other things, developing powers of visual or aural perception and attention, learning to notice subtle differences in the light throughout a room or the notes within a chord. Similarly, value perception requires development on the part of a person. We might all have a basic palette of emotional experiences, but in order to notice and attend to the subtle variations within one's emotional field, we must have a sufficiently tutored heart. Doing this requires becoming familiar with a wide range of values. Stein says:

> He who never meets a person worthy of love or hate can never experience the depths in which love and hate are rooted. To him who has never seen a work of art nor gone beyond the walls of the city may perhaps forever be closed to the enjoyment of nature and art together with his susceptibility for this enjoyment. Such an "incomplete" person is similar to an unfinished sketch.[17]

Emotional development requires that we have subject matter that will evoke a broad range of emotions and the energy to attend to the various experiences, as well as tutoring to help us notice relevant differences and distinctions. Most human beings develop basic emotional responses relatively easily, but the emotional sensitivity necessary to recognize fine details between different values and recognize complex value structures might require a great deal of emotional development.

Children have a relatively simple appreciation for taste; they tend to like strong simple tastes: sugar, peanut butter and jelly, hamburgers, etc. In contrast, one must have a relatively mature taste palette in order to appreciate fine wines and sophisticated sauces. In an analogous way, we might say that, although it does not require a great deal of emotional maturity to recognize that dogs or cats should be valued differently than carpet, it does require a relatively sophisticated emotional life to recognize other value distinctions.[18]

More sophisticated versions of emotional development are both difficult to cultivate and time-consuming. We have many capacities as human beings, and all of them require time, will, energy, and decent conditions in order to cultivate. If one lives in a culture, for example, that values science more than literature or business more than art, there are simply fewer resources and incentives to cultivate emotional capacities, and the society as a whole may be little poised to train large segments of its population to perceive values in very fine or detailed ways.[19]

Second, Stein claims that value perception is a more intimate affair than other kinds of perception. Anyone who has tried to go to sleep or to concentrate on some task when suffering a mildly intense pain can agree that sensory pain can absorb our attention. Despite this, few of us think that such physical pain is worse than the pain of being rejected by a loved one or fundamentally betrayed by a close friend. Such psychological pain is personal and intensely private in a way that physical pain is not.[20] Because our receptor for value, that is, our heart, is closer to who we are as persons than our receptors for colors and sounds, there are risks involved in value judgments that are not involved in other judgments.[21]

Perceiving certain values requires that we open ourselves up to them. This is true in all perception. We cannot see what is outside us without opening our eyes nor feel a baby's new skin without touching. It is possible that we can get hurt when we open ourselves up to certain kinds of perception. If we open our eyes in particularly bright lights or touch a hot stove, we will be injured. Also, in the emotional realm it is possible to be hurt if one attends to certain values. Because the pain involved in perceiving certain values is particularly acute and personal, we often understandably desire to avoid that pain and consequently refuse to open ourselves to those values.

Further, because an inability to respond to certain values can reveal a hardness or immaturity of heart, and because few of us value hardness of heart or immaturity, there is an incentive not to appear as such and not to give the opportunity to reveal—either to ourselves or to others—that we are either. Stein says: "The fact that it's egoic data which constitute values for us, the fact that these values decisively influence our inner life and have an entirely personal meaning for us—this is what makes it understandable that they're so often made out to be 'merely subjective' or 'private.'"[22] The values that we feel intimately reveal who we are.

Like all perception, value perception requires something of the perceiver; it requires a certain level of development, discernment, and attention. In contrast to seeing and hearing, the kind of development required to appreciate values necessarily implicates the I and who we understand ourselves to be.[23] There is no shame in being blind; there might (although perhaps not justly) be embarrassment, but not shame, in such a state. In contrast, failing to feel appropriately might involve not merely embarrassment but also shame.

Conclusion

There are certainly understandable reasons for critics to be distrustful of emotions and suspicious of allowing that objectivity might include such capricious things; still, I am not yet convinced that those are ultimately sufficient reasons. While I am sympathetic to the difficulties involved in developing right affective responses, I do not think that the difficulties require us to discount our emotions as truly perceptive and, as such, part of an objective understanding of reality. Instead, the difficulties are a call to take seriously the task of becoming mature, especially emotionally mature, people.

Notes

1. Fyodor Dostoyevsky, *The Brothers Karamazov*, trans. Constance Garnett, rev. Ralph E. Matlaw (New York: W. W. Norton & Co., 1976), 212.

2. There can be cases in which differing emotional responses are both fit and right; thus, some differences in emotional perception might be appropriate. Because Stein ties our emotional responses to a truly objective perception of value, not all differing emotional responses can be right.

3. I have chosen the language of perception, which might seem to imply certain models of the way experience of objects works. In particular, we might be tempted to think of all experience, especially knowing, on a spatial model, as a relation between a subject here and an object over there. Edmund Husserl and his followers make clear that they do not think that knowing is like, or should be modeled on, sensation. Knowing involves intentional relations that can be built on and use the material given in sensation but should not thereby be confused with mere sensation. It follows that all perceiving, even of the most simple objects, involves constitution. Stein follows the basic Husserlian account of knowing, and her analogy is not meant to undermine or conflict with that account but to develop it.

4. See, for example, Stein, "First Treatise: Sentient Causality" in *Philosophy of Psychology and the Humanities*, trans. Marianne Sawicki and Mary Catharine Baseheart, CWES, vol. 7 (Washington, D.C.: ICS Publications, 2000), introduction.

5. See Stein's development of this point in, among other places, *Philosophy of Psychology and the Humanities*, pt. 1, sec. 2. I am grateful to Michael Sharkey, both for drawing my attention to this distinction and for providing so many examples.

6. For more on this distinction, see especially Jean-Paul Sartre's work on bad faith in *Being and Nothingness*.

7. See especially Stein, "Individual and Community," in *Philosophy of Psychology and the Humanities*, 157–167.

8. Stein attended a number of Scheler's lectures in Göttingen, Germany, and was clearly influenced by his work on value, as is made explicit in the final chapter of her dissertation, *On the Problem of Empathy*, trans. Waltraut Stein, CWES, vol. 3 (Washington, D.C.: ICS Publications, 1989). Certainly the claim that emotions are affective responses to value and the analogy with perception owe their inspiration to Scheler; however, there are important differences between Stein's and Scheler's developments of these points.

9. One might ask about the metaphysical bases for this perception, that is, how values are present *in* things and whether something like a natural law is an appropriate model for thinking of the nature of these values. Stein does not directly address these questions in *Philosophy of Psychology and the Humanities* and is interested, rather, in how we come to experience values.

10. See Stein, *Philosophy of Psychology and the Humanities,* 157–165; 226–232.

11. Presumably various chemical imbalances work in a similar manner. Depression, for example, might lead one to feel less fully what is, in fact, a genuine and deeply joyful emotion. A manic stage might lead one to feel intensely a nonintense emotion. This distinction between the emotions themselves and the feeling of the emotions adds both nuance and complication to Stein's account.

12. See Stein, "Second Treatise: Individual and Community," in *Philosophy of Psychology and the Humanities,* 160.

13. Ibid.,227.

14. One might be tempted to object that this is merely a matter of convenience: it is inconvenient to step on a dog and deal with the resulting mess, whereas there is no such inconvenience involved in stepping on the carpet; however, consider the emotional difference between accidentally kicking over a glass of Kool-Aid and accidentally kicking a dog. Although the first might involve a great deal more inconvenience and thus be quite frustrating, most of us still feel less disturbed about kicking Kool-Aid than dogs.

15. We could compare Stein's claim with Martin Heidegger's argument from *Being and Time* (1928), pointing to mood or attunement as one of the basic structures of all human beings. There are, though, some differences between Stein's and Heidegger's accounts, the most significant of which is Stein's sharp distinction between life feelings and emotions proper.

16. Stein says, "A value-constitution goes hand in hand with every object-constitution. Every fully constituted object is simultaneously a value-object" (Stein, "Second Treatise: Individual and Community," *Philosophy of Psychology and the Humanities,* 160.).

17. Stein, *On the Problem of Empathy,* 111.

18. One might point out that children are all too willing to treat pets much worse than carpet. Does this not suggest that children fail to make this simple value distinction? I take it that children can be so cruel precisely because they recognize the animals as distinct from the carpet. If dogs and cats did not have such value, it would not be nearly so much fun for children to torment them.

19. I am grateful to Kathleen Haney for raising questions about the conditions for emotional development. Although Stein certainly thinks

that a culture might encourage one not to develop emotional capacities and, as a result, fail to develop a rightly nuanced and mature value perception, I am not sure that it can encourage a wrong development. If we follow the analogy with other types of perception, although one might fail to distinguish various tastes or might be encouraged to overlook certain critical distinctions, one's conditions probably still could not lead one to think sweet is sour or basil is dill. One might simply fail to make the distinctions (and thus use language that obscures these distinctions), or one might lack, for whatever reason, the ability to taste certain flavors, but it is not clear that one can have both a cultivated taste palate and substantially mistake sweet for sour and vice versa. (Basil or fennel might be off-putting to one person but not another, but, once again, one could not cultivate a taste faculty that even when fully cultivated consistently misperceives.) I do not know whether Stein would push the perception analogy far enough to make a similar claim regarding emotional perception.

20. One might object that this is not a fair comparison. Certainly, mild physical pain is better than intense psychological pain, but as methods of torture show, there are a few who will betray even their closest friends when given enough incentive. I am not sure that in such cases the person believes that the physical torture is worse than the psychological torture, but instead thinks that the physical pain is worse than another's psychological torture. Further, even if the opposite were shown to be true on some occasion, we would still need to ask whether some particular act of succumbing to torture arose from something more like weakness of will than the persistent judgment that sensory pain is worse than psychological pain. Stein says, "Sensory pain and sensory pleasure come over the ego from its periphery on down. They seize possession of it so exclusively that nothing else has room besides, but they don't get into its depths and they never attach to the ego itself" (See Stein, "Second Treatise: Individual and Community," *Philosophy of Psychology and the Humanities*, 163).

21. See "Second Treatise: Individual and Community," *Philosophy of Psychology and the Humanities*, 164.

22. Stein describes this slightly differently in *Philosophy of Psychology and the Humanities* and her earlier *On the Problem of Empathy*. In *On the Problem of Empathy*, she says, "In 'theoretical acts,' such as acts of perception, imagination, relating or deductive thinking, etc., I am turned to an

object in such a way that the 'i' and the acts are not there at all. There is always the possibility of throwing a reflecting glance on these, since they are always accomplished and ready for perception. But it is equally possible for this not to happen, for the 'i' to be entirely absorbed in considering the object. It is possible to conceive of a subject only living in theoretical acts having an object world facing it without ever becoming aware of itself and its consciousness, without 'being there' for itself. But this is no longer possible as soon as this subject not only perceives, thinks, etc., but also feels. For as it feels it not only experiences objects, but it itself. It experiences emotions as coming from the 'depth of its 'I''' (*On the Problem of Empathy*, 98). In contrast, in *Philosophy of Psychology and the Humanities,* Stein de-emphasizes the differences between theoretical and emotional acts. This shift may indicate, in addition to a slight change in her view of value constitution, a further shift in her view of the pure versus empirical egos.

23. A version of this paper was first presented at Notre Dame's Center for Ethics and Culture conference on Formation and Renewal, October 4, 2003. I am grateful for my Philosophy Department colleagues' comments on an earlier draft of this paper, the suggestions from those present at the conference, and Kathleen Haney's helpful prodding and questions.

5

EDITH STEIN'S METAPHYSICS:
Body, Soul, Spirit

JOHANNA VALIQUETTE

Edith Stein has become known perhaps more for her striking and sometimes controversial life story than for her philosophy. While her relentless, uncompromising search for truth is no doubt inspiring for many, the dramatic events of her life might have overshadowed interest in her philosophical contribution. Because of that, this essay is one of the first attempts to introduce Stein's philosophy and, more specifically, her metaphysics to a wider audience. While admittedly a daunting task, I have endeavored to stay very close to her text so that the reader is introduced faithfully, albeit rather incipiently, to the power, beauty, and logic of Stein's thought.

Edith Stein's metaphysics, as seen most completely in her *Finite and Eternal Being*, could be a starting point for any number of avenues of investigation. One could look at the influence of phenomenology on her method, or the philosophical compatibility of traditional realism and phenomenology, or many other subjects. But I have selected three distinguishing aspects of her philosophical theory. These are (1) a metaphysics that explains the structure of all things living, inanimate, rational, and non-physical; (2) a phenomenological as well as a traditionally realist way of doing philosophy that is unique; I would call it "Steinian"; (3) a metaphysics whose first principle may accurately be called love.

To my mind these three subjects are high-priority items because they define, in part, her contribution to philosophy as a discipline. To understand her philosophy, like anyone's, one must attempt to grasp its method and read it through this lens. Stein uses her own version of Edmund Husserl's method, apparent in her writings as early on as her doctoral dissertation. All the while she incorporates classical philosophical terminology, but only after having analyzed it and understood it through phenomenological analysis, thus making it her own.

For those whose frame of reference is principally phenomenology or classical realism (or other), the result can be disconcerting because the meanings in one and the other are made Steinian. Until one knows the language it can be as frustrating as trying to understand someone speaking to us in a thick and irritating accent. Although we might be tempted to disregard the message, the payoff for diligence in learning her language is rich philosophical understanding.

Although it is open to discussion, I will refer to Stein's metaphysical writings in *Finite and Eternal Being* as philosophical rather than theological. The object of Stein's investigation is not God but, instead, the being of contingent beings, and for this reason it seems she is principally doing philosophy. Still, one might argue that she does take her first principles from theology. As Aristotle would agree, just because two sciences share some principles, that does not mean that the two sciences are, in the end, the same science. Just as the physicist who studies light waves uses mathematical principles to calculate the focal point of a parabolic mirror, so Stein employs the principles of a higher science (theology) to formulate the structure of beings: body–soul–spirit.

———

There comes a point as one reads *Finite and Eternal Being* at which there are sparse footnotes to other authors or philosophers. This is where we see what is most Steinian. What I am explaining now is for the most part where the footnotes dwindle and end.

The basis of Stein's entire metaphysics is a threefold structure, body–soul–spirit, that pertains to all things, animate as well as inanimate, although in different ways. Stein displays, in true phenomenological style, the disposition of things in such a way that we glimpse what holds true about them. She incorporates classical philosophical terms such as "essence" and "form" without distorting them to fit her methodology. Neither does she attempt unnecessary, strict interpretations of them; rather, she takes a *prima facie* acceptance of these terms, then unfolds their implicit meanings as they pertain to the structure of things: body–soul–spirit. This is part of what I mean by a philosophy that is "Steinian."

Another aspect of being Steinian has to do with completeness. Stein seems bent on not leaving out anything relevant to the discussion, daring to include discoveries taken from her early studies in psychology; even self-awareness, the subconscious, and the ego are objects of metaphysical explanation. The context of the discussion includes a perceiver of being, the human person, whose experience of being has different levels. For Stein, those levels should be objects of philosophical study since the experience of them makes known their status of relevance and their meaning. Stein shows that by engaging newer discoveries about the person, classical philosophical terms can be rarified. For example, by analysis of the "I," she concludes that "[t]he 'I' is neither equivalent to the soul nor to the body."[1] In sum, she uncovers a real world, a contemporary world, the meaning of which can be found and penetrated inside and out under the tutelage of a single, felicitous formula.

My third claim has to do with a theological principle that is at the same time legitimately used by Stein as a philosophical one: "the meaning of the image is determined by the archetype."[2] In this case the archetype is the Creator. The image is understood to be all created things that are structured with that same basic structure found in the Creator. Stein has a passion for continuity, unity, and completeness. The Creator as a structure is tripartite and one at the same time. As all spiritual, he gives himself and yet remains. This common structure is but one layer of unity in her philosophy; spirit and meaning are the others. Here we seem to encounter some of the philosophical benefits of being in the hands of a woman: continuity, unity, completeness, and, therefore, perhaps meaning.

Stein knows well that what she attempts is a thoroughgoing challenge: "the archetype (the Creator) and the image (creation) are separated by an infinite distance." Still, she is unflagging: "Yet this distance and the incomprehensibility of the archetype cannot shake the certainty that the meaning of the image is determined by the archetype."[3] In other words, the only means of arriving at the sense of something is through its source, regardless of the difficulty in uncovering that source. Stein shows us the meaning of the image, created things, through the structure and meaning of the archetype.

Stein's metaphysics is complete, although not fully developed. I say complete because the outline she has left of it for us is sufficient to grasp its fundamental principles, its most significant conclusions, and its philosophical methodology. The essential structure or blueprint of her metaphysics is there, yet Stein did not have the time to flesh it out. Unfortunately, she was killed at the age of fifty-one in a gas chamber at Auschwitz. We have only her first attempt at expounding philosophy. With frank humility, she regards her magnum opus of philosophy as "by a beginner for beginners."[4] She was only beginning to enunciate her philosophy, but her powerful mind, her expertise in confronting philosophical questions, and the integrity of her discipline belie her self-appraisal.

———

Stein proceeds systematically. She sets up the problem of how to explain the relationship of Creator to creation in being. She proposes a first principle: the meaning of the image (created things) is determined by the archetype (the Creator). She analyzes what attributes seem most in evidence about God: first, that he is spiritual, contained in himself in a nonspatial way, and living. Then she proceeds step by step through the various orders of things: inanimate, animate, rational, and spiritual, applying this tripartite structure derived from the tripartite archetype.[5] She ascends to divine being "by starting out from creaturely being and by proceeding from the finite and conditioned to the infinite and unconditioned author and archetype."[6] In this way we go from the Creator through creatures and back to the Creator.

God is spirit, Stein explains, and a "going out of itself pertains to the spiritual essentially."[7] All other forms of being have their primordial archetype in this realm of spirit. All other forms of being have the spiritual-like quality of being able to go out of self while remaining themselves because of their likeness to God who is spirit; moreover, they all share in this first Being as "predesigned in it."[8] That is to say, all created things were designed by the Creator before they came into actual existence. The Creator, according to Stein, while wholly spiritual can be understood through other dimensions as well. These dimensions pertain to God primarily and to other things[9] because he is their archetype.

Surprisingly, Stein says, "God has a proper body," and she hastens to qualify, "not a material body, of course, but a spiritual body [*Geistleib*]."[10] Her assertion seems oxymoronic until we enter her analysis, which while phenomenological (it makes meanings explicit) also employs classical terminology and brings it to newly attempted meanings implicit in its own definitions. "We speak of 'bodily' being wherever an existent owns its nature in a 'born-out' form"; thus, God can have a body because "[God] owns the total plenitude of his nature in a fully actualized, manifest, luminous form—a form which though infinite, is enclosed with and by his own self, because he holds himself completely in the possession of his own self."[11] Such analyses are Stein's philosophical trademark.

Yes, we realize that God must possess his full form, his full self, as "born out" or actualized. If we think of the definition of nature as the actualization of an essence in its operations, then we see that God would certainly contain in himself his nature or actualized essential form. God would contain himself in a nonspatial way but contain himself, nonetheless, in a born-out way, and consequently have a body.

Perhaps we never thought of form or body in this way. Stein did, though, because she understood in the definition of form its implicit meanings; she analyzed it phenomenologically. If something has a form, the form is forming something that has itself. Before we physical things had bodies, it seems that God had a "body." We note that this is not a case of anthropomorphizing God; rather we understand that the primary model of ours and all physical bodies is God.

This is one example of Stein's variance with St. Thomas Aquinas, who holds that things other than rational ones are not an image of God but rather a mere vestige of him.[12] As Stein explains: "(Aquinas) speaks of *vestigium* (*Spur*) where merely *causality* of the cause can be inferred from the effect (as fire may be inferred from the phenomenon of smoke), and he speaks of *imago* (*Abbild*) only where we find in the effect a representation of the cause (as the statue of Mercury represents Mercury)."[13] For Aquinas, nonrational creatures are mere vestiges of God, whereas rational creatures are images of him. Stein sees that all created things bear the stamp of the Creator Spirit in a more vital way. Even the physical, in its born-out form of the physical body, is an image of the body of God. Of course, Stein does not hold for matter or potentiality pertaining to the body of God. These contingent manifestations of body seem to have accrued to body in our physical realm of existence.[14]

Aquinas, like others of his tradition, saw in reason that dimension of the human person that is most like God. Understandably, he and other realist philosophers became a bit enamored of reason, because they beheld its capacity for accurately penetrating reality; however, it may be true that the seedbed for the great and sometimes distorting rationalist philosophies of the Enlightenment was an overconfidence in reason spawned initially by the Greeks and sustained into the Medieval ages by the Scholastics. Stein suspends the potentially destructive or distorting forces of reason by holding it accountable to meanings as they are experienced. She sees in all creatures a spiritual dimension, a capacity to go out of self while remaining in self, that images at different levels (inanimate, animate, personal) the going-out-of-self of the Blessed Trinity, which is love.

God lives and is the source of all living. This being-the-source-of-life-and-giving-life can be attributed to him. We know that in things that live it is the soul that is the source of life, its unifying element. When some unified living thing loses its integration and unity, it is said to be dead or no longer with a soul. Since God is the one who lives and gives life in a primordial way, God seems to exemplify the primary instance of soul. Whereas his life, his soul, may be far removed from the life and soul we know, we claim that both are living. There is a commonality between the notions of life and God, the source of which points to one thing: soul. So, in God there is body and soul.[15]

Stein establishes the structure of body–soul–spirit based on the structure of the Creator, then she reveals how this plays out in the world we know, the world of physical as well as nonphysical realities and animate as well as inanimate ones. Here again, we note Stein's passion for unity and meaning; the true meaning of something cannot be found by separating its essential elements from one another, even for the sake of analysis, if those elements are not reunited since the whole appears to be greater than the sum of its parts. That is to say, its meaning is greater than the sum of the meanings of its parts taken individually, since the true meaning can only be seen in its completeness: body–soul–spirit.

Even what constitutes the spiritual is for Stein an area of experience: "No experience of things spiritual would be possible if there were not implicit in human experience as such a certain understanding of what constitutes spirit and spirituality."[16] In other words, we could not even locate the spiritual as a concept if we had not experienced the spiritual. In Stein this has absolutely nothing to do with the paranormal and has everything to do with the normal, our ordinary lives, since meanings of whatever kind are conveyed through the spiritual.

Once the structure of body–soul–spirit is established, Stein shows what these mean in the different orders of being. She tells us that, for different things, "body–soul–spirit (are) used with different connotations." In human beings the soul is "the supra-material [*stoffuberlegen*] form which animates a body, molding it from within, in accordance with the specific essence, in a temporal process." Its physical body is formed by the soul, but soul has a triple function unique to human beings: "the forming of the body, the forming of the soul, and the unfolding in spiritual life."[17] Like Aquinas, Stein perceives in the human person a kind of representation of all forms of being; "owing to the fact that human nature presents a union of spirit [*Geist*] and matter—the whole of creation appears to be epitomized by it."[18] Stein also sees a function of soul in impersonal animate beings: "That which is efficaciously operative in the formation of animate beings and exercises its efficacy as the 'center' or 'core' of structural unity we have designated as a supra-material form, living form, or soul."[19]

Perhaps the most unforeseeable element of Stein's theory is the third part of the structural triad: spirit. We could have understood how animate things have body and soul, with their counterparts, matter and form, in the case of inanimate objects. How is it that all things have spirit? This is perhaps her most Steinian contribution to philosophical theory, and some find it most compelling. This notion of spirit unifies her metaphysics, since it is a property that she holds is possessed universally by all things and ultimately likens them to their Creator.

Stein wants us to understand that a thing, personal or not, has and communicates its spirit, that is, goes out of itself when it makes itself known, conveys its meaning. Clearly, in the case of nonpersonal things, this going out of self is not something consciously willed. When we know a thing, we grasp it because it conveys its meaning to us; it goes out of itself while not losing itself. Stein says we

> characterize the spiritual as the non-spatial and non-material, as that which possesses an "interiority" in an entirely non-spatial sense, and which remains "within itself" while going out of itself. This going-out-of-itself pertains to the spiritual essentially. It is indicative of its being completely "selfless," not indeed in the sense of having no self but rather in the sense of a total self-surrender without any loss of self, a self-giving in which the spiritual reveals itself completely.[20]

Naturally, Stein does not hold that inanimates be considered spiritual in the sense that humans are spiritual, since they have no freedom or self-reflective capacity; however, she insists that even inanimate objects make themselves known, make their meanings known while not knowing themselves, by "enunciating [their] meaning with the aid of sensible appearance."[21]

Stein understands that even a lifeless creation has meaning (*Sinn*) and thus it "is therefore in the broader sense of the term a spirit-filled (*geisterfullt*) structure and thus a structure through which the Creator Spirit speaks to the created spirit."[22] It is in the enunciation of its meaning that Stein sees evidence of the spiritual in the inanimate being. The phenomenon that will convince Stein of the spiritual dimension of nonliving things is what she calls the "enunciation of its meaning." Through this enunciation the thing "steps outside itself [*ghet aus sich heraus*] and has some amount of *spiritual being*."[23]

This spiritual property of going out of self to enunciate the proper meaning of a being is for Stein the clearest sign of the *imago* of God in all beings, including nonpersonal ones. This property common to all beings mirrors the going-out-of-self-without-loss-of-self that is the essence of love, the essence of God who is love. While the Trinity is in itself a communion of persons in love, Stein attributes this "spiritual radiance" and "essence or nature"[24] of created beings, especially to the Holy Spirit, who is love personified. He is the archetype of creation, which because it is made in the image of love possesses the power of being, of unfolding its nature or enunciating its meaning, that is, of giving itself.

In Stein's words:

[B]ecause God's creative will [and] his existence-creating and life-imparting love have from eternity apportioned to creatures their *power of being* [*Seinsmacht*], the *power* of unfolding their essence or nature, the Holy

Spirit—as the person of life and love—is the archetype of all creaturely life and efficacious action as well as that spiritual radiance of their essence or nature which is a property even of material structures.[25]

Stein says it with different emphasis in another passage. The primary archetype of all things is spirit since God is spirit, but spirit for Stein means above all else this going out of self while remaining in self; the kind of selfless movement that is a property of love, of God who is love:

[T]he spirit in its purest and most perfect actualization is found in the total self-giving of the divine Persons, a self-giving in which each person totally divests itself of its nature [*wesen*] and yet totally retains its nature, in which each person is totally within itself and totally in the others. The triune Deity *is* the authentic "realm of the spirit." . . . And all the spirituality or spiritual endowment of creatures denotes an elevation, of a "being lifted up" into this realm, albeit in varying modes and degrees.[26]

Here again, the fundamental image of God in creatures is spirit; self-communication, self-revelation, self-gift, which when we are talking about creatures who are persons means love.

Stein holds that the one God abides in a relationship of persons, Father, Son, and Holy Spirit, whose inner life and outward expression is love: "God is love and that love is a free self-giving of an I to a Thou and a union of both

in a We."[27] This love is the Creator of all and the archetype of all, since all, and especially the human person, is
made in his image. According to Stein, his tripartite unity
is imaged in everything created and in a threefold way:
body–soul–spirit. Stein is not advancing a brand of pan-
theism nor polytheism. Love is not creation; instead, Love
as the author of all things created, is reflected, especially
as spirit, in creation. Stein's philosophy can thus truly be
called a Christian philosophy, since it takes its axioms
from Christian theology, that is, trinitarian theology. The
theory that all things resemble the triune deity as spirit,
this going out of self while remaining in self, is the most
characteristic feature of Steinian metaphysics.

Now that we have a grasp of her teachings about the
nature of all kinds of being, we can consider some further possibilities based on these teachings. Stein's metaphysics gives grounds for what could be the basis of a
Steinian epistemology. For example, we grasp a thing as
"tree" because it gives itself as tree; that is, it enunciates its
meaning sensibly and we are equipped to acknowledge its
meaning. We can intend it as tree because it makes itself
known or knowable as a tree through a natural enunciation of its essence.

We might ask where in Stein's personal inner work-
ings did this potent explanation of being originate? It
seems likely to have been the confluence of an intellectual
endeavor that had marked her soul profoundly—as does
the dissertation of any serious student of philosophy—
and her faith in love. The topic of her doctoral dissertation was empathy: a going out of self to make one's own

something which is primordially experienced in another. Her analysis of empathy reveals evidence contravening radical rationalistic selfishness, solipsism, something of great concern to her camp of Husserlian phenomenology. The going-out-of-self characteristic of love may have reminded her of the going-out-of-self essential for empathetic experience.

On a more critical note, we can observe something rather seductive about Stein's philosophy. Is it compelling because it is true or because everything would make such lovely sense if it were? If it were true and accurate, that would mean that the world gives itself to me in its manifold meanings; moreover, it does so through its semblance to love. A starting point like this one is rife with possibilities for self-understanding and personal meaning. One can understand oneself as a personal enunciation in a chorus of meaningful self-utterances, the meanings of which all image love and point to love.

Notes

1. Edith Stein, *Finite and Eternal Being: An Attempt at an Ascent to the Meaning of Being*, trans. Kurt Reinhardt, CWES, vol. 9 (Washington, D.C.: ICS Publications, 2002), 374.

2. Ibid., 359.

3. Ibid.

4. Ibid., xxvii.

5. Ibid., 355–467.

6. Ibid., 418.

7. Ibid., 360.

8. Ibid.

9. Ibid.

10. Ibid.

11. Ibid.

12. St. Thomas Aquinas, *Summa Theologiae* I, q. 45, a. 7.

13. Stein, *Finite and Eternal Being*, 596.

14. Ibid., 360–61.

15. Ibid., 361.

16. Ibid., 382.

17. Ibid., 422.

18. Ibid., 363.

19. Ibid., 424.

20. Ibid., 360.

21. Ibid., 423.

22. Ibid.

23. Ibid.

24. Ibid., 418.

25. Ibid.

26. Ibid., 360.

27. Ibid., 419.

6

IMAGES OF THE UNSEEN:
Stein's Semiotics of Mystical Theology

KATHLEEN HANEY

St. Teresa Benedicta of the Cross, neé Edith Stein, was a twentieth-century philosopher who studied with the father of modern phenomenology, Edmund Husserl, and served as his first assistant. In that capacity, she edited Husserl's early manuscripts on the constitution of time and the personal world. She became a Christian at the age of thirty-one, converting from the atheism she had adopted after rejecting the Jewish faith that her mother taught her as a child. After her conversion, she became interested in the great writers of the Christian tradition. She even translated St. Thomas Aquinas into German. Her conversion eventually led her to the cloistered order of the Discalced Carmelites, where other Catholic mystics such as Sts. Teresa of Ávila and John of the Cross found their home. Stein studied their works, too, and, of particular interest to this exposition, those of Dionysius the Areopagite.

Stein was called upon to experience and express the unspeakable, as well as the *in*effable, though it was the latter about which she wrote substantially. She contemplated, and then theorized, the semiotics of mystical theology, as based in the writings of the Pseudo-Dionysius. I begin this study with a poem that shows his influence on Stein. Her niece, Susanne M. Batzdorff, provides the translation that replicated the rhyme of the original and thus involved the rearranging and recasting of the original.

"In his anguish he (Jesus) prayed even more earnestly" (Luke 22:44).

Aphorisms in the Month of June 1940

I.
The Lord is stomping grapes,
And blood red is his gown.
He sweeps with broom of iron
Through hamlet and through town.
Proclaims in the storm's resounding
That he will come again,
We hear the awesome pounding.
Our Father alone knows when.

II.
Within Your heart lives peace eternal.
You want to pour it into our hearts.
And into each of them You want to flow,
But there is no opening where You can go.
When You knock gently, they give no ear.
A hammer's blows they will surely hear.
When the long night is past, morning will dawn,
In painful labor Your kingdom's born.

III.
From night to light who'll be our guide?
How will the horror end?
Where will the sinners be justly tried,
When will our fortunes mend?
From the Mount of Olives His anguished plea
To the Father in Heaven He hurled.
His agony gained Him the victory,
Determined the fate of the world.
There prostrate yourselves and pray, and then
Ask no more: Who? How? Where? or When?

IV.
Judge not lest you be judged in turn,
Appearances cloud our view,
We guess at the truth, but only learn
God alone knows what is true.[1]

Stein employs graphic images of sensible things in order to evoke allegories with supernatural matters. In this practice, she follows the Areopagite's analysis of positive theology, which is preliminary to the development of mystical theology. Stein's aphorisms take place against the historical background of Europe during World War II. Stein was familiar with war; she had served as a combat nurse in World War I. The second war was worse, though. Stein's own people were particularly targeted in the merciless conflict. Kristallnacht, of great infamy, was in 1938: "The Lord is stomping grapes," shattering fecund spheres, doing violence to turn food into drink.

"And blood red is his gown." The Lord makes no secret of what he does. He wears his deeds for all to see. His costume displays his intentions: "He sweeps with broom of iron." Paris fell to Hitler's armies, armaments, and tanks. The Soviets took over Estonia, Lithuania, and Latvia, "Through hamlet and through town." The Lord "[p]roclaims in the storm's resounding/That he will come again."

Stein joins her three metaphors of stomping grapes, sweeping with an iron broom, blowing winds and rains into uncanny, incessant "awesome pounding." "We hear the awesome pounding," the ineluctable, uncanny beat. He is coming. "Our Father alone knows when." The loving parent, the Lord, is making wine and cleaning house. The brutal weather announces a front, which will bring another horizon with it. The kingdom of God will appear. Her firm faith invokes an unseen meaning, lost on many who despaired of God and man.

Through these graphic images of auditory experiences, the roar of the war sounds Stein's experience of God. He wants to pour his eternal peace into the hearts of his people, but they are not open to his bounty. God hesitates to go where he is not sought. "But there is no opening . . ." We can see tea or coffee in the pot ready to be poured. We can see the small being filled up by the great. We can see tributaries of the rivers in our mind's eye. They bring moisture ever fresh and clean, flowing, not dammed up. The Lord pounds with a hammer so that his people can hear his call. The knocking of the God who wants to visit his people is too tender, too quiet. June 1940, "When the long night is past, morning will dawn"; the watch and the wait will end. The painful labor that was one of Eve's punishments will result in new life. The Lord's "kingdom is born."

How to find a way "from night to light" and "who'll be our guide?" How can the injustices and the terror end? How can we endure them? Stein returns us to the line from St. Luke's Gospel with which she began. Even Christ threw his entreaty for mercy at his Father, but by enduring he endured and carried the day. Let us go to the Garden to plead for mercy so that, like Christ, we can endure and carry on. Let us go to the Garden and say with Christ, "Thy will be done." The good God permits these incomprehensible horrors. But how can he?

Yet, after all, even appearances, even phenomena, can block the light.

> Only someone whose spiritual eyes have been opened to the supernatural correlations of worldly events can desire suffering in expiation, and this is only possible for people in whom the spirit of Christ dwells, who as members are given life by the Lord, receive his power, his meaning and his direction. Conversely, works of expiation bind one closer to Christ, as every community that works together on one task becomes more closely knit and as the limbs of a body, working together organically, continually become more strongly one.[2]

Stein's last line summarizes philosophic faith: "God alone knows what is true."

Though he was rarely mentioned in the work of her day, Stein reacquaints us with the philosophical legacy that the Pseudo-Dionysius the Aeropagite left behind for a semiotics of mystical theology. Stein considers his work to be among the three major intellectual currents that shaped Western thought in the Middle Ages (along with the Greeks and St. Augustine): "[H]e dominated Western thought from the ninth to the sixteenth century, and the church recognized his authority from the sixth century and looked upon him as a leading figure."[3]

Although his writings did not begin to appear until the end of the fifth century, they were attributed to the Areopagite whose conversion we read about in the Acts of the Apostles. The Pseudo-Dionysius may have deliberately fostered the confusion since he sets his reports during the time period of the early church, addressing them to the contemporaries of the apostles. With the advent of humanism, the writings became suspect since by then most scholars placed them at the end of the fifth century rather than in the first century. The identity of the Areopagite remains quite a controversial matter. In the best philosophical fashion, Stein avoids all versions of the ad hominem fallacy, concentrating instead on the Areopagite's thought and his significance in intellectual history.

The late Husserlian Thomas Seebohm, in his masterful study of hermeneutics, implies that the mystery concerning the identity of Pseudo-Dionysius has to do with an effort to assuage the church's concern with pagan sources, particularly Neoplatonism. By the fifth century, the church admitted only typological interpretation, since it alone was sanctioned by the New Testament itself.[4] "The application of allegorical interpretation was suspicious and even condemned by the church if the goal was to find a hidden neo-Platonic or other meaning behind the verbal sense."[5] Though not a Neoplatonist himself, the Areopagite's writings disclose Plato's influence within an orthodox version of Christianity. Finally, the church did provide some leeway for the restricted use of allegorical interpretation in order to make sense of the sign. In more contemporary terms, Jacques Derrida argued that allegory, as a kind of extended metaphor, functions as the condition for the possibility of metaphysics. Even so, as Walter Benjamin reminds us, allegory was not always taken to be a closed system as the moderns would have it:

> Even great artists and exceptional theoreticians, such as Yeats, still assume that allegory is a conventional relationship between an illustrative image and its abstract meaning. Generally authors have only a vague knowledge of the authentic documents of the modern allegorical way of looking at things, the literary and visual emblem-books of the baroque. . . . Allegory . . . is not a playful illustrative technique, but a form of expression, just as speech is expression, and indeed, just as writing is.[6]

Allegories are not mathematical equations. The way that x can be substituted for y is not the allegorical structure that generates a new recognition. Stein and Dionysius recognize that allegory is also a condition of the possibility for a symbolic theology. According to the Areopagite, God sets forth his revelation in Holy Scriptures, and theology properly speaking is this body of inspired knowledge. Theologians for Dionysius are those who are seized by God and brought into his presence to hear his Word. God, as source, must be the primary theologian. In Stein's presentation, the Areopagite's account of the communication of theological revelation analyzes how symbols can express a personal experience of the ineffable.

Stein's phenomenological mystical theology shares the structure that Charles S. Peirce sketched for signs. The process of transferring the meanings of words that refer to sensible things to those that evoke the divine requires, as its foundation, signs that evoke interpretants that stand "for something, its *object* . . . not in all respects, but in reference to a sort of idea, which I have sometimes called the *ground*."[7] God, then, is the ground of mystical theology, but the idea of the presence of God necessarily includes his absence.[8] Though presence can provide an intuition of the God who has drawn near, no human intuition can draw the All into itself. Immaterial body or not, God eludes being held in grasp. The intention that recognizes God's presence always has the caveat that in order for God to be, a theologian who follows along the *via negativa* must admit presence and absence. Only in second order hermeneutical understanding can the experienced God evoke the transcendent God, beyond experience, as the meaning of the idea of God. Interpretation along these lines will show how Stein's semiotics of mystical theology extends Peirce's categories.

Peirce contemplates iconic images that resemble or symbolize ideas. Stein's study of the Areopagite's theology amplifies Peirce's view that the icon joins a word-presentation to a mental image of an object so that his notion can refer to objects that cannot exhibit themselves directly, for instance, God. In addition to the Pseudo-Dionysian account of the science of theology, not as commentary, but as direct revelation, Stein adapts his version of symbolic theology: "image-language about God."[9] This image language suggests Peirce's notion of the icon, the basic channel for both direct and indirect communication. Often we think of the icon as pictorial, although words may also perform an imaging function. The problem for this philosophical doctrine is the problem of this study. How is it possible to specify the transcendentally necessary conditions for making images of God? Especially if God is, as the Areopagite stressed, importantly unknowable?

Peirce and Husserl both held that experiences of presence are feelings that can be put into words and those words meaningfully repeated. "Stein describes the core of mystical experience as an inner certainty of 'feeling' that one is touched by God in one's innermost being."[10] Someone else's grasp of the meanings closes the circle when, say, the prophet's hearer returns a response that indicates he shares a meaning, even when he interrogates or disagrees with it. Finding interpretants becomes a matter of translation into the language of a subject's personal experience, as expressed in an intersubjective, shared language. Still, the other's freedom determines one's communicative intentionality. Openness is prerequisite for this or any "person to person encounter." When communication of God's Word occurs, Peirce's shared object and Husserl's shared meaning are God's partial revelation of himself. Clearly, the icon that serves as the vessel of divine revelation must be a more complicated image than that which delivers an empirical resemblance.

We see that the definition of theology that Stein adopts from the Areopagite, God's Word as written by theologians, now the sacred writers, includes difficulties that a more traditional treatment glosses over since the Ur-theologian is God speaking his word.[11] For this reason, the sacred writers and mystics are theologians who recognize and repeat the Word of God. God is the utterly other who finds those who seek to draw close to him. As Husserl reminds us, these free movements are the striking feature of all real otherness. "I can only find them; I cannot create others that shall exist for me."[12] The likes of Moses or the great Carmelite saints repeated the Word of God as they had heard Him speak it. "[T]hey *speak of God* because *God has taken hold of them* or *God speaks through them*,"[13] yet this God must remain ineffable. What we consider as the different fields included within theological science are, in this telling, but "*different manners of speaking of God* and . . . *different ways or manners of knowing God* (or not-knowing him)."[14] Stein's early investigation of empathy makes clear that an encounter between any persons can only be partial. The I cannot fathom its depths completely and entirely, much less those of another or of the Other.

When the prophets are enjoined by God to speak his word to others, they report to us concerning that which they have seen and heard. They translate inexpressible presence well beyond words into a Peircean interpretant. The experience evoked in the prophet's audience entails grasping a sign of God. It "stands to somebody for something."[15] The subjective sign that expresses the prophet's experience makes way for its audience to grasp their evoked experience in another interpretant (though it may be a more developed sign). Prophetic interpretants are intuitive grasps of the Word of God. Recall, though, that God often speaks in parables, which further complicates the task of understanding.

Communicating an interpretant to another by evoking an image in the other initially functions in passively receptive, primal consciousness in the genetic phenomenology that Husserl analyzed in *Ideas II* (which Stein edited) as well as in his later work. Husserl finds that obtrusion motivates an intentional regard through stirring or awakening receptivity. He looks underneath the relations of sign/signifier/signified in order to point to the origin of signification in the passive receptivity that motivates it. The passive, primal ego submits to what is coming in through the spoken or written interpretant of the theologian, be he or she primal theologian or prophet. Husserl uses obtrusion rather than the more customary intrusion in order to emphasize that the ego is provoked, not forced, to go out to grasp what is before it. The ego is not stormed; rather, it intentionally opens the doors of its citadel; its receptivity determines its assent. The sign as an obtrusion addresses somebody who acts to construe it as another sign, an interpretant. The first speaking, the word of the Ur-theologian, remains the object of the referent; thus, God can speak to his prophets and his prophets to their people, although his difference from his hearers limits his self-disclosure.

Words that hearken to inner, outer, and life experience can call up something unfamiliar; in the service of mystical knowledge, words can bridge presence and absence. Positive theology, according to the Areopagite, uses graphic images as signs that lead from the immediate world we know to the God who mysteriously reveals himself through his creation. If we liken this kind of sign to Peirce's icons, we see the need for images that precede the verbal as its necessary foundation. Verbal signs can deliver some of these images, which amplify Peirce's notion of the icon. Verbal image language makes present an evoked experience that can lead to alternative icons. This aspect of Peirce's triad of icons, indices, and symbols can be generalized into a theory of the semiosis of mystical theology that may have broader implications. The icon does more than resemble its conceptual object; some icons bring their ineffable referents to presence. This notion of icon enriches the possibility of the triad that Peirce first describes. The symbol restricts its referents to a general class of things, but the icon that recognizes the transcendent God points to a unique experience. This use of the word "icon" enhances Peirce's usage by its emphasis on its capacity to evoke, to bring about experience of the unseen, so that icon includes the literally recognized and that which can be glimpsed through it.

Significant similarities between Peirce's schema and classical phenomenology include the use of signs, presences as grasped in interpretants, meanings that evoke an object, a *noema*, within the consciousness of somebody, some subject, a transcendental ego. To switch terminologies again, the signifier, signified, and sign (as a dynamic relationship of self and other) present a figure of the dyad experience/expression (whether of the world or of an idea of the divine) that we saw in Stein's poem.

The identifying moment of obtrusion can piggyback on classical semiosis as well to lead into the dimension that is missing in general semiotics. Positive symbolic theology presents a graphic image, which the final consumer sees in the mind's eye, after first sensing it in some kind of bodily milieu. This organ, since it combines imagination and intuition, in fact, serves the mind/body function that René Descartes attributes to the pineal gland. We have two chains, two repetitions of the sign/interpretant/object structure that Peirce theorized. One chain leads from God to prophet, another from prophet to people. Prophet and people squeeze that which gave itself as presence into interpretants that include undetermined objects.

Stein focuses primarily on the process of the grasp of the interpretant, rather than the ineffability of the divine, yet she writes, "Perhaps the best translation of 'mystical theology' may be secret revelation." God discloses himself, and "the spirits to whom he reveals himself pass on the revelation."[16] "But the higher the knowledge, the darker and more mysterious it is, the less it can be put into words. The assent to God is an ascent to darkness and silence."[17]

The ineffable may not be knowable, but the nonknowing is quiescent. Stein's attitude is one of acceptance, not of rebellion, although even self-knowledge as well as God's revelation is at stake.

When God speaks, prophets must produce their interpretant in one of the natural languages. The difficulty here is that experience, though it may be evoked through words, is itself, as we have seen, initially preverbal. Phenomenological hermeneutics, which we shall consider in more detail later, makes a distinction between first and second order understanding. God, the speaker, the primal and primordial eternal, is active as he instigates the movement that brings the prophet to search for him. When God speaks his word, the prophet recognizes God's signs. With such recognition, the prophet also wants to speak about the idea, the object, the Word that was given to him.

Husserl's doctrine of preliminary, passive receptivity prescribes that typically the subject turns toward that which awakens him. Some awakenings may be sudden or violent; most involve gradual, continuous turning toward, with increasing desire for that which obtrudes. Consciousness, in this capacity, experiences what it has not as yet named. Its level of understanding seeks to articulate its nondiscursive experience, although it remains the essential moment in the transaction. "What the prophet hears and sees is as it were the great school of symbolic theology where images and words become available to the sacred writer so that he may say the unsayable and make the invisible visible."[18]

That is the trick, but how is it done? More primary than the language of symbolic theology is the experience of God's presence/absence. The reasons that Stein makes this claim are not exclusively theological, though she seems confident that "God gives his theologians the words and images that enable them to speak of him to others."[19] We shall discuss later the problems with receiving the interpretant hermeneutically, that is, making meanings correlated to the original as presented by the prophet.

Typically the person of faith, Stein traces Moses's career as illustrative; he witnesses God and feels his presence when he reveals himself. On the mountain, Moses had an experience of the divine that he reported as an unconsuming fire. The prophet grasps his experience of the divine by means of icons, graphic images: these "*noemata*," as Husserl calls them, must be acts of one's own imaging (*noeses*). Peirce would say that the prophetic word gets passed along to somebody else who will provide another symbol by his grasp of the object. Likewise, the followers of Moses have an interpretant for unconsuming fire in their ordinary experience. The extension of the transfer of meaning that the metaphor negotiates is into Eternal Fire that persists in its changing appearances. Stein comments that this image conjures the almighty power of God and his mysteriousness as well, so positive theology might not be quite as straightforward as we had assumed. The iconic image language can deliver more than it initially reveals and more than Peirce realized.

Self-evidence, derived from reflection on the meaning of bestowal, lives as fulfilled intention, including its unintended consequences. The graphic image of fire suggests fires that all have seen and heard but evokes the might and majesty of God. Awesome power, such as raging fire, frightens, as it did Moses when he directly experienced the ineffable God. Both hearers and readers of Moses grasp what he saw through their images of what Moses pictured. After all, not everyone conjures up the same idea. The word "dog" brings to mind for some a cocker spaniel or to others perhaps a Labrador. Also, each person must image an all-consuming fire for one's self. As Stein points out, no reality corresponds to an all-consuming fire.

The experiences we have all had of fires must be extended into the counterfactual fire that beckons us to envision God. The acts of imaging bring Moses's audience into their own encounters with Moses's experience of the Godhead. Hearers translate the prophet's images into their own private symbolic systems so that all may grasp the meanings as they each can understand them. Passing along Ineffable Being makes it intersubjective, maybe even sinking eventually into ordinary being in the world, seemingly effable being can lose its mystery in the ordinary categories that deliver it. Yet, an excess of meaning distinguishes Stein and the Pseudo-Dionysius from Peirce. Their iconography does not link x to y; rather x moves beyond itself to the z of which we were unaware.

Positive theology, as science, rests its possibility on its hearer's or reader's translation of the prophet's words that (s)he formed as a graphic image. Once the obtrusion of the communicated interpretant has brought the other out, (s)he can express reception of the intention of the prophet's work in the particular vocabularies of intersubjective language that the hearer's listeners or readers understand in their images. "The meaning structure of nouns, and of other words in a language known in elementary understanding, can be taught and learned because it is a system of linguistic expressions for well-known artifacts and their system."[20] Surely Stein's analysis of the image language that calls up an idea of God depends upon ordinary usage though its object transcends the monotony of the mundane, but, wait: We might say tenderness rains from God. God makes deserts come alive and jungle flowers burst forth with his gentle moisture. Nature opens itself to God's gifts. Stein would explain that this image of its Creator comes from nature, and natural theology is only a stepsister to faith, yet inextricably interconnected with other intentions that point beyond themselves toward transcendence.[21] After all,

> effects go forth from God into the created world that harbors some of his essence within themselves (that is, they are "divine") and make "divine" whatever takes them in . . . and merges them with God into the oneness of the Kingdom. . . . This must be made accessible to us, who are bound to the world of natural experience, through images from the world we know.[22]

The possibility of understanding the image, not as an image of itself (we recall René Magritte's famous painting of the pipe, which is not a pipe) but as an image of the unseen God, rests in what Seebohm takes to be the

function of higher understanding. "Elementary understanding is an understanding of how to do things; higher
understanding can be characterized as an understanding
of what things are."[23]

Reminiscent of the distinction between calculative and
meditative thinking that Martin Heidegger makes, particularly in his *Discourse on Thinking*, Seebohm continues,

> Higher understanding occurs, e.g., in the understanding
> involved in the creation of a narrative, of religious con-
> texts, of a scientific theory, of a painting, or of a poem.
> The subsequent understanding of such creations, their
> re-living, as [Wilhelm] Dilthey says, is the task of sec-
> ond-order higher understanding."[24]

Thus, first order understanding associates the meanings
given in a natural language, a lingua franca, for represent-
ing things.

> [While] acts of higher understanding are essentially acts
> of free imagination, i.e., what was called divination or
> revelation in traditional hermeneutics. The creations
> generated by higher understanding through imagina-
> tion belong to first-order higher understanding, while
> the understanding of such creations belongs to second-
> order higher understanding."[25]

Stein's symbolic practice in her poetry as well as in her
philosophy of symbolic theology allows the opportunity
to defer or to defy understanding. The ineffable is not
domesticated, thus "the assent to darkness and silence."
Ineffability is not the last word, though. Stein's semiotics

breaks through the clouds, not to make the invisible visible, but to point to it. In this way, Stein's semiosis reverses or complicates the usual process in its dual movement toward and away from understanding and vision. This is how her mystical theology signifies. The first order semioses of the prophets are prime examples of this amplified signifying process: thus, a matter of degree of envisioning/understanding on the part of the prophets rather than kind, so that the prophets' special role might be generalized into a notion of an icon that allows itself to be seen through. In this way,

> Understanding the intention of a text—not the author—and practicing hermeneutical adequacy is in principle not a problem in some genres. The intention is either explicitly mentioned or implicitly indicated in the text as the intention of the text itself. Even eminent texts in the field of the law, science, historical reports, and certain types of philosophy have to state clearly what their intention, [*sic*] is and can be criticized if such statements are missing. . . . The intention of the author is explicable as the intention of the text in the text itself.[26]

Although Seebohm does not include poetry among the genres that necessarily discourse on their intention, I think that Stein's poem makes its intention clear. The title "Aphorisms June 1940" suggests a concise formulation of a truth or sentiment, in this case, God's providential care underlying the mayhem and chaos of a bloody month in early summer of a horrific war. Sister Teresa Benedicta died in Auschwitz three years later, in August 1942.[27]

Notes

1. Edith Stein, *Selected Writings*, trans. Susanne M. Batzdorff (Springfield, Ill.: Templegate Publishers, 1990), 72–75.

2. Edith Stein, *The Hidden Life: Essays, Meditations, Spiritual Texts*, trans. Waltraut Stein, CWES, vol. 4 (Washington, D.C.: ICS Publications, 1992), 93.

3. Edith Stein, *Knowledge and Faith*, trans. Walter Redmond, CWES, vol. 8 (Washington, D.C.: ICS Publications, 2000), 83.

4. Thomas Seebohm, *Hermeneutics: Method and Methodology* (Dordrecht, The Netherlands: Kluwer Academic Publishers, 2004), 23.

5. Ibid., 29.

6. Walter Benjamin, *The Origin of German Tragic Drama*, trans. John Osborne (London: Verso, 1977), 162.

7. Charles S. Peirce, *The Collected Papers of Charles Sanders Peirce*, 8 vols., ed. C. Hartshorne, P. Weiss, and A. W. Burks (Cambridge, Mass.: Harvard University Press, 1931–58), CP 2.228.

8. See Michael Andrews, "Paradox and Prayer," chap. 7 of this volume. Andrews provides an excellent discussion of the effect of the structural absence and presence of God in prayer according to Stein.

9. Stein, *Knowledge and Faith*, 108.

10. Marian Maskulak, *Edith Stein and the Body-Soul-Spirit at the Center of Holistic Formation* (New York: Peter Lang Publishing, 2007), 110.

11. Stein, *Knowledge and Faith*, 87.

12. Edmund Husserl, *Cartesian Meditations*, trans. Dorion Cairns (Dordrecht, The Netherlands: Martinus Nijhoff, 1960), 141.

13. Stein, *Knowledge and Faith*, 87.

14. Ibid.

15. Winfried Nöth, *Handbook of Semiotics* (Bloomington: Indiana University Press, 1990), 42.

16. Stein, *Knowledge and Faith*, 87.

17. Ibid.

18. Ibid., 108.

19. Ibid., 117.

20. Seebohm, *Hermeneutics,* 112.

21. Stein, *Knowledge and Faith,* 108.

22. Ibid., 95.

23. Seebohm, *Hermeneutics,* 117.

24. Ibid.

25. Ibid.

26. Ibid., 162.

27. Many thanks to Professor Lois Zamora for her suggestions for improving this paper. She enabled me to see my topic more clearly and to explain it more coherently.

7

FAITH AND PHENOMENON:
Edith Stein on the Paradox of Prayer

MICHAEL F. ANDREWS

Introduction

In turning to the philosopher-saint, we encounter a most provocative set of images: a distinctly modern woman of intellectual prowess, of prayer and deep faith, of tears, driven by suffering and a passion for truth.[1] Edith Stein was a prolific and gifted philosopher, even by Edmund Husserl's exacting standards. Instructed by Husserl himself in his newly established phenomenological method, Stein served as Husserl's assistant from 1915 to 1918.[2] Although she remained deeply loyal to Husserl and to her phenomenological formation throughout her entire life, Stein's most mature scholarly works were profoundly theological in nature. Focusing on questions of grace, redemption, suffering, and the heavy cost of Christian discipleship,[3] Stein drew effortlessly on the writings of saints Thomas Aquinas, Teresa of Ávila, and John of the Cross, as well as those of her philosophical contemporaries. One could say, without exaggeration, that Stein was a citizen of two worlds: the world of apodictic phenomenology[4] on

145

the one hand, and the world of apophatic Christian theology[5] on the other.

Stein's phenomenological description of prayer attempts to reconcile these two distinct approaches to the question of truth and, in so doing, reflects her rather enigmatic and precocious personality. Born into a devout Jewish family in Poland, Stein declared herself an atheist at the age of sixteen. Years later, on New Year's Day 1922, she was baptized and confirmed a Roman Catholic. Following a decade of teaching and lecturing, Stein entered the contemplative Order of Discalced Carmelites in Cologne, Germany, in 1933, taking as her religious name Sister Teresa Benedicta of the Cross. Like a modern-day (Jewish) Queen Esther, Stein lived as a foreigner in a strange land. She felt more at home praying in her adopted Latin than in her ancestral Hebrew. She was a Jew without Judaism, a philosopher who sought nearness of God amidst signs of God's absence, a Christian mystic who grasped God's incomprehensibility as a gift of incommensurate grace.

Through the language of eidetic phenomenology, Stein described Christian prayer as she experienced it, that is, in terms of a dialogical relationship between Lover and Beloved. Stein reminds us that God is both Epiphany and Cloud of Unknowing. God as Wholly Other cannot be wholly known. Such a creaturely grasp of the God beyond being entails an interior subjectivity very much at home in the apophatic tradition of Pseudo-Dionysius and those other mystics, like John of the Cross and Teresa of Ávila, who also attempted an ascent of Mount Carmel.

In this essay I am interested in exploring the complex relationship between prayer and knowledge to which Stein alludes in her enigmatic essay on Pseudo-Dionysius. The manuscript, "Ways to Know God," was probably composed between 1940 and 1941 and should be read in light of two other major and much longer works on which Stein was working at the time: *Science of the Cross* and *Finite and Eternal Being*. These three texts together comprise Stein's most theologically rich analysis of the phenomenology of religious experience. They represent a culmination of disciplined, intellectual reflection. Originally intended as an article for a North American audience, "Ways to Know God" remained unpublished until it appeared in *The Thomist* in 1946.

"Ways to Know God: The Symbolic Theology of Dionysius the Areopagite and Its Objective Presuppositions" represents the emergence of a new paradigm, characterized by an attempt to break the hermeneutical circle of intellectual inquiry. Beginning in classical Scholastic style, Stein investigates the order of being and knowledge according to various approaches in negative and positive theology. Turning to patristic and medieval texts, she examines the sources of symbolic knowledge according to three distinct stages of the mind's ascent to God: first, symbol as image; second, image as understanding; and third, image and natural knowledge of God as science.

There is a fourth stage that Stein describes: supernatural experience of God that includes symbolic theology. Stein describes such genuine encounter with God

as a "concealing veil." In effect, symbolic theology conceals God instead of revealing him and so constitutes, in
a phenomenological sense, the impossibility of the giving of God's [pure] presence. In effect, Stein retains the
mystical-experiential context of apophatism, assigning
it two senses (apophatism on the level of discourse and
apophatism of the experience). Consequently, apophatic
discourse is a transcendental experience, that is, it serves
as a prelude to, and the language accounting for, every
condition of possibility of authentic experience of God.
For this reason, Stein speaks of prayer as darkness and
incomprehensibility, while maintaining that every experience of prayer, insofar as it can be understood as a genuine phenomenal appearance, manifests a constituting
moment of authentic selfhood. Religious apophatic experience, most notably in the form of negative Christian
mysticism, marks a particular comportment or attitude of
praise toward the Creator.

Stein's task is a bold and inventive undertaking: She
seeks to understand religious experience and access its
various forms of rational expression. For Stein, prayer
is essentially dialogical in nature; it moves the self to an
infinite horizon of nonthematic givenness. Speaking of
prayer in this way, Stein pushes the hermeneutical circle of intellectual inquiry, including the phenomenology
of prayer, to its breaking point. What the I-as-subject
encounters in and through genuine prayer is an eman-
cipation from the *via positiva*, situated at the level of
linguistic repetition, thus, usable as a tool for academic
discourse. The experience of infinite alterity exceeds every

phenomenological horizon and every mental grasping of God as an object of consciousness. For Stein, the phenomenology of prayer renders comprehensible the very structure of knowledge itself. Authentic Christian prayer and genuine human knowledge remain intersubjectively and inextricably connected.

Prayer: A Passion for the Infinite

Prayer, as we learn from the Desert Fathers, is filled with signs of contradiction, not the least òf which is the risk of false pride.[6] For this reason, Jesus instructed his disciples to shut the doors to their rooms whenever they prayed and to pray in secret; otherwise, so the gospel reminds us, we run the risk of praying like the Pharisees, who pray in order to be seen at public feasts and festivals. From the ancient wisdom tradition of the apostolic church, we can thus note that authentic Christian prayer consists of four primary attitudes: praise, thanksgiving, petition, and repentance. Prayer as "disinterested delight," Evelyn Underhill reminds us, "is the perfection of worship."[7] As such, genuine prayer cannot be exhausted by limitations imposed upon it by (human) knowledge.

The attitude of prayer demands an infinite capacity; it must remain always open to a most generous acceptance of the whole of reality. In this sense authentic prayer, as distinct from Pharisaic prayer, finds its grounding in the experience of transcendence. For Stein, the contemporary loss of the experience of transcendence is one of the most haunting catastrophes relegated to the benighted twentieth century. Classically formulated in terms of spiritual crisis, the loss of transcendence often gets falsely addressed as an opposition between the sacred and the profane. Such radical dualism, I submit, does not adequately depict Stein's concern or her deep, penetrating insight into the phenomenology of prayer. For her, the spiritual problem of our age lies in our inability to pray, that is, in our apathy about acknowledging the loss of transcendence as such.

For Stein, prayer announces the infinite; it makes possible the experience of transcendence. In what sense can a human "I" ever claim to know God, the infinite and transcendent? If God is given as an experience of infinity, of transcendence, then in what sense can it be said that God can be known as a matter of creaturely experience? Conversely, to what extent can the notion of prayer be true to itself if it does include God? Can prayer include what both announces and hides itself? In an essay on which she was working near the end of her life,[8] Stein hints at just such a possibility—or, rather, *im*possibility—concerning the essential structure of authentic Christian prayer. Reflecting on her experience of Carmel, Stein describes genuine Christian prayer (mystical union with God) similarly to how she described *Einfühlung* [empathy] and the constitution of the alter ego in her much earlier work, *On the Problem of Empathy*.[9] In both cases, Stein notes that one's primordial experience is led by an encounter with the radically Other, with what is foreign and beyond any strictly cognitive grasp.

Authentic prayer involves an encounter with transcendence. In principle, authentic prayer never apprehends the infinite through understanding alone. Stein notes the following: Seeing with the eyes or in the imagination does not necessarily have anything to do with prayer *as prayer*. When both are absent there might still be an inner certainty that it is God who is speaking. This certainty can rest on the feeling that God is present; one feels touched in his innermost being by God, by the One present. Stein calls such experience of God "prayer" in a proper sense. It is the core of all mystical living experience: the person-to-person encounter with God. "This world with all it discloses and all it conceals," Stein notes, "is just this world that also points beyond itself as a whole to him who 'mysteriously reveals himself' through it. It is *this* world, with its referrings that lead us out beyond itself."[10]

Following in the footsteps of Dionysius the Areopagite, Stein likens authentic prayer to silence, to a withdrawal of presence, to what John of the Cross called a journey through the dark night of the soul. Johannes de Silentio, Søren Kierkegaard's disciple of postmodern prayer par excellence, also endured the deafening, silent withdrawal of presence in his maddening attempt to comprehend Abraham's actions at the summit of Mount Moriah.[11] Stein insists that genuine prayer, even for the most faithful seeker, is wrought with divine absence amidst a sense of loss and spiritual impoverishment. One might even be tempted to add that, in the spirit of Carmel, Sister Teresa Benedicta defines prayer as a nonexperience, as experience of felt absence, as experience beyond experience.

Prayer, then, is a matter of infinite concern. It announces the impossible; it brings to light what can be known by faith alone.

How (Not) to Speak of God

In her essay "Ways to Know God," Stein recounts two very different ways that the Areopagite speaks about God, one positive and the other negative. Human discourse can affirm God's self-revelation to his creation. The kataphatic affirmative theology describes, albeit metaphorically, both the proximity to and the remoteness of creatures from God. Divine knowledge is always mediated and thematized according to orders or degrees of greater and lesser perfection. As a science of order, positive theology entails what Thomas Aquinas calls the journey of all human beings to and from God. In effect, Dionysius mirrors St. Augustine's maxim from the *Confessions*, namely, that "God is more interior to me than my inmost self." *Noli foras ire, in Te redi, in interiore homine habitat veritas*: "Do not go outside, return within yourself; truth dwells in the inner man." Essentially, God is no more available to precise description than is the innermost self.

According to Pseudo-Dionysius, language and thought are confined to the realm of created existence; hence, the only valid affirmation of God is, strictly speaking, that God is nonbeing. This paradox is essential to Stein's phenomenology of prayer. God is beyond being (and, as such, correctly described as nonbeing), precisely in the sense that God is the cause of being. Following

Dionysius, Stein argues that apophatic discourse about God as nothing, that is, "no thing," is not antagonistic to the experience of purification, illumination, and union but is, rather, the condition sine qua non for genuine experience of and philosophical discourse about God. In other words, God is the cause of being yet nonbeing insofar as God is beyond being. The so-called names of God should not be understood as attributes that determine divine essence but as linguistic expressions that describe different levels of the human experience of God.

Prayer, then, does not issue from what we can say about God, but precisely from what *cannot* be said. Pseudo-Dionysius is, of course, not an atheist. He calls this way of speaking about God negative theology. In a manner characteristic of apophatic theologians, the *via negativa* (negative way) of Dionysius points to an insurmountable tension in every cognitive attempt to describe God exclusively in terms of a philosophy of presence. In his effort to distinguish genuine prayer from the limitations of human discourse about prayer, Dionysius uses the biblical image of Jacob's ladder. He describes the ascent and descent of human meaning vis-à-vis divine attribution. Jacob, of course, was the Hebrew patriarch whose name means "He who overreaches." His dream linked the human and the divine, the heavenly and the earthly communities. Jacob's ladder thus describes a genuine hermeneutics by which prayer engenders a dialogical relationship between the thought we grasp and the sense we feel.

All theological language, of course, must be analogous in some sense, since we can speak of God and describe the divine attributes only in relation to the created things that we know.[12] The fathers of the Fourth Lateran Council (1215), for example, declared that "no similarity can be found so great but that the dissimilarity is even greater." It is important to note that for the Areopagite, as with Aquinas, negative theology does not eradicate affirmative theology; rather, negation purges all theoretical structures and delineates all perceptual attributes that affirmative theology naïvely consigns to God. Human discourse does not define God as the object of prayer; instead, it points to the ambiguity that underlies all genuine prayer as an experience of transcendence as such. Language exposes the limitations of prayer; it marks (every) prayer's finite capacity to preserve the transcendence of its encounter with the God beyond being.[13] Every genuine dialogue or conversation is constituted between subjects. In prayer, God is encountered as a subject who shares in the conversation, not its object.

A God who is radically and Wholly Other cannot be constituted cognitively. If this were the case, God would be reducible to the limitations of human cognition; that is, God would no longer be God. What Stein seems to be saying is that the order of experience precedes the order of knowledge. If it were otherwise, that is, if knowledge were principally understood as science about God and things divine, then the other, every other (even God as the [W] holy Other) would first have to be constituted cognitively as a concept within the confines of human intellection. In effect, Dionysius's description of God as nonbeing means to speak of the impossible, but in a particular kind of discourse. God is beyond being not in terms of what is manifest to human intellection, but in describing the divine being-producing processions of the divine names. In other words, one can speak legitimately about God, but such discourse is fundamentally directed toward and has its limits in being. Stein correctly contends that Christian prayer—which seeks authentic union with God, with nonbeing, with that which is beyond being—remains, humanly speaking, an impossible experience, an experience of infinite impossibility, a dark encounter that "lacks the evidence of insight."[14]

Here, I submit, Stein is speaking not only about prayer but also about faith. As an extra-linguistic dialogue, we might say that prayer helps bridge the gulf between self and other, but dialogue does not give the other to me; it does not make the other comprehensible. Just as conversing with another person helps lead to a fuller and more complete (though never fully exhaustive) knowledge of that person, so, too, prayer leads me to God without my ever being able to comprehend God. To pray to God means to sacrifice God as a concept or reference point of understanding. Indeed, following Stein, we might even say that prayer is precisely the horizon of expectation that awaits the unexpected. It reveals and withdraws transcendence in much the same way that every authentic conversation reveals and at the same time withdraws the other person as a subject similar to me, yet different.

Authentic Christian prayer is without why. It seeks for unity always beyond its grasp: "not my will, but Thine be done." It is a reply to a call whose origin is completely gratuitous, an amazing grace. Prayer elicits a response, it speaks: *me voici* [Here I am!]. As a reply to a call that originates from outside the self, prayer announces the revelatory epiphany of a source that is foreign, strange, alien, unknown, unexpected. Of course, such a radical experience of prayer remains, in principle at least, utterly impossible (though with God all things are possible). What prayer gives is the experience of pure presence, that is, that which is impossible for human knowledge ever to grasp or comprehend fully. Prayer thus violates the strict, cognitive laws of object constitution.

The God of prayer, the God who is beyond being, remains outside every such object constitution. We should note, then, that genuine prayer admits no homage to supra-rationalism. On the contrary, Stein argues, prayer is both a constituting as well as a constitutive event. Through prayer, the human subject fully comes to rest in a kind of still, contemplative repose outside every horizon of expectation. Much like the lilies of the field that neither toil nor spin, prayer does not admit of a principle of sufficient reason. Of course, such a moment of prayer, of silence, of restfulness is not without language. What is spoken in prayer is precisely what cannot be said or, better still, what is left unsaid: "God's speaking in its most proper sense is that before which human speech must grow dumb; it finds no place in the words of man, nor in the language of images. God's speaking seizes the person whom it addresses, and demands personal surrender as a condition for hearing him."[15]

Stein describes genuine, full, supernatural faith as a dark light. She asks, "How is it possible for us, starting with the things of experience, to reach something lying beyond all experience?" In other words, is it possible to speak meaningfully of prayer if prayer reveals the incapacity of experience to grasp or name that which knowledge seeks? For Stein, prayer announces the impossible experience of such nonexperience. "God" signifies a nonexperience, an experience of absence, an unimaginable, unthinkable, and absolutely incomprehensible expectation; hence, the language of prayer can never accurately describe the one who is above all meaning and beyond all determination. "In the end," Stein tells us, "[language] must abolish itself, since denial no more applies to [God] than does affirmation."[16]

In phenomenological terms, prayer means to be seized by God, to be brought into immediate contact with "something quite different and yet . . . something that makes the expression-relation possible and enables the expression to be understood."[17] Classically formulated as the dark night of the senses, Christian prayer functions for Stein as a sort of icon: it allows what is visible and tangible to point to the indiscernible, to what is not there. The visible does not make present what is not there. What is made present through prayer is the absence of presence, that is, God as Wholly Other, God as that which or, rather, the one Who precisely cannot be made present. Prayer points beyond itself to what remains essentially disclosed and concealed.

According to the Areopagite, the writers of Sacred Scripture and the mystics and saints are theologians who recognize the Word of God and repeat it as they heard

God speak it. Stein concurs and notes that "all speaking of God presupposes God speaking";[18] nevertheless, this God must remain ineffable, concealed, veiled. In fact, for Stein prayer both presupposes and at the same time undoes the very conditions that make prayer possible. The more cogent one's experience of God in prayer, the less such experience can be described adequately in words. Every authentic experience of prayer is at the same time an illumination of the poverty and limitations that saturate human knowledge. Conversely, such obscurity of knowledge in the order of experience constitutes an ascent in the order of genuine human knowing. Stein argues that, for the novice, prayer is often clear, evocative, and sensually expressive. As human knowledge grapples with its humility and emptiness before the ineffability of God, the language and imagery of prayer become ever more vague and unclear. Symbolic theology climbs Jacob's ladder much as Augustine searched for God amidst the creatures of the world in book 10 of *The Confessions*. At each higher stage, theology acknowledges that the Creator is not to be found there: "I am not God, God is the One who made me."

According to Aquinas, any similarity drawn between creature and Creator results from the analogy of being. In order to say that the creature enters into union with the Creator, one must first experience the dis-association between creature and Creator. In Aquinas's view, negative theology rests on knowledge that alongside similitude lies a major dissimilitude. No genuine experience of prayer, no matter how enlightening, involves an experience of knowing God completely. Just as the finite cannot comprehend the infinite, so human consciousness cannot fathom what remains outside its lived stream of conscious life: that which is known must be adequate to the knower. Through prayer, the mystery that is unveiled is the incomprehensibility of the mystery itself. Unlike intellective forms of knowing, prayer does not entail a strict, cognitive relationship between the knower and a known.

Following Aquinas, then, Stein holds that images and words used to describe God are by nature symbolic. Prayer leads to a different, noncognitive kind of knowledge of what must remain unknown and unknowable in order to be what it is. A symbol does not give meaning; it makes present meaning's absence and inaccessibility. Likewise, prayer does not give God to cognition. On the contrary, genuine prayer points toward the insufficiency of human reason to speak of God. Prayer constitutes every genuine experience of God as Wholly Other. For Stein, prayer violates the formal meaning of the infinite: Prayer announces the primordial experience of what is, and must remain, unfathomable and ineffable, yet this speaking together brings the creature closer to its Creator.

The Prayer of the Church: Image and Icon

Prayer reaches beyond what is here and now given to the senses in the everyday attitude. Through the use of images and signs, we are led from the immediate world we know to the God who is revealed through his creation. In effect, the world is an icon or image that precedes every linguistic attempt to describe it. The image *pre*-sents discourse about the image as its necessary foundation. The structure of prayer is iconic; that is, prayer constitutes an apperception of things hoped for. Prayer seeks forgiveness; it longs for a messiah and a kingdom always yet to come in its fullness but visible, nevertheless, as in a glass darkly. Stein reminds us that the structure of prayer resembles the structure of empathy, in that prayer grasps what is not given along with what is given. Thus her notion of prayer is iconic. Like the icon, prayer combines imagination and intuition; it gives more than what appears. Such excess of meaning makes intersubjectivity possible. Consequently, what is given by the icon is not an image of the ineffable, but ineffability as such. Similarly, the icon thematizes what gets lost in translation, specifically what remains inaccessible to the world of natural experience.

The phenomenological attitude points beyond itself toward transcendence, much as the icon points beyond itself to that which lies beyond being. Phenomenologically speaking, prayer is always *ek*-static. What is given in prayer is precisely what remains hidden and concealed or, as St. Paul says, "In the same way, the Spirit too comes to the aid of our weakness, for we do not know how to pray as we ought, but the Spirit himself intercedes with inexpressible groanings" (Rom 8:26). Similarly, Stein writes about the Areopagite in order to preserve and reaffirm the viability of the traditional Christian paradigm of theology as purification, contemplation, and union. Her attempt to describe the phenomenon of prayer in its pure essence or givenness in fact reiterates the contemplative experience of Teresa of Ávila: the goal of Christian prayer is union with God, the deifying vision of the Trinity. Ultimately, according to Stein, it is the desire for union with God that teaches the saints negative theology, not the reverse.

In effect, Stein wants to free prayer from every accident of appearance while, at the same time, preserve apophatic theology from dangerous misunderstandings. Prayer places into radical question the extent to which I encounter God precisely in God's inscrutability, as *mysterium tremendum*, but without reducing God to being merely a conceptual or rationalist construct of human knowledge. Along with the possibility of understanding the image of the icon as an image of natural experience is the possibility of understanding the icon as an image of the God who is beyond being. The distinction between the two different ways of seeing is reminiscent of the distinction between what is given in a natural language and what Husserl characterizes as meditative thinking or the phenomenological attitude.

Stein's description of prayer presents an act of second-order higher understanding that stands outside the limit and sufficiency of reason. It calls for believing in the impossible, that is, communication between the human and the divine. Even so, her phenomenology of prayer assents to darkness and silence without allowing ineffability to have the last word. Stein's phenomenological description of prayer does not make the invisible visible but points to it. As the Areopagite notes, prayer is a condition of possibility that shatters all horizons and makes the ineffable, the impossible, temporal. Similarly, the icon makes the God beyond-being present within being. Prayer may thus be described as a journey into a dark night without words, without images. It announces a rupture in representational thinking. It demands that the God of my prayer be at one and the same time intimately more present to me than my inmost self, yet remain always outside every conscious attempt to define such givenness in strictly rational or cognitive terms.

Prayer functions as a kind of icon for Stein. What is perceived in prayer always points to something beyond its comprehension. Stein is clear on this point: I cannot experience God except as a constituted phenomenon, yet God himself is never phenomenally given. Through prayer I approach the divine Other as transcendent mystery, as an experience of what cannot be experienced, as a matter of revelation. By virtue of prayer, God is experienced as veiled, hidden, *mysterium tremendum*. If it were otherwise, that is, if I could have primordial access to what lies hidden and unknown in the depth of divine mystery, then God would merely be a rationally designated entity consumed within an economy of sameness. Divine invisibility becomes accessible only through an apprehension of what is visible but hidden. Stein adds that prayer is the revealing or unfolding of God as "totally other," namely, as divine incomprehensibility:

> [H]uman ideas are a bridge to thoughts about God. But they go beyond to the "totally other," other than anything their experience encounters or can encounter

in the world. And this they allow to move them to accept the teaching of supernatural revelation as the fulfillment of what they at first grasped in but empty fashion as the "totally other," and as the answer to the riddles that experience itself poses without ever being able to solve them. In this case passing from the world of natural experience into the world of supernatural faith comes about as a matter of course and almost imperceptibly.[19]

The Areopagite seeks union with God, not mere knowledge about God; hence, authentic prayer emanates from a response to a call that comes from outside the self, from a primordial experience of alterity that is not grounded by the order of sufficient reason, from a nonprimordial experience that announces a primordial one. It is a calling, a responding, a being claimed without intention, without limit, without cause or sense, without reservation. This experience is what Stein describes by the phenomenology of prayer. It requires that God first lay claim to me before I can ever begin to imagine how I could possibly respond. Prayer requires divine grace and human acquiescence.

Following Pseudo-Dionysius, Stein argues that the essence of prayer is not knowledge about God but a sense of interiority "transformed in that new way of knowledge." Whereas René Descartes and the moderns believe that God must somehow be thought within the horizon of creatureliness, Stein argues that the condition of the possibility of prayer is that God must remain hidden precisely in order to be encountered. Christian prayer therefore requires that I who am finite must relate intimately to the infinitely Other, without providing sufficient reason for doing so. Such is the paradox of prayer: it is excess, supplement, joy, a desire without concern for itself. Prayer always prays for the impossible. It hopes all things, loves all things. It gives expression to a unitary, reciprocal exchange between the visible and the invisible, the kataphatic and the apophatic, the secular and the sacred, what is Caesar's and what is God's.

We can thus infer that for Stein it is precisely the impossibility of prayer that makes prayer possible. To pray to a God who hides in the negation of experience means to remain faithful to a future that never quite arrives, to an eternal advent, to a Messiah who is present and yet-to-come. Prayer remains hopeful even as it exposes the radical incongruity of the whole of reality. Through prayer I learn to trust the unknown and to keep one eye always on the invisible. Genuine prayer makes present what both is and is not at one and the same time; it manifests what in principle remains silent, absent, and mysterious; hence, no cognitive or linguistic description of the experience of God can be adequately justified by mere sufficiency of reason. What Stein discovers is that prayer both shatters and constitutes at one and the same time every horizon of expectation.

The prayer of the church is a topic of extreme importance to Stein, but somewhat beyond the scope of this paper; nevertheless, it is vital to note that prayer for Stein is never merely an individual, egoic activity. For Stein, prayer manifests a universal phenomenon in the life of faith; it draws every isolated individual into a community of reciprocity and grace. She notes that "every true prayer is a prayer of the Church; by means of that prayer the Church prays, since it is the Holy Spirit living in the Church, Who in every single soul 'prays in us with unspeakable groanings.'"[20] When Stein speaks of prayer, she has in mind the prayer of the whole church, that is, ways in which persons and whole communities are able to express themselves verbally as well as through bodily movement. This is true regardless of the form or type of prayer being expressed: sung, meditative, liturgical, intercessory, scriptural, petitionary, supplicative, or confessional. As a mode of discourse, Christian prayer is inherently liturgical; the prayer of the church is praise of the divine names of God but, as Stein and Pseudo-Dionysius agree, praise of the God beyond-being necessarily includes apophatic discourse. The paradoxical contemplation of God transforms the language of prayer into apophatic experience. It does not merely bring language out into the open, but seeks to express and communicate that which, cognitively speaking, remains inaccessible and incomprehensible. The hymnic prayer of the church gives witness to the apophatic experience of divinity beyond being, it corrects what has gone amiss from the Scholastic transformation of theology into *scientia*.

Since the prayer of the church is never isolated but manifest always in community, the prayer of the church seeks the kingdom here, now, even in our midst; it says, "Arise!" and believes that the dead shall be raised. Prayer discloses a phenomenon that is not constituted by a lonely, isolated Cartesian ego but that, in fact, constitutes the "I" as a source of intellective human subjectivity. The prayer of the people of God is a call of response, of gratitude. It makes a claim upon me, it calls me to infinite responsibility. Responsibility to whom? To the other. Which other? Every other. Stein's description of prayer offers a resounding "Yes!" to Cain's question, "Am I my brother's keeper?"

Prayer is both ethically constitutive and, at the same time, constituted nonphenomenally as neither the object nor the subject of human intellection. As St. John reminds us, love is also a name of God, since God is love. Stein concurs: "As for what concerns our relations with our fellow men, the anguish in our neighbor's soul must break all precept. All that we do is a means to an end, but love is an end in itself, because God is love."[21] God as infinite love is the name of that which remains most intimately present to my inmost self, yet paradoxically is that which can never be fully present or cognized in thought. Experience of God can never be given without violating the sine qua non condition of possibility of its own givenness. This is why the Areopagite and Stein similarly describe the prayer of the church as an experience of divine love, as the experience of a hidden light and dazzling darkness. By operating in the blind, so to speak, prayer violates every condition of empirical knowledge abstracted from the natural attitude. Just as divine love remains blind to self-interest, so the phenomenology of prayer exposes a certain blindness in every act of faith; it reveals a lack of insight in every appresentation; it posits a certain sense of absence as a condition of possibility of divine Presence.

Following the Areopagite's critique of theology as merely a primarily intellectual enterprise, Stein argues that prayer disprivileges the role of cognition in every genuine act of transcendence. The phenomenology of prayer describes how transcendence both appears within a given frame or horizon of reference and, at the same time, points to what remains hidden or outside its grasp. Prayer exposes that which is excess in every act of givenness. As a condition of possibility of faith, prayer renders present precisely that which cannot appear phenomenally, namely, the triune God who is beyond being.

Concluding Thoughts

"Experience of God," Stein reminds us, remains "even in its greatest conceivable perfection essentially fragmentary."[22] The subjectivity of human finitude finds its perfection only in relation to Eternal Being, a perfection that remains outside every earthly grasp. Accordingly, the God who is encountered through prayer remains beyond being, concealed, veiled in language. Just as the icon points beyond itself to an excess that is not fully recognizable in it, so, too, prayer points beyond itself to that which is never fully given in discursive speech. The phenomenology of prayer reveals an attitude, an orientation that transforms and interprets human subjectivity apart from all a priori conceptions of it. As an experience of God, prayer both rises from and points toward the church's liturgical hymn of praise to the divine names. Phenomenologically speaking, then, prayer is dialogical, reciprocal, relational. What gets expressed through such discursive dissonance is a subject-to-subject encounter by which language grasps God precisely by recognizing that it can never grasp God. This is prayer's distinctive grace: it renders imperfect every attempt by human language to express divine perfection; it seeks God without ever grasping God; it affirms the nature of God's inscrutable and incomprehensible nature. In its ascetic-mystical context, Stein's description of prayer speaks of the unspeakability of God, much as the icon makes present an epiphany that exceeds every human attempt to grasp and contain it. Prayer announces an experience of impossible expectation, of ineffability, yet of intimate presence and absolute gift; it lies beyond every cognitive effort to comprehend it.

Notes

1. Edith Stein was declared a saint by Pope John Paul II on October 11, 1998.

2. Stein received her PhD under Edmund Husserl's direction. In the years immediately following, she edited a number of Husserl's texts, including *The Phenomenology of Internal Time Consciousness* and what was posthumously published by the Husserl Archive in 1952 as *Ideas II.*

3. These works include *Finite and Eternal Being: An Attempt at an Ascent to the Meaning of Being,* trans. Kurt Reinhardt, CWES, vol. 9 (Washington, D.C.: ICS Publications, 2002); *The Science of the Cross,* trans. Josephine Koeppel, CWES, vol. 6 (Washington, D.C.: ICS Publications, 2002); and an essay, titled "Ways to Know God," in *Knowledge and Faith,*

trans. Walter Redmond, CWES, vol. 8 (Washington, D.C.: ICS Publications, 2000), 83–117.

4. For Husserl, phenomenology was the culmination of Greek thinking, its goal to restore to philosophy the precision and apodicticity lost to philosophy by the crisis of European sciences.

5. By apophatic theology I mean the *via negativa* of Meister Eckhart, Dionysius the Areopagite, John of the Cross, et al., as opposed to the positive theology of the kataphatic tradition, which speaks of God in terms of positive attributes.

6. Several modern spiritual writers concur, including Thomas Merton and C. S. Lewis.

7. Evelyn Underhill, *Worship* (New York: Harper and Row, 1936), 5.

8. See Stein, "Ways to Know God," in *Knowledge and Faith*, 83–117.

9. Stein's dissertation, *Zum Problem der Einfühlung (On the Problem of Empathy)*, as well as her twin habilitation essays, *Beiträge zur philosophischen Begründung der Psychologie und der Geisteswissenschaften (Philosophy of Psychology and the Humanities)*, explore questions concerning the constitution of the self [*das Ich*] and the Other [*der fremde*] in light of Husserl's phenomenological reduction.

10. Stein, *Knowledge and Faith*, 99.

11. Søren Kierkegaard's Johannes de Silentio is struck dumb by the same *mysterium tremendum* that shatters Abraham's faith as he ascends Mount Moriah with his beloved son Isaac, filled with "fear and trembling."

12. One could here make the even more striking statement that all human knowledge is, at heart, analogous.

13. Several contemporary French philosophers have attempted to explore the implications of ontotheology phenomenologically, most notably in terms of the manifestation of the God beyond-being. See, for example, Jean-Luc Marion and Jacques Derrida.

14. Stein, *Knowledge and Faith*, 114.

15. Ibid., 116–17.

16. Ibid., 39.

17. Ibid., 38.

18. Ibid., 116.

19. Ibid., 127.

20. "Edith Stein." *BrainyQuote.com*. Xplore Inc, 2010, accessed April 11, 2010: *http://www.brainyquote.com/quotes/quotes/e/edithstein198684*. Also available at *http://ocarm.org/en/content/ocarm/edith-stein-quotes*.

21. "Edith Stein." *BrainyQuote.com*. Xplore Inc, 2010, accessed April 11, 2010: *http://www.brainyquote.com/quotes/quotes/e/edithstein198683.html*. Also available at *http://ocarm.org/en/content/ocarm/edith-stein-quotes*.

22. Stein, *Finite and Eternal Being*, 26.

PART II

In Dialogue with Moderns and Postmoderns

8

EDITH STEIN AND RENEWAL:
"The New Spirit Already Exists and Will Prevail"

JOHN SULLIVAN, O.C.D.

The words chosen as the subtitle of this essay were penned by the young Edith Stein, PhD, during World War I to assure her sister that it is worth hoping and worth working through current crises toward a better, a renewed future. Stein offered that encouragement in a letter on July 6, 1918, as her answer to a foreboding missive (now lost) from her favorite sister, Erna Stein (Biberstein).[1] Although the new spirit she touted to Erna was not then for her *the* Spirit that Christians adore and denote with a capital "S," it is very interesting to see the future saint refer to a power abroad in the land that went beyond her sister's doubts and her own relative inexperience. Their land was Germany: a country heading for final defeat at the eleventh hour of the eleventh day of the eleventh month of 1918; then moving toward a subsequent revolution that would force the parliament to transfer from the capital Berlin to the city of Weimar; and lurching further into such national turmoil that the Nazi Party would take power before another block of eighteen years passed from the twentieth century.

In spite of the darkness, Edith Stein (1891–1942) made an appeal to recognize that better things would also be coming their way because a new spirit had come already, was at work, and would win out in the end. Brave sentiments, indeed; clairvoyant, perhaps; good solace for her sister certainly. One can derive reassurance in the initial decades of this subsequent century, provided, like Stein, one desires to be renewed in the Spirit to benefit the current scene.

The purpose of this essay is to demonstrate how Stein, that is, Sister Teresa Benedicta of the Cross (Carmelite nun and now co-patroness of Europe) went resolutely ahead beyond that moment in her life to find ways of renewal in the Spirit-dominated realm she could see at work as it unfolded. Like other trusting individuals, she was capable of forging onward as an agent of renewal precisely because she relied on Spirit-filled trust. Such people are able to effect renewal (the first part here contains some renewal activities she undertook) because they rely on a higher power to move ever forward; the second part illustrates how she drew on the Spirit's inspiration.

Pursuit of Renewal in Edith Stein's Life: Contributions to Philosophy

Professor Ludwig Landgrebe, a contemporary of Stein and also an assistant to Edmund Husserl as she had been, has synthesized for us the role she played in the philosophical ferment of phenomenology that she helped promote. He gave the following testimony in the docudrama TV film *Edith Stein, Stations of an Extraordinary Life*, distributed in the United States by the Eternal Word Television Network (EWTN):

> What does renewal mean? In Husserl's sense? It means requiring a return to the immediate and original, practical knowledge that human beings had about themselves and about the world, even before there was any science—before such science was known to them; everything [is included] that appeared to them as immediate certainties and truths that were accepted by them. Among these must be counted not only those that deal with life in the world, but also the question about the forces that rule therein, the questions that touch upon the matter of religious belief and its various forms. These are the data for humankind that can never be retrieved [or "caught up with"]. Therefore, Husserl was also convinced that religious, really living, certainties of faith belong to those original experiences that can never be surpassed, or improved upon, or changed, but which rather precede all thought and reflection and all scientific endeavors. So she [Edith] never saw philosophy as a competitor of religion, but as a critic of the demands of the sciences, of all which—really—we are moved to clear up altogether and grasp.[2]

One deduces from Stein's application of her beloved master's approach that we apply in the present useful principles and truths from the past. For her, renewal, even at the stage of philosophy, would always involve Christ's Gospel description of "the good scribe who knows how to bring out of his/her storehouse, things new and old" (Mt 13:52). In today's quest for meaning, our contemporaries can still recognize the perennial wisdom detected by previous generations where it has stood the test of time.

The very nature of the effort Stein devoted to philosophy as a career was significant: it was one of renewal. With Husserl (1873–1938) in the lead, she knew that the dominant idealism in the philosophical endeavor at the time led to a dead end; so people needed some new method to come to grips with reality. The phenomenology of Husserl that she was able to deepen through her thesis, *On the Problem of Empathy*, was a new breath of fresh air in the world of ideas. She would show a preference for new ways in other phases of her life too.[3]

Her intellectual searching, once she became a Catholic in 1922, involved learning the principles of Thomism and uncovering points of intersection between its realist vision of things and that of phenomenology. From this emerged two kinds of valid contributions to the ferment among Catholics for a Thomistic revival in the first half of the twentieth century: through both her writings and her personal exchanges and contacts.

On occasion authors draw up dream pieces of imaginary dialogues between personages who lived at entirely different epochs of world history. Stein created one such dialogue in 1929. She devised a comparison of some of the tenets of Thomism with those of phenomenology in an exchange of views between St. Thomas Aquinas and

Husserl. Titled "Husserl and Aquinas: A Comparison," it appears in the volume *Knowledge and Faith* in the two versions she drafted.[4]

After that she did a two-volume translation from Latin to German of Aquinas's work *Disputed Questions on Truth*. Both this and the previous small original piece were published while she was still alive. On occasion she would refer to this lengthy translation as "my Thomas," meaning her rendition of the thought and expressions of the medieval theologian/philosopher who was considered the great mentor of Catholics. A few of the chapter headings of what she put into modern German were: Truth (1), Providence (5), The Book of Life (7), The Teacher (11), Ecstasy (13), Faith (14), Knowledge of Christ's Soul (20), God's Will (23), and The Grace of Christ (29). She found inspiration from those questions of the Angelic Doctor and through them provided access for her readers to a useful manual of Christian thought.[5]

In *Finite and Eternal Being* she examined the concept of a perennial philosophy, one that runs the centuries and stays valid at the heart of philosophical systems and vindicated Thomism's place among them as she laid out Aquinas's teaching on being in the second half of the book. She evoked themes suitable to the spiritual lives of believers. For instance, part seven bears the title "The Image of the Trinity in the Created World"; then she concluded part eight (and the whole treatise) with "The Unity of the Human Race: Head and Body, One Christ." She aimed her reflections at shoring up new avenues of Christian commitment for the troubled times of the third decade of the twentieth century.[6]

At that time in the first half of the twentieth century, Catholic thinkers were busy at reviving Thomistic philosophy and using it to come to terms with current problems that asked for answers from people of faith. In a part of his encyclical *Fides et Ratio*, on the Relationship between Faith and Reason, the late Pope John Paul II recommended familiarity with writings in this direction by modern thinkers from both Western and Eastern Christianity. He listed the following names: John Henry Newman, Antonio Rosmini, Jacques Maritain, Etienne Gilson, and Edith Stein. The two persons listed before Stein were participants in the neoscholastic movement.[7] Stein both corresponded with Maritain and spent a full day with him at an encounter that took place near Paris on September 12, 1932, between Thomists and phenomenologists.[8]

Education for Women

Several events mark Stein's strivings for renewal in the field of women's education. Soon after her arrival among doctors of philosophy in the summer of 1916—and with top honors, *summa cum laude*—she wrote to the Prussian Minister of Science, Arts and Popular Education to complain that women doctors were barred from teaching in universities in positions commensurate with their high academic achievements. She did not obtain a job for herself as an immediate consequence, but the minister circulated an official letter to rectors of universities to investigate and remedy the situation. A history marking the fiftieth anniversary of women teaching in university faculties placed

Stein's name not in first place on the list, but in the book's Prologue with the claim that had it not been for her intervention the list would have begun much later.[9]

One way the Second Vatican Council (1962–65) showed the church's desire to spread the good news of Catholic teaching was its Decree on the Means of Social Communications [*Inter Mirifica*]. The renewal desired by the bishops in communion with the Pope Paul VI would rely on things such as television and other electronic media for widely displaying its message. Stein considered radio a useful new format for informing her contemporaries. Welcomed by Bavarian State Radio she appeared April 1, 1932, on "The Woman's Hour" and addressed the maternal art of raising children.[10]

Church Renewal Movements

Although Stein believed that all professions should be open to women, she frequently stressed the role of women in the religious formation of children and young people. Acknowledgment of the contribution she made to the renewal of the church takes the form of many schools dedicated to her in Germany today. In this she sided with other forces at work busy seeking church life renewal in the German-speaking world between the two World Wars. That topic is broad and varied and has been commented on in studies about the currents that led to the renewal council of Vatican II.[11]

Afterward her pupils echoed with admiration the reassuring investment they could see her making. Why would they not? They knew from up close someone who wrote thoughts like these to another teacher:

> Surely the children who attend convent schools should gain there the strength to form their lives in the spirit of Christ. Surely it is most important that the teachers truly have this spirit themselves and vividly exemplify it. At the same time they also need to know life as the children will find it. Otherwise there will be a great danger that the girls will tell themselves: "The Sisters have no notion about the world"; "They were unable to prepare us for the questions we now have to answer"; and the [danger] that then everything might be thrown overboard as useless.[12]

Earlier that same year (1932), she gave a speech to a convention of young women in Augsburg whose title is more descriptive in the original German than what appears in the ICS translation: "Woman's Task of Leading Young People to the Church."[13] For a woman to do this she, like Stein, would have to pay her dues in the struggle to come up with new answers for questions that, by definition, were new because they were being posed by a new generation. The replies would have to be new too, renewing the expression of the valid truths the church has to offer in the name of Christ who is and remains the Way, the Truth, and the Life.

The insight from that letter finds many parallel expressions in her other extant writings. She tried to be on the cutting edge of what is generally sought after today, namely, a Catholic culture, but ostensibly one for her time and one devised in terms that aimed to proclaim the truth in an up-to-date format.

One sees this happening, too, in the way she was conversant with some centers of the liturgical movement. Two names come quickly to mind: the Archabbey of Beuron where she spent time making retreats full of intense prayer, either in the abbey church chanting with the monks or in meditation, and the Abbey of Maria Laach. The latter was the final stopover she made en route to her home city, Breslau, Poland, in the summer of 1933, before entering religious life in Cologne in mid-October of that year.

Her aspirations for renewed liturgical practice did not stop once she joined the Carmelites. At Carmel she wrote a short study that put things in perspective among liturgists and more individualist devotion-centered persons. She wrote "The Church at Prayer" and published it in 1937 to recommend peaceful coexistence between often opposed quiet/meditative types and praise-filled liturgical devotees. What she wrote then still makes much sense today and has stood the test of time, all the more so for the confirmation that Vatican II has given to healthy liturgical piety.[14]

Inspiration to Renewal for Edith Stein

Rooted in Trust in Providence

To believe in renewal as a possibility, to dedicate oneself to being an instrument of renewal (just as St. Francis of Assisi asked to be "an instrument of your peace"), one must also believe that God is in charge of things and always wants them to get better than they have become, thanks to the tarnishing tendencies of sinners. The creation account of the first book of the Bible shows God viewing the world and declaring it was good; what happened subsequently in the original sin of our forebears brought darkness upon it. Ever since, the task has been to heal creation, and thanks to the redeeming work of Christ, we are on the road to full recuperation. St. Pius X, who was pope early in the twentieth century when Stein was a teenager, placed a phrase to that effect on his papal coat of arms: "*Instaurare omnia in Christo*" or "To renew all things in Christ," as the words borrowed from Ephesians 1:10 are usually translated.

Renewal, then, presupposes willingness to abide by change so long as it remains in line with God's plans. We discern the presence or not of God at work in evolving events, and then we are able to find peace in the midst of transformation. In spite of our reticence to let things as we know them gradually fade into the past out of the present, we know deep down that oncoming developments according to the Lord's wishes are well worth embracing even as they take the place of favorite ways of doing things. Stein took this trust in God at work as the key to serenity in accepting the new. Not to act with trust in God's providence would be to substitute for it empty human agitation. She offered this advice: "Every change in the external circumstances of life can easily lead to a disturbance of inner tranquility. Therefore one should never seek a change which God does not decree."[15]

Stein once crystallized this truth in her crowning work, *Finite and Eternal Being*, when she affirmed that "what was not in my plan, lay in God's plan."[16] This oft-quoted and popular maxim was coined by Stein, not to describe her life as such but—as we know from reading its context in *Finite and Eternal Being*—to propose a hypothetical case for explaining the question of chance and happenstance. As such it can be applied to everyone directly, not just to her and what might have emerged in her life. When we look back ourselves, we sometimes ruefully agree that to follow God's call forward would have been much better than the course of action we adopted.

As a further inducement to imitate her trust in God's providence we can accept the words she attributed to St. Ambrose in a translation she shared with another Carmelite nun: "God does all things at the right time. Whatever He does is not outside of time but rather at the most opportune moment and comes at the right time for me."[17]

Springing from Love for a Loving God

Like the saints, people usually wonder which verse of Scripture would be the favorite inspiration of their spirituality. Until completion of the new German scholarly edition that will replace what Dr. Lucy Gelber tried to organize in the series *Edith Steins Werke*, we await a cumulative scriptural index to assist our search. Still, I would offer as a prime candidate the following verse. Stein always derived from it much consolation as she sought to confront the changing, new situations of life that called her to apply her faith in Providence. Taken from the letter to the Romans, it reads: "We know that for those who love Him, God turns everything to the good"(Rom 8:28). The nature of this renewal-oriented verse of Holy Writ is evident: "God *turns* everything to the good" in the midst of his plan for the betterment of creation.

Its appeal comes, not just from the fact that those words were coined by the convert Paul, someone who had stood opposed to the Lord and who was able to formulate a thought likely to attract the attention of a former atheist convert like Stein who was filled with appreciation for the mysterious dispensation of God's grace, though that probably helped. The heart of the matter lies elsewhere. Edith Stein cherished that verse from the letter to the Romans especially for the central word "love."

For those "who *love* him, God turns everything to the good." Stein came to love God finally through reading the life story of one of the greatest women lovers of God, St. Teresa. The "flaming heart" of Ávila espoused in her famous "Bookmark" the inspiring challenge: "Nothing is lacking to those who possess God/God alone suffices." Stein, later Sister Teresa Benedicta, recognized in St. Teresa someone who accepted unflinchingly the Gospel message that the law of God is a law of love. We fulfill it by showing our love in the first place (even before works of repentance or of praise), since the God who proposed a law of love is deserving of love before all else. The simple reason why this works is the identification of law with the lawgiver: both are sources of love in the world. God is love, by nature.

With this in mind (and in heart) those who love him also take for granted that what he provides for them are always proofs of his love. Nothing coming from God could be anything but love. Then, by embracing whatever is accurately assumed to be God's disposition, one comes to see that it turns to the good. As a practical outcome, those who love him will allow God to lead them forward and not fear for the results; they will be able to take on the new set of coordinates they engage in as just one more expression of his loving plan. Sister Teresa Benedicta even found a place for Paul's words in her meditation on Advent and Christmas, *The Mystery of Christmas.* In the section on the Mystical Body of Christ she left us these programmatic words: "Wherever that will lead us on this Earth we do not know and should not ask beforehand. Only this do we know: that for those who love the Lord, all things work out for good."[18]

As a result, Stein relied on the verse of St. Paul to keep herself receptive of the tensions served up by new life stages without her seeking them. The key occasion to demonstrate this was the death of her mother. She had a premonition the night before her mother died that the final hour was fast approaching. On September 13, 1936, she wrote the following confidence to a dear friend:

> [E]very bulletin from Breslau [Stein's hometown] reports a worsening. I must be prepared to hear the worst any day. The "Scimus, quoniam diligentibus Deum . . ." ["We know that, for all those who love him, God turns everything to their good" (Rom 8:28)] will surely apply to my dear mother, too, since she truly loved "her" God (as she often said with emphasis). And,

with confidence in him, she bore much that was painful and did much that was good. . . . That phrase I quoted from the Letter to the Romans afforded me the greatest comfort and joy during the summer of 1933, in Münster, when my future was still shrouded in total darkness. Never have I prayed the Divine Office of the Martyrs, which recurs so frequently during the Easter cycle, with greater fervor than I did at that time. Now, it must be my support again.[19]

How beautiful was the inclusiveness she expressed: Stein felt the words of Paul applied to her mother, the Jewess loyal to her faith to the very end; they also applied to herself as a mantra of sorts that previously helped her decide in 1933 to change her life's calling from the classroom to Carmel, and also now as she was readying herself to face separation from her mother on this earth. She truly loved her God—Mother Stein, that is, loved "her God"—and Edith Stein loved that God, too. May people follow her as their example and see how surely they can pass calmly through what challenges them.

Resilient in Hope

Our imagination would like to capture, for its inspiration, the persona and life of a saint in one special virtue that he or she stood for as a member of the pilgrim people of God while still *in via* on this earth. In the case of Stein it was hope. Hope fed her willingness to seek renewal; hope was her stay throughout the many abrupt changes that emerged from life's stages.

Whereas the media claim she had an extraordinary and an exceptional life, it was, for all its fascinating facets, a hard and troubling life. A veritable litany of the potholes and hurdles she had to traverse would include early loss of her father as a child; shift from a religious to an atheistic outlook; interruption (although voluntary) of her doctoral studies by World War I; denial of a university post after a brilliant doctoral defense; anti-Semitic persecution in her homeland; dismissal from her teaching position because of discriminatory Nazi laws; disappointing velvet-glove treatment for her courageous intervention to warn Pope Pius XI,[20] that is, no direct reply but some verbal remarks only from her spiritual director; flight from Germany soon after *Kristallnacht*; separation from her family as they, too, took flight; worries over her family either emigrating or under house arrest back home; loss of citizenship while in exile in nearby Holland; eventual arrest, deportation, and murder by the SS [*Schutzstaffel*]. Through them all, she held high her hope.

The kind of hope meant here is nothing less than hope as a full theological virtue, not some hollow and superficial optimism. It must be hope taken to be a resilience that almost drives the person forward through adversity, not an escapist maneuver that leads one around it, nor can one just switch the focus away from the present to a rosy future. Hope is placing one's hand in God's hand, in the knowledge that by it as a theological virtue one is united to God no matter what happens. A person is convinced that if, as Stein's great mystical master, St. John of the Cross, once said, "Hope obtains from God all it hopes for," then one can go on hoping with hope, not against hope. A person can't foresee the other side of the trouble he/she is in, but trusts that God will bring him/her beyond it to a new day.

Such hope, then, is the mainspring of Christian renewal. This really happened in Stein's case because the writings she left behind never betray any traces of despair or discontent, even though she described life's difficulties to friends and family alike. Aided by unflagging hope, she did prevail just as she had predicted the "new spirit will prevail" in those beautiful words she wrote to her sister Erna. She leaned on hope willingly. It helped her be renewed and move ever forward as she asserted in one of her letters: "The story of a soul is hidden deep in God's heart. And what we sometimes think we understand of our own soul is, after all, always just a fleeting reflection of what remains God's secret until the day when all is revealed. My great joy is the *hope* for that future revelation."[21]

Convinced that Change Can Be Handled

The following two sentences display well the conviction that committed Christians will courageously face change and thus engage in renewal: "The Church as the Kingdom of God in this world should reflect changes in human thought. Only by accepting each age as it is and treating it according to its singular nature can the Church bring eternal truth and life to temporality."[22]

As in so many other passages of her writings, Stein placed in fruitful tension realities that oftentimes appear to be opposed yet are fated to coexist and can coexist peacefully if embraced by faith: kingdom of God and world, age and singular nature, and, finally, eternal truth and temporality. That is to say, for those who recognize the fact that we are alive here and now through a design of God, the dull and often daunting drama of human existence is open to redemption, not doomed to a downward spiral into despair. Even though we cannot escape being subject to the attrition of the passage of time (the years fly by, as the saying goes), we, with Stein, can take it in our stride. Inevitable passages out of one stage into another serve up different coordinates in the overall picture of the human scene, and yet one thing remains: God set it all in motion so as to draw all creatures into the orbit of his everlasting love. God remains serene in his eternity, supreme in his truthfulness, but he wants us to share in it ultimately and, in the meantime, be drawn gradually into it. The church as the kingdom of God in this world is his preferred instrument for helping people come to terms with life's puzzlements and discover that he is the origin and goal of all their longings. Eternal truth is brought to temporality by a church aware of its mission as it refines the perennial message it has to deliver: God is with us, God will be with us because God has been with us from the beginning. Nothing escapes God's benign design. Move ahead: God won't let us down.

Tension derives from weaving in and out of the developments of evolving human reality, as everyone well knows, but the children of God need not think they are alienated for their faith. Quite the opposite: they are an indispensable leaven within the dough that rises and heaves and moves. We belong to something better and must let our reliance on the solid verities we have learned from other believers make a difference. Stein promises us calm in the midst of it all when she states: "The imperturbability of the Church resides in her ability to harmonize the unconditional preservation of the eternal with an unmatchable elasticity of adjustment to the circumstances and challenges of changing times."[23] By doing this, we will promote the coming of the kingdom; it is yet to arrive, so changes are still on the way.

We pray daily, "May your kingdom come." May we realize we pray for it to come into this struggling world, for its transformation, for changes for the better. The kingdom is not supposed to take form anywhere else. Jesus died for the life of the world, the changing world that can fill us with nostalgia, but a world that has been designated the theater of God's operations. We can be at peace with change in this scheme of things, because the outcome will be new things converging into renewal by God's standards.

Notes

1. Stein to Erna Stein, July 6, 1918, letter 24, in *Self-Portrait in Letters, 1916–1942*, trans. Josephine Koeppel, O.C.D., CWES, vol. 5 (Washington, D.C.: ICS Publications, 1993), 27; hereafter *Letters*.

2. Text rendered by Sister Josephine Koeppel, O.C.D., in an unpublished typescript. See the recent study of Stein's early philosophical output, Alasdair MacIntyre, *Edith Stein: A Philosophical Prologue, 1913–1922* (Lanham, Md./Oxford: Rowman and Littlefield Publishers, 2006).

3. See Stein, *On the Problem of Empathy*, 3rd rev. ed., trans. Waltraut Stein, CWES, vol. 3 (Washington, D.C.: ICS Publications, 1989).

4. Stein, "Husserl and Aquinas: A Comparison," in *Knowledge and Faith*, trans. Walter Redmond, CWES, vol. 8 (Washington, D.C.: ICS Publications, 2000), 1–63.

5. The work remains untranslated into English.

6. See Stein, *Finite and Eternal Being: An Attempt at an Ascent to the Meaning of Being*, trans. Kurt Reinhart, CWES, vol. 9 (Washington, D.C.: ICS Publications, 2002), 355–468 and 510–27.

7. See "Edith Stein in the Encyclical 'Fides et Ratio,'" in *Holiness Befits Your House, Canonization of Edith Stein—A Documentation*, ed. John Sullivan (Washington, D.C.: ICS Publications, 2000), 20.

8. See Stein to Sister Adelgundis Jaegerschmid, O.S.B., August 28, 1932, letter 120, *Letters*, 118.

9. Her exchange of letters is given in the new German edition of her correspondence *Selbstbildnis in Briefen I 1916–1933*, Edith Stein Gesamtausgabe, vol. 2 (Freiburg: Herder, 2000); hereafter ESGA. See Edith Stein an Konrad Haenisch, December 12, 1919, Brief 26, in *Briefen I*, vol. 2, 50–51; and Konrad Haenisch an Edith Stein, February 21, 1920, Brief 30 in *Briefen I*, vol. 2, 55–56. In this connection we would amend the assertion of Theresa Wobbe where she says Heinrich Becker was the minister for education ("The Complex Modernity of Edith Stein: New Gender Relations and Options for Women in Early-Twentieth-Century Germany," chap. 6, in *Contemplating Edith Stein*, ed. Joyce A. Berkman [Notre Dame, Ind.: University of Notre Dame Press, 2006], 125). At the time Edith Stein presented her letter of protest, H. Becker served Konrad Haenisch, the minister, as state secretary, and Becker became minister only later in the 1920s; see Stein in *Briefen I*, 56n3.

10. German text available as "Miltterliche Erziehungskunst," in Stein, *Die Frau, Fragestellungen und Reflexionen*, ESGA, vol. 13, 4th ed. (Freiburg: Herder, 2000), 115–26.

11. In her monographic study, Gerda Brockhausen, *Espiritualidad en Alemania, Corrientes modernas—Edith Stein* (Madrid: EDE, 1968), identifies several renewal movements, in the fields of "liturgy"; "Christocentric" [theology]; "biblical and patrology" [studies]; "Marian" [studies]; and "mystical" [theology]. To them we would add renewal movements of the laity, of youth, and of missiology.

12. Stein to Sister Callista Kopf, O.P., October 20, 1932, letter 123, in *Letters*, 122–23.

13. See Edith Stein, "The Church, Woman, and Youth," chap. 6, in *Essays on Woman*, 2nd rev. ed., trans. Freda Mary Oben, CWES, vol. 2 (Washington, D.C.: ICS Publications, 1996), 237–51.

14. See John Sulllivan, "Edith Stein Challenges Catholics," in *Edith Stein, Testimone per oggi, Profeta per domani*, ed. Jean Sleiman (Roma: Ed. del Teresianum, 1999), 353–56. Simposio Internazionale su Edith Stein, Teresianum, Roma / 7–9 Ottobre 1998.

15. Stein to Elly Dursy, November 25, 1936, letter 230, in *Letters*, 242, taken from Susanne Batzdorff's rendition of an entry for January 25, in *An Edith Stein Daybook* (Springfield, Ill: Templegate Publishers, 1994), 14.

16. Stein, *Finite and Eternal Being*, 113.

17. Stein to Sister Maria Ernst, O.C.D., presumably beginning of 1937, letter 233, in *Letters*, 245.

18. Edith Stein, *The Mystery of Christmas*, trans. Sister Josephine Rucker (Darlington, England: Darlington Carmel, 1985), 9.

19. Stein to Mother Petra Brüning, O.S.U., September 13, 1936, letter 225, in *Letters*, 234–35.

20. For the full text of her letter to the pope see the newly re-edited biography by her novice director and prioress Teresa Renata Posselt, O.C.D., *Edith Stein: The Life of a Philosopher and Carmelite*, trans. Susanne Batzdorff and Josephine Koeppel, O.C.D., ed. John Sullivan, O.C.D. (Washington, D.C.: ICS Publications, 2005), 312–14.

21. Stein to Sister Maria Ernst, O.C.D., May 16, 1941, letter 320, in *Letters*, 331.

22. See Stein, "Problems of Women's Education," chap. 5, in *Essays on Woman*, 169.

23. See Ibid., 161 (slightly amended). Stein goes on to offer us this good advice on page 169 of the same essay: "The concept which assumes that everything in the Church is irrevocably set for all times appears to me to be a false one. It would be naïve to disregard that the Church has a history; the Church is a human institution and like all things human, was destined to change and evolve; likewise, its development takes place often in the form of struggles."

9

A Purely Formal Conclusion:
"God Exists"

WALTER REDMOND

Et ecce intus eras et ego foris[1]

Potency and Act

Edith Stein seems to have had some misgivings about getting beyond her inwardness when, at the age of fourteen, she deliberately and consciously gave up praying; her search for what lay beyond came to define her life.[2] There were actually two beyonds that escaped her: not only God but also the world outside of her awareness. In her work *Potency and Act*, she broke out of her consciousness toward God and toward the world, and in a way toward herself.[3]

Stein's framework here was three worlds or spheres or realms: the world-within is the immanent sphere of inwardness, defined by the category of consciousness.[4] The other worlds are transcendent, beyond awareness. The first world-beyond is the world-without of things and of other persons; the second world-beyond is the world-above: absolute being, God. Her reasoning goes from her world-within to the worlds-beyond.

Stein was working within formal ontology, following the reduction (or *epochē*) of her master, Edmund Husserl, the founder of phenomenology, who bracketed out the existence of things to focus on their essence. She bracketed out not only the world-without and the world-above but her own world-within as well. She was thinking formally: inside immanence, that is, within what belongs to the subject (herself); however, she was not content to remain within her immanence; she went on to recognize the transubjective reality of herself, of things and people, of God. Her argument for God's existence is thus embedded in her search for reality.

Stein hoped to access the world-without when she studied philosophy at the University of Göttingen [Germany] under Husserl, who was, indeed, promising to get back to things beyond his reduction. After reading his *Ideas* (1913), she doubted that Husserl made it back to things and decided she had to find her own way out of her consciousness.[5]

Stein found God in a personal way when, after reading the *Life* of St. Teresa of Jesus, she declared, "This is truth," and became a Catholic, but her search for God was also philosophical. Indeed, three paths, she said, lead to the world above: faith (open to anyone), mystical contemplation (compelling but not universal), and

> the way of natural knowledge which any reasonable person could take. Why this does not happen, why not only dull or indifferent people but even those having a theoretical interest do not take this path or stop along the

way, and why so much energy has been spent to prove that this path cannot be traveled—is as unfathomable as the very mystery of the being itself that lies outside the divine or is opposed to the divine.[6]

Her conclusion was that pure, true absolute being exists: I wish to claim that we must come to this conclusion *by thinking*, and that the basis for an argument of God's existence is given in the sheer fact of being.[7]

Stein's breakthrough from consciousness into the world and toward God, a single movement of thought, will rest upon this fact of her-being (*schlichte Seinstatsache*).

Potency and Act is the second of three works in which Stein endeavored to fulfill her proper mission in philosophy, her life's task: relating the phenomenology of Husserl and the Scholasticism of St. Thomas Aquinas. More than critically comparing these two ways of thinking, she wished to fuse them into her own philosophical system, seeking that perennial philosophy lying beyond ages and peoples common to all who honestly seek truth.[8] The first of these works was a play wherein Husserl and Aquinas appear on stage to discuss their agreements and differences; it later (1929) appeared as an article in the *Jahrbuch* of phenomenology.[9] The second was *Potency and Act*, written in 1931 but published for the first time in 1998. The third was her major work, *Finite and Eternal Being*, written around 1935 and also published posthumously in 1950.

These last two works are quite different in content; *Finite and Eternal Being*, she said, contains "only a few pages" from *Potency and Act*;[10] however, her argument for God's existence in the former work is clearly related and complementary to the one we shall now consider.[11] Also, in both works she offered a critical response to Heidegger's *Being and Time* (1927); "the strong impression the work made on her," she said, "may linger in the present work," *Potency and Act*.[12]

Stein made two approaches to the world-above; these will be considered first, then her defense of realism, and, finally, her distinction of the two absolutes.

The World Above: A First Approach

Stein began by analyzing her world within. When I reflect upon my being, she said, I meet a series of ideas that come not from things outside myself but from my inwardness.

My Being

The starting point of my reflection is a certainty-of-being (*Seinsgewißheit*), the fact-of-me-being (*Seinstatsache*).[13] Here, Stein was following St. Augustine, René Descartes, and Husserl. Augustine's stance against skepticism was expressed in his famous maxim that even if he is wrong, he is. Descartes, after doubting his world, reconstructed it from the principle that he is because he thinks. Husserl sought a basis for his thinking that he could not doubt; however, I do not *infer* that I am, Stein insists; I do not say with Descartes that I think *therefore* I am. That I am is rather an immediate awareness given before I think at all, a primal certitude from which I cannot retreat further.

It is important to understand "being" in Stein's sense. In English we speak of being as existing and of *a* being (as in human being); Stein used *Sein* of being (or *esse* in Latin) and *seiendes* of *a* being. Being will have the first sense here; however, there are a number of ways of being, and Stein often connected an adverb to *Sein*, such as being-actually.

Not Being

When pondering my being, I come upon several other ideas. With Husserl and St. Augustine, T. S. Eliot, and Martin Heidegger,[14] Stein pondered how my time-bound being involves not-being. My being is act, a now-flowing between two kinds of not-being: a no-longer-being harking back to a past that I recall and a still-not-being heralding a future that I expect. My being springs from darkness, crosses a ray of light, only to fade into darkness. I cannot isolate my instantaneous being-now from my lasting through time (as I cannot conceive of a point apart from a line).

Stein here understands act *formally*, that is, remaining inside her immanence. At this point in her argument she was not claiming any outside existence. From her inside viewpoint act means conscious life, living-aware, spiritual stirring (*Regung*).

My act of being is stretched between two not-beings: a past that was but is no longer and a future that will be but is not yet. It is a lasting, a duration, but as instantaneous, fleeting, my act of being is wanting (*mangelhaft*) and frail (*hinfällig*).

From the fact of me-being through time, then, I acquire by contrast the idea of not-being, indeed, of two ways of being: actually and non-actually or potentially.

Being Absolutely

Now, when I think of my time-bound being, another contrast is forced upon me. I feel my being, passing and changing, to be opposed to being-timelessly. My frail being contrasts with full being, lacking past and future, unmixed with not-being, with potentiality. I thus gain the idea of pure act, being-absolutely (*schlechthin*), without coming to be, from ever, being always all it is. This way of being is being-absolutely.

The relation between my timeful being and timeless being in immanence mirrors Aquinas's analogy of being; me-being-in-time is an analogue of being-absolutely.[15] Stein stresses that I discover the "it" within myself at the very beginning of my philosophizing.

At this formal stage in her argument, Stein could not assume any relation of origin between being-timelessly and being-in-time suggested by the theological words "Creator" and "creature"; she did not claim that being-absolutely brings about frail being. Here, Stein called absolute being God, but she took the word in its ontological meaning. By her analysis she wished to understand being; she was doing ontology here, not theology.

Upholding

I have acquired three ideas: being, not-being, and being-absolutely. Stein now returned to her starting point: to the fact of me-being, the *Seinstatsache*. In the fact that *I* am, I find myself, the "me" (*ich*) that remembers my past and faces my future that lasts yet varies over time. Even though my "what now?" (*quale*) is constantly shifting and I am no longer what I was, still I retain my uniqueness. I am perhaps also different from other people. Stein said "perhaps" here because at this stage in her argument I may not consider people or things outside of my consciousness.

My being-actually is wholly instantaneous as it arises from one potential being (what I was able to be) and passes over into another (what I shall be able to be). I realize, still in my idea, that my actuality upholds (*halten*) what is potential; the actual gives purchase (*Halt*) to the potential (not conversely). Stein then asked: [W]hat upholds me in my temporally discrete existence between being and not-being? When I have pressed ahead into the transcendent sphere, I may conceive of the substance evinced in my flowing actual being as the bearer of this being.[16]

She was thinking ahead of when she would speak of the world-without; from this outside viewpoint, the flow of me-being-actually discloses myself as a substance that bears my being between being and not-being.

I cannot grasp my substance directly; I meet it in my ongoing self-awareness as something there (*Dasein*) at the bottom. I sense it in the immediate certainty of my act, in me-being, as well as in what is happening within myself.

Pointing Beyond

Stein next suggested that substance is "the first direction whither immanence points beyond itself and whence it obliges us to set out."[17] I discover the idea of substance in my inwardness, but my consciousness itself is not substantial; strictly speaking, the word applies only to things that transcend, lie outside, my inwardness. The "me" category on the other hand, Stein said with Husserl, applies only to my world within, although I do speak of "me" as transcendent. The substance category, since I find it within but may properly attribute it only to what is without, is a kind of bridge leading from immanence to transcendence: "substance points into the transcendent sphere, and in the immanent sphere it has no place."[18]

The idea of substance then gives me the idea of another sphere, outside the one wherein I dwell, beyond my world within, and I gain the idea of a transcendent sphere of things beyond my awareness, a world without. This first transcendent sphere of substances, the world without, heralds itself (*ankündigen*) in my innerness, and this heralding counts as evidence of the existence (*Existenzbekundung*) of these substances.

Another World Beyond

Next, Stein asked if God himself is a substance. Clearly she did not think that he is a substance as creatures are substances; nevertheless, she did formulate her own definition of substance, which is applicable, presumably by analogy, both to God and to creatures: "a something whose being stretches over a duration and which activates what it is in certain effects."[19] In God the duration is eternity and the effects are not distinct, temporal acts: whatever God is, is ever in effect.

God, then, is a substance and since being a substance is proper only to what lies beyond my awareness, Stein concluded that "we shall have to posit the sphere of absolute being as a second transcendent sphere," a world above, radically different from the other worlds, since it is being-absolutely.[20]

Stein, starting from the simple, immediate fact of me-being, had reasoned to the three spheres of being; however she insisted that so far she was thinking only formally: the world above discloses itself (*en*) only in my idea.

The World Above: A Second Approach

In her second movement toward the divine sphere, Stein came to a purely formal conclusion about the existence of God.[21] She began by explaining three senses of act and potency. The first has been explained: act is the now, the pitch of being (*Seinshöhe*), spanning the potentiality of no-longer-being and not-yet-being. In another sense, act means action and presupposes the potency to act.

The third sense of act and potency is the chief one in this context: being-in-act (*in actu esse*) or being-actually (*aktuell*), and being-in-potency (*in potentia esse*). Being-in-potency presupposes, goes back to (*hinweisen auf*), being-in-act.[22] Since being-in-act lends being to potential being

(not conversely), it is fully real (*wirklich*); it is self-sufficient in that it is not referred (*verweisen*) to another
being. Being-in-potency is needful (*bedürftig*) because it
is referred to being-actually; furthermore, what is-actually
must be an individual; being-in-potency merely points to
an individual.

Stein then arrived at the fullest sense of being-in-act:
being-actually-without-qualification (*schlechthin aktuell*),
pure act. I acquire this idea, again by way of contrast,
with not-being. Being-in-an-absolutely-actual way lacks
being-no-longer and being-not-yet, even being-able-not-
to-be.[23] What is-actually in this way also is an individual.

Stein then drew her conclusion: "[O]ur—purely
formal—conclusion, then, is that only a perfectly simple
whole can be absolutely actual. This can only be an individual whose being is no longer separate from what it is,
an individual wherein all basic forms coincide, the being
absolutely (*das Seiende schlechthin*)."[24]

Her three basic forms are: (1) object or something
(what-is: *id quod est*); (2) content, being-thus (what-it-is:
quid id est, essence); and (3) being, existence (*esse*, existence). In God, something, essence, and existence are one;
Stein obviously was recalling Aquinas's teaching: God is
his being; "what He is" is "that He is."[25]

Her second approach to the world-above ends in
this way: "Here again we encounter the idea of God in
what is purely formal, the equation of *actus purus* and
being-absolutely."[26]

Breakthrough

There remains a certain ambiguity in these passages. In some, Stein seemed to leave her consciousness behind to affirm the existence of the world of objects and the divine world. But later she would say:

> We have envisioned three realms from the immanent point of view: the world-within (the immanent world), the world-without (the transcendent world), and the world-above. We may say that all possible being is contained therein, insofar as we cannot conceive of anything except as something that belongs to the subject itself, something that the subject runs up against outside itself, and something that becomes evident both within and without as beyond. But as we do this, we are grasping everything from one particular point of view, namely, the relationship to the subject. And what the three realms signify in themselves remains open.[27]

Obviously, her argument depends for its validity on the transubjective reality of the three realms, and this she proceeded to establish.

Stein did, indeed, come to state unequivocally what the three realms mean: she interpreted them realistically. She did this in a remarkable "Excursus on Transcendental Idealism."[28] By transcendental idealism she meant Husserl's ontology, as she interpreted it in his work *Ideas*: her master, she feared, was stuck in immanence and never got back to things.

Her "*Excursus*" is a spirited defense of realism: we do indeed access the three worlds. She said of Husserl:

[W]hile Kant clings to a "thing-in-itself" as the basis—real yet in itself unknown—of transcendental forming and of the world of appearance, the idealistic interpretation that Husserl gives his own teaching on the transcendental constitution of the objective world seems radically to do away with this last vestige of "naïve realism." For Husserl, "thing" and "the world of things" is now nothing more than a label of networks for acts [of the] subject. . . . Hence to speak of a thing which appears, something of which falls upon the senses, becomes a pure *façon de parler.*[29]

It is most important to understand that Stein began her critique of idealism within immanences, for "any attempt to do this will tell against transcendental-phenomenological arguments [for idealism] only if the attempt itself is made in a phenomenological reduction—as far as it is actually admissible."[30] Of course, it will not be admissible—that was the point.

The First Absolute

Husserl did admit that we may attribute an absolute being or existence to other subjects, people, but not to material objects. This appeared strange to Stein. She rejected both claims: (1) that the being of other subjects is absolute, and (2) that we lack access to material things.

First, she distinguished two senses of being-absolutely. In the first, I alone am the only absolute being; my being is absolute as a fact (*Faktizität*). Stein explained in a way reminiscent of Descartes, Heidegger, and Husserl, that when I awaken after first coming to self-consciousness, I already find myself set into existence.[31]

This simple fact of me-being (*Seinstatsache*) grounds Stein's argument: I cannot separate my being from myself, from my own "me." I can imagine that I do not exist and I can be deceived about other people and things (taking a dummy for a man, for example). I cannot be wrong about me-being, and it is in this sense that my "me" is absolute, unconditioned, original. On the other hand, the being of other people is absolute for them, but not for me; as far as I am concerned, people in this regard are the same as nonhuman objects.

She continued her argument in this way. Since for myself neither subjects nor objects are absolute, then, if I may accept the existence of other people, there is no reason why I cannot accept the existence of everything falling upon my senses. Husserl accepted the existence of persons, why not things? In her *Excursus*, Stein worked out a careful defense of the objectivity of the world-without: I can get beyond my own me both to a community of people and to material objects around me; indeed, I can know the world in another way: "that view of the being of things as interpreted in the creation account and church teaching."[32]

The Second Absolute

In the second sense of absolute, I am not absolute, unconditioned, or original. Stein used the notion of freedom to show how I am conditioned. I am free in my intentional activity, that is, in my thinking, imagining, recalling, etc., only up to a certain point. My freedom is limited by two things: (1) what falls upon my senses, what affects my sensation from outside myself; that is, the objects that I know through my senses; and (2) what my mind brings to my knowledge, that is, the laws regulating my intentional activity, indeed, my own "me" grounding this activity.

These two things, both what I know and my own "me," are precisely what idealism cannot explain. The very idealistic notions of thing and being are inadequate. Here, Stein used surprisingly harsh language: the thing about idealism that

> gives us pause is not only the conception of thing and being that lies in the original approach here, but the fact that this transcendental idealism itself ends up with a leftover—unsolved, unsolvable, and totally irrational—I mean, the material of sensation presupposed to all constitution and the fact of the constitutive function. Here all spiritual living—which amounts to all being, since spiritual living is the only absolute being—appears to dissolve into a meaningless game.[33]

I get beyond in two directions: not only toward the things out there but also toward a being that is-absolutely, in that other sense: absolutely without qualification or condition. This being is the principle (*Prinzip*) that grounds both things-being and me-being: the world-without and my world-within. I am absolute compared to the persons and things I know but not compared to this principle. In other words, in my living in awareness and freedom, beyond my subjectiveness I reach the objectiveness of the world, and beyond subjectiveness and objectiveness I reach the base of them both.

This is a cosmological argument for God's existence, resting on the fact that we, the world and I, are really. World-being, itself needy and frail, is referred to (*verweisen*) a principle, being-absolutely in the unqualified sense. Stein would further treat this referring relation (*Verweisung*) of frailty to the absolute principle upholding it (*halten*), especially in "Ways to Know God," her work on Dionysius the Areopagite, that she wrote at the end of her life before *Science of the Cross:* "This world with all it discloses and all it conceals, it is just this world that also points beyond itself as a whole to him who "mysteriously reveals himself" through it. It is *this* world, with its referrings that lead us out beyond itself, that forms the intuitive basis for the arguments of natural theology."[34]

Stein denied that her argument infers the real existence of God starting from the idea of God.[35] Her argument is rather cosmological: being-frailly entails upholding. She did, of course, begin in immanence, where I am led from the fact of my-being to contrasting ideas (time-bound/timeless, changing/changeless, wanting being/full being, etc.) and to those of substance and upholding. The point is that I must break through to the reality of myself, of the world and of God.

Stein saw two rational approaches to the world-above: the way of St. Augustine from the world-within and the way of Aquinas from the world-without.[36] She combined both in *Potency and Act.*

Notes

1. "And behold, Thou wert within but I without" (St. Augustine, *Confessions*, 10:27).

2. Edith Stein, *Life in a Jewish Family: An Autobiography, 1891–1916*, trans. Jospehine Koeppel, O.C.D., CWES, vol. 1 (Washington, D.C.: ICS Publications, 1986), 148.

3. Stein, *Potency and Act: Studies Toward a Philosophy of Being*, trans. Walter Redmond, CWES, vol. 11 (Washington, D.C.: ICS Publications, 2009), esp. 19–13; from immanence, 20–21; a formal approach, 52–58; and for finding the world, 360ff.

4. Ibid., 17–18, 70–98.

5. Edmund Husserl, *Ideen zu einer reinen Phänomenologie und Phänomenologischen Philosophie*, Husserliana, vol. 3, no. 1, ed. J. Schuhmann (The Hague: Martinus Nijhoff, 1976); *Ideas Pertaining to a Pure Phenomenology and to a Phenomenological Philosophy*, book 1, trans. F. Kersten (The Hague: Martinus Nijhoff, 1983). Stein had been impressed by Husserl's *Logische Untersuchungen*, Husserliana, vol. 19, no. 1 (The Hague: Martinus Nijhoff, 1984); *Logical Investigations*, trans. J. N. Findley (London: Routledge & Kegan Paul Ltd., 1977).

6. Ibid., 22. For "opposed to the divine" see Walter Redmond, "A Nothing That Is: Edith Stein on Being Without Essence," *American Catholic Philosophical Quarterly* 82, no. 1 (Winter 2008): 71–86.

7. Ibid., 21. Stein continued: "This does not mean, however, that the certainty of the existence of absolute being lies immediately in the sheer fact of being. I *do have* this certainty the moment I *believe*; then I am reaching for the absolute hold and by it I feel myself upheld. But the certainty of faith is blind certainty; believing is not seeing. Indeed, it is doubtless possible to be conscious of God's actual being without making an act of faith in it or even to have faith in but a non-actual way. There is also a certainty of being upheld absolutely, a certainty of the presence of God, that goes beyond the certainty of faith and is no longer blind; any mystic can tell of it. But mystical awareness of God is not inseparably connected with the sheer fact of being. Were it so, there would no longer be any place for faith."

8. *Verschmelzung* as well as *Gegenüberstellung* or *Auseindersetzung*. "Her personal concern was to seek the meaning of being and strive to fuse

medieval thought with the vital thought of today," Stein said in her preface to *Finite and Eternal Being: An Attempt at an Ascent to the Meaning of Being*, trans. Kurt Reinhardt, CWES, vol. 9 (Washington, D.C.: ICS Publications, 2002). *Potency and Act, she said, "is growing into my 'philosophical system,' which of course is a give-and-take between Thomas and Husserl"* (Stein to Ingarden, March 9, 1932, in Edith Stein, *Briefe an Roman Ingarden 1917–1938*, Edith Steins Werke (ESW), vol. 14 (Freiburg: Herder, 1991). The final allusion is from her preface to *Finite and Eternal Being*, xxviii (cf. German editor's introduction to *Potency and Act*, xxiii).

9. The article appeared in the *Festchrift Edmund Husserl zum 70 Geburtstag*, supplement of the *Jahrbuch für Philosophie und phänomenologische Forschung* (Halle, Germany: Max Niemeyer, 1929), 315–38, hereafter referred to as *JPPF*; the manuscript was published in *Erkenntnis und Glaube, "Was ist Philosophie? Ein Gespräch zwischen Edmund Husserl und Thomas von Aquino"* (Freiburg: Herder, 1993), 19–48. Both versions appear in opposing columns in *Knowledge and Faith*, trans. Walter Redmond, CWES, vol. 8 (Washington, D.C.: ICS Publications, 2000), 1–63.

10. Stein, *Finite and Eternal Being*, xxviii; for differences in the works, see *Potency and Act*, viii–ix.

11. Cf. Karl Schudt, "Edith Stein's Proof for the Existence of God from Consciousness," *American Catholic Philosophical Quarterly* 82, no. 1 (Winter 2008): 105–25.

12. Stein, *Potency and Act*, Foreword, 4. Heidegger suggested that Stein revise her play for the *Jahrbuch* and was one of the readers of *Potency and Act* when she presented it as part of her application for a teaching position at the University of Freiburg in 1931. See Antonio Calagno, *The Philosophy of Edith Stein* (Pittsburgh, Penn.: Duquesne University Press, 2007), chap. 7.

13. Stein, *Potency and Act, 9–10.*

14. St. Augustine, *Confessions*, 11:18:23–24; T. S. Eliot, "Burnt Norton," in *The Complete Poems and Plays: 1909–1950* (Orlando, Fla.: Harcourt Brace and Company, 1971), lines 1–10, p. 117.

15. Stein said of Aquinas's *analogie entis* that his "entire system of basic concepts is bisected by a radical dividing line that splits each basic concept, starting with being, into two faces, one turned here below and the

other pointing beyond: nothing can be said in the same sense of God and creature" (*Potency and Act*, 6).

16. Ibid., 20.

17. Ibid., 17.

18. Ibid., 18.

19. Ibid., 7, 18, 19.

20. Ibid., 22.

21. Ibid., 51ff, in the section "Potentiality and Actuality from the Perspective of Formal Ontology: Forms and the Origin of Becoming. The Aporia of Ideas and Creation."

22. Ibid., 52.

23. Ibid., 54.

24. Ibid., 52.

25. Ibid., 38. St. Thomas Aquinas, "Deus enim est suum esse," *Summa Theologiae* I, q. 2, a.1 ; also I, q. 3, a. 4; "Hoc ipsum quod Deus est [est] suum esse," *Summa contra gentiles*, I, beginning of chap. 11; "ac si idem sit quod respondetur ad quaestionem 'quid est' et ad quaestionem 'an est,'" *Contra gentiles*, chap. 10, third argument; in God "idem est 'an est' et 'quid est,' ut dicit Avicenna," *De Veritate*, q. 10, a.12, corpus. Stein gathered that there is but one such individual, because otherwise the what would be separate from the things that instantiate it. See Redmond, "La rebelión de Edith Stein: La individuación humana," in *Acta fenomenológica latinoamericana* of the Latin American Circle of Phenomenology (CLAFEN), vol. 2 (Lima: Catholic University of Peru, 2005): 90–106.

26. Stein, *Potency and Act*, 52.

27. Ibid., 97–98, 70.

28. Ibid., 360–78. See Stein, *Excurso sobre el idealismo transcendental*, trans. Walter Redmond, Opuscula Philosophica, vol. 20 (Madrid: Ediciones Encuentro, 2005).

29. Stein, *Potency and Act*, 360.

30. Ibid., 361.

31. Stein usually writes "set into existence" (*ins Dasein gesetzt*); Heidegger, "thrown" (*geworfen*).

32. Stein, *Potency and Act*, 377. For an analysis of Stein's reasoning, see Redmond, "Edith Stein, Santa Teresa Benedicta de la Cruz/Una defensa del realismo," *Acta fenomenológica latinoamericana, CLAFEN*, vol. 1 (Lima: Catholic University of Peru, 2003), 123–41.

33. Stein, *Potency and Act*, 360.

34. Stein, *Knowledge and Faith*, 99.

35. Stein, *Potency and Act*; Stein thus interpreted St. Anslem's reasoning (in his *Proslogion* and the *Librum apologeticum contra Gaunilonem*); the ontological argument, however, is usually not understood in this way.

36. Ibid., 22–23.

10

EDITH STEIN
AND MARTIN HEIDEGGER:
On the Meaning of Being

METTE LEBECH

Appended to Stein's "spiritual testament" *Finite and Eternal Being: An Attempt at an Ascent to the Meaning of Being*, we find a long essay entitled: *Martin Heidegger's Existential Philosophy.*[1] A shorter essay on the *Castle of the Soul* by Teresa of Ávila is also appended.[2]

An appendix is always an awkward thing to analyze because its status remains somewhat unclear. The author deemed the appendix important enough to append it to the main work, yet it was not directly included in it. It is clear from a letter to Conrad-Martius that the appendices were written after the main work was completed;[3] however, to judge from the level of importance the other appendix has for the understanding of Stein's thought, this one should also provide insight into an important aspect of it. The appendix on Teresa of Ávila's *Interior Castle* gives an analysis of the soul's experience of its own depths in the context of mystical life, which confirms Stein's early phenomenological analyses. If the Heidegger appendix gives us something of equal importance, what is it?

The following essay will discuss the reasons Stein had for writing about Heidegger, after which it will turn to Stein's discussion of Heidegger's project. The discussion will conclude by outlining Stein's and Heidegger's alternative phenomenological inheritance and their relationship to the meaning of being.

Why Did Stein Write about Heidegger?

The appendix provides a key to *Finite and Eternal Being*, which can be read, because of it, as a response to Heidegger's *Being and Time*;[4] such a reading on its own, however, would not do the work justice, since its investigation of the meaning of being points to the meaning of being itself for its meaning. Reading the work as a reply to Heidegger must remain an afterthought, since the positive content of the work does not directly concern Heidegger's work. When the thought inevitably occurs, it is because *Finite and Eternal Being* answers the same question concerning the meaning of being addressed by *Being and Time* but, in contrast with the latter, retains a focus on being as such and not only on the human being in its ascent to the meaning of being.

Stein had first met Heidegger at the Husserls' in Freiburg, then later on several occasions while she was working as Husserl's assistant. She had found him charming, but had also noticed that his writings contained "unmistakable digs at phenomenology."[5] She understood

Heidegger to take the phenomenological inheritance in a direction that led away from Husserl's original insights, and she warily observed Husserl placing his full trust in Heidegger.[6] As she associated herself with Husserl's vision for phenomenology as the foundation for future collaboration in philosophy, she saw Heidegger's "digs" as an attack on what she had found most valuable in phenomenology.[7] Writing about Heidegger was an opportunity to speak for phenomenology against the direction in which he took it. It was also an opportunity to address the question of being as Hedwig Conrad-Martius and Roman Ingarden had done.[8]

Heidegger's turn toward being or toward the meaning of being was a turn toward *Dasein* as the meaning of being, in prolongation of Husserl's transcendental idealism. To Stein, the subordination of eidetics to transcendental phenomenology in Husserl's later philosophy, in contrast, constituted a problem. She saw the essential structures and the consequent foundation of a science of phenomenology as necessary for the Cartesian starting point to be of any consequence, and understood the possibilities for future research into axiology and the normative sciences to rely on this. The investigation of essences took up a prominent place in Husserl's early philosophy: formal ontology was understood to determine the regions of the various regional ontologies, in the same way as the science of essence (*Wesenswissenshaft*) was a necessary presupposition for the sciences of reality (*Tatsachenwissenschaften*). That formal ontology should rely on the constituting function of the transcendental ego for the constitution of the formality it obeyed was clear to Stein in the sense that the constituting function is required in order to identify this formality; that this formality, however, should rely on the constituting function of the transcendental ego in order to be what it is *in itself* could be possible only if this ego were infinite. If conceived as temporal, the idea was parallel to Heidegger's reduction of being to *Dasein*, and of being to time. Discussing the meaning of being—finite and eternal being—would allow one to clarify this and to focus on being and its meaning without reducing it to the human being.

Stein's Discussion of Heidegger's Project

Stein's essay is divided into four sections, each concerned with one of Heidegger's (until then) published works: *Being and Time, Kant and the Problem of Metaphysics, The Essence of Reasons,* and *What Is Metaphysics?* About two-thirds is taken up with an analysis of *Being and Time*, again simply divided into an "Outline of the Argument" and an "Evaluation." The latter part of this critique addresses three questions: "What is *Dasein?*"; "Is the Analysis of *Dasein* Accurate?"; and "Is it sufficient for adequately addressing the Question of the Meaning of Being?" The remainder of the analysis of Heidegger's work is concerned with testing whether the attempt at carrying through the threefold reduction outlined below is continually adhered to in Heidegger's subsequent work.

Stein initially characterizes Heidegger's investigations as "often truly enlightening"[9] and as accurate "in a certain sense"—"in the sense namely that [they] reveal something of the basic constitution of the human being, and [he] sketches a certain way of being human with great clarity." She says she knows "of no better expression for this way of being, which he calls *Dasein* and understands to pertain to all human beings, than *unredeemed being*."[10] It is unredeemed in both of its two different modes of "everyday" and "authentic" being, and although she describes Heidegger's description of the alternation between these modes as "masterly,"[11] she also regards it as flawed: "the human way of being as such is caricatured despite its being elucidated in its ultimate depths."[12]

She points to Heidegger's omission of any references to an I, subject, soul, or person as particularly critical. It results from his attempt to go beyond the "what" of the human being, but the lack of identification of important elements of the human being inevitably leads to an inexcusable confusion of ontology with anthropology, and of existence with *my* existence.

Stein understands Heidegger's project as an attempt to accomplish three impossible reductions: (a) reduction of the meaning of being to the human being; (b) reduction of the human being to its finitude; and (c) the reduction of being to time.

(a) The Attempt to Reduce the Meaning of Being to the Human Being

Heidegger starts as Aristotle did, by asking for the meaning of being,[13] yet, instead of concentrating on the meaning of being, he enumerates the *conditions* for asking for the meaning of being. The condition upon which he focuses in particular is the being for which its own being is in question—*Dasein*—literally "existence," but which it can hardly be doubted that Heidegger employs to refer to the human being. He does that "without opposing the being, as 'that which is,' with being itself,"[14] and this enables him to claim for the human being two things that are generally reserved for God: "the identity of essence and being," and that it is that "from which alone information about the meaning of being is to be hoped for,"[15] yet "the human being does not simply mean being, but a particular way of being, in contrast with which there are others: the present-at-hand and the ready-to-hand";[16] and also the *being* of *Dasein*.

The identification of *Dasein* with the source of the meaningfulness of being[17] as well as with a particular kind of being among others accomplishes the assimilation of *Dasein*'s inability to be defined with being's inability to be put in any genus. That the two kinds of being opposed to *Dasein*—being present-at-hand and being ready-to-hand—are understood to be dependent in their being on *Dasein* from whom they hold their relevance, situates *Dasein* on a par with being simply. That *Dasein* is simultaneously understood as a *kind* of being is underlined by the fact that Heidegger often talks about the *being* of *Dasein*, distinguishing it from *Dasein* itself.[18] It is this being (simultaneously a kind of being and being simply) that has determinations (existentials). They must on the one hand remain very abstract in order to fit the dimensions of being in general and on the other be disconnected from the human reality of body and soul, the limitations of which they reflect.

(*b*) *The Attempt to Reduce the Human Being to Its Finitude*

Stein objects not only to Heidegger's reduction of the meaning of being to the human being, but also to the human being being reduced to its finitude. Although Stein conceives of experience as laid out in the "now" of time—deploying itself in past, present, and future—she insists that experience is experience of *something* and that the human kind of experiencing is also *something* that we can and do identify by constituting it. Heidegger's rejection of engaging with *what Dasein* is leads him to understand the constituting function (experiencing itself as constituting in time) as the ultimate source of the meaning of being, and as the essence of the human being (*Dasein*),[19] but for *Dasein* to disclose the meaning of being adequately, we must have an understanding of the whole of it; this we are supposed to have in death.[20] Death, in Heidegger's understanding, is the end of *Dasein*, but in such a manner that it leaves undecided whether there is a life after death. How can death be the end of *Dasein* if we cannot be sure that death is the end of *Dasein*? How can death provide us with a perspective that enables us to grasp *Dasein* in its entirety because it is the end of *Dasein*, particularly if we are not certain that it is the end of *Dasein*? If we are not sure that death is the end of *Dasein*, we are still lacking a feature that will enable us to understand *Dasein* in its entirety and, with that, an element of the meaning of *Dasein*. This makes *Dasein's* being-towards-death insufficient for understanding the meaning of being. Death, or finitude in other words, cannot be the whole, or the end, of *Dasein*, nor can it be the meaning of being, if *Dasein might* continue to exist or might indeed exist as finalized by something else than death.

Other features of *Dasein's* finitude do not serve us any better to understand it as a whole. Authentic *Dasein*, marked by resoluteness and concern, understands its own possibilities and throws itself forth to meet the demands of the situation and the moment.[21] Although this marks a relative independence, the momentary existence of *Dasein* depends on something beyond it: "In the moment . . . something meets us that perhaps no other moment will offer. To 'bring it out,' i.e., to take it up completely into one's own being, we must 'open' ourselves to it and 'hand ourselves over' to it,"[22] but that means that it comes with *something* for which we must be open, and that it comes to *something* that can be actualized or diminished by it. The moment, inseparable from the concern present in it, is—rather than a manifestation of *Dasein's* wholeness in finitude—a sign of the human being's openness to other kinds of being and, in particular, to the eternal fullness of being to which it can abandon itself in the present. Far from being the meaning of being, finitude is a characteristic of the human being experiencing itself as open to the eternal meaning of being.[23] As a result, finite beings and finitude cannot be understood in themselves without reference to eternal being, just as constitution is unintelligible without that which is being constituted. Heidegger's attempt to reduce the human being to its finitude is intelligible only as an impossible attempt to derive what is constituted from constitution itself.

(c) *The Reduction of Being to Time*

Heidegger's attempt to reduce the meaning of being to the constituting function of *Dasein* reveals his desire to identify what lies before the "what," but it also entails that being as such is conceived according to the mode of being it has in the human person: being that is in time. To Stein it is significant that Heidegger never actually wrote the last section of *Being and Time*, which should have accomplished the reduction of being to time, but refers to it in several places as an aspiration to which the work as a whole tends. Some attempt to finish the project (upon which the rest depends) can be found in *Kant and the Problem of Metaphysics.*[24] She interprets Heidegger to say: "The human being must, in so far as it is, be able to *let be*, and for this it must 'have already projected that which he encounters as a being.' Existence (i.e., the human way of being) 'is in itself *finitude* and, as such, is *only possible on the basis of the comprehension of being. There is and must be such a being only where finitude has become existent.*'" Insofar as Heidegger is attempting to derive being from finitude without it either being or authentically becoming a "what," he must understand nothing to be prior and original to being. He has, in fact, a tendency to go all the way and identify the being of *Dasein* with the nothingness it

experiences in its finite being.[25] Not only does he thus identify the being of *Dasein* with nothingness, but also "being
itself," the being whose meaning we are seeking. "If we take
all the passages quoted together [Stein says], and moreover remember what was said about original time, no other
interpretation remains possible than that by nothingness is
meant a being's constitution of being, which is projected
with understanding by human beings, i.e., being itself."[26]
Stein compares this distinction between a being's constitution of itself on the one hand and being itself on the other
with the distinction between essence and existence, which
she sees worked out in the *analogia entis* [the analogy of
being]. Heidegger's reduction of the meaning of being to
nothing remains severed from the Scholastic insight that
existence is nothing in the sense that it is distinct and different from essence. Stein, in contrast, while sympathetic
to the idea that being is no thing and also understanding
how this nothing could be seen to be the temporalization
inaugurated by the finitude of human experience, cannot extend this same finitude to being as such nor to the
meaning of being, as the experience of it includes within
it reference to different kinds of being that are not finite
in the same way—Infinite Being, which is what it is, i.e., is
its own essence, and also essences and essentialities, whose
being is not temporal, although they are limited.

Two Versions of Phenomenology

The alternative proposed by Stein to Heidegger's contin-
uation of phenomenology is one in which eidetics plays

a role complementary to constitutional or transcendental phenomenology, and in which analysis of the essence of constituted beings is necessary for the completion of the constitutional analysis. Put in terms closer to Heidegger's: the meaning of being (and of the being of *Dasein*) cannot be nothing *full stop* and still retain our attention; it must be a fullness in which our desire for meaning can find rest.

We can sketch the difference between Stein's and Heidegger's alternative continuations of phenomenology by contrasting ideas of theirs that play comparable roles, as well as looking at some shared ideas that come to play opposite roles. The role of the *eidos* in Stein's version of phenomenology can be seen as parallel to the *existentials* in Heidegger's (a); the function of constitution can be seen as comparable to the idea of projection (b); Stein's understanding of the I, self, soul, and person parallels Heidegger's *Dasein* (c); her understanding of empathy his *Mitsein* (d); interpretation, in contrast, bears for both a relationship with values, which is of importance to Heidegger's opposition of authenticity and inauthenticity, and for Stein's opposition of sentient contagion and rationality (e). Death, likewise, and in particular the experience of the death of the other, is understood by the two authors to play opposite roles for the understanding of the meaning of being (f).

(a) Eidos and Existentials

Heidegger's existentials—the structures of the being of *Dasein*—mark the dimensions of *Dasein* and explain its involvement with the world. They explain the world as much as they explain the being of *Dasein*, insofar as they constitute the meaning of the world as *Dasein* opens it up or clears it by or in its being. The existentials—concern, being-in-the-world, and being-towards-death—reveal the world in its truth as projected with them and as dependent for its meaning on their projector, *Dasein*. Existentials structure the world, and it is in this capacity that they play the role played by essence in Stein's view. To Stein, essences are understood to be dependent for their translation into mental being of an I, but in themselves their being is essential, a priori, and not reducible to mental being. What they are constituted *as* can be the object of an eidetic analysis (an analysis of a particular understanding of something), but it remains distinct from an analysis that investigates them as such, i.e., investigates what pertains to them and what does not.[27] Heidegger's existentials, although having the same function of being that in terms of which experience is intelligible, cannot really be said to be of a kind of being distinct from that of *Dasein*. *What* they are is thus neither more nor less difficult to define than *Dasein*, which we seem to be prohibited from not identifying with nothing.

(*b*) *Constitution and Projection*

The world is, for Heidegger, dependent on *Dasein*, whether as deteriorated or as authentic. It is projected by *Dasein* as either by virtue of *Dasein*'s own possibility. The projection is itself projected with the self-initiation that belongs to *Dasein* in the same way as constitution is itself constituted by the constituting function of the I according to Stein. The constitution of things is consequently dependent on the I in the same way as the world is dependent for its projection on *Dasein*, but the things themselves, in what they are, i.e., in their essences, are co-constituted by others and a priori meaningful. Constitution and projection are, according to both authors, fundamentally structured by intentionality, but whereas Heidegger's projection emphasizes the dependence of the projected on the projector, Stein's constitution emphasizes the dependence of constitution on its constituting something objective. To her, only a type of constitution that is infinite can be unlimited by what it constitutes. We can know about such constitution from the possibility of negating the finitude of our own constituting activity, but the fact that we must negate it shows that it is not simply our own.

(c) I, Self, Soul, Person, and Dasein

It is the fundamental differentiation between my I and other I's, regarded by Stein as requisite for the inauguration of (human) experience as we know it, which makes me able to access the objectivity of the constituted and puts my ability to access the *a priori* in relief. It is also this differentiation that enables the I to constitute itself as *an* I, one among others, experiencing itself as embodied, and as visible to others as being beings of a certain kind.[28] These embodied, animated beings constitute their world and are motivated by it. This means that they constitute values to motivate them, which they might share with others, and which energize them in characteristic ways closed to beings who do not constitute the same values to motivate them. The dimension of openness to the realm of values is according to Stein what makes us constitute human I's as persons. As human personal I's experience themselves as embodied, the feeling of the energy of the values resonating in the psyche opens up a space of depth, which she calls the soul. The constitution of the human person as a personal I having a body and a soul is for Stein warranted by experience as we know it. Her account contrasts with Heidegger's account of *Dasein*, which supposedly does not constitute itself as one of a kind, nor as anything specific at all; in its world projection it is neither a person nor even an I, and it does not have a body or a soul. Such ontic designations would compromise its universality as the meaning of being.

(d) Empathy and Mitsein

As *Dasein* is not one of a kind, Heidegger's *Mitsein* (being-with) designates an existential which structures experience, but it does not open the possibility for another self to make itself manifest as *other* and as *like* me, nor does *Mitsein* make me constitute myself as an I who is another I for someone else. For Stein, in contrast, empathy enables the I to constitute itself as one among many, and it also enables the I to test, confirm, and enrich its own perspective by that of the other. *Mitsein* for Heidegger is a semi-inauthentic state of *Dasein* in which it co-sees the world with others, but not with others who, like it, are themselves *Dasein* and can correct my worldview by opening a space of objectivity. This air of inauthenticity makes it different from Stein's understanding of empathy as an act that is indispensable for the full constitution of the individual I and the person, one's own as well as that of the other, without which authentic objectivity or science is impossible.

(e) *Interpretation, Authenticity, and Rationality*

The contribution of empathy toward the constitution of individuals whose experience is open to one another enables Stein to conceive of values as motivating objectivities, i.e., as spiritual forces of direction available to all. Values manifest themselves on the one hand in the feelings of the individual human person and on the other as explanatory factors of the emotional life and the character of others, who, like myself, are exposed to their motivating power. Stein understands interpretation as the explanation of the motivation of a text, event, object, or institution (itself in turn motivated), in contrast with Heidegger who considers interpretation to be projected by *Dasein* as its own possibility—the mediation of values being subsumed into *Dasein*'s possibility, hence losing their objectivity and consequent intelligible availability as objective for others, who could also want to realize them. The only measure of the authenticity of the interpretation is, according to Heidegger, whether responsibility for the projection is assumed. To Stein there are other, more important, criteria: an interpretation has to do justice to what is being interpreted, i.e., account for the motivations that govern it. There is a way to remain below the level of taking responsibility for the interpretation, and that is when opinions are absorbed by sentient contagion and no longer personally tested for their rationality.

Not having an understanding of value-objectivity and its importance for explaining social cohesion, Heidegger will see all collective normativity as an assault on personal independence and an occasion for inauthenticity. *Das Man* is the fallback position of inauthentic *Dasein*, in which it drowns responsibility in unconscious behavior. In contrast, Stein maintains the possibility of adequately corresponding to the motivating power of values, thus being rational, no matter whether these values are valued by others.

(f) Death and the Meaning of Being

For Heidegger, death is the end of *Dasein*, i.e., the end of being-in-the-world (irrespective of the question of a life after death). It is the transition from being *Dasein* to no longer being *Dasein*, and it can be undergone only in my own case because *Dasein* is always mine; it cannot be experienced as it is the transition from experience to non-experience. In contrast, my possibility of not-being is experienced in anguish. An understanding of the totality of *Dasein* is not advanced by the death of the other, thus the understanding of being cannot be completed and we cannot advance toward the meaning of being, except provisionally, by existential analysis which in principle cannot be finished except perhaps at our own death. The awareness of the possibility of not-being has a sobering effect in that authentic living is being-toward-death in resoluteness or un-guaranteed self-investment, whereas fleeing in front of death leads to inauthentic hiding in "the they."

For Stein, death is not the proper end of the human being, although it is the occasion for its facing finally the question of "being or not being." Death can be experienced in my own near-death experiences, such as in anguish, severe illness, or imminent threat to my life, and it can also be experienced through empathy for the death the other is experiencing, or even from seeing the other already dead. The experience of the different types of death of the other: the fight, the victory, and quiet glory shining through, might contribute to our experience of the meaning of being.

The meaning of being cannot for Stein be answered simply by *Dasein*, no matter how well explained it would be in terms of its existentials. Being, for Stein includes different kinds—finite and eternal, personal and non-personal— and reducing being to one of its types is an answer that mistakes a part for the whole. Such a mistake is bound to ignore important features of being as we experience it, first and foremost essence, but also the independent being of natural being, personal individuality, values, community, and eternal being.

Notes

1. As the new, complete English translation of *Finite and Eternal Being* has not yet been published, I refer to the page numbers of the German work *Endliches und ewiges Sein* (*EES*) from the German series Edith Stein Gesamtausgabe (ESGA), vols. 11/12 (Freiburg: Herder, 2016), although I quote from my own translation of the Heidegger Appendix (HA) published in the *Maynooth Philosophical Papers*, 2007 (*http://eprints.nuim .ie/1005*); hereafter referred to as *EES, HA. Finite and Eternal Being* was written in the years 1935–36, just after Stein had finished her novitiate in the Cologne Carmel. It is an extensive revision of her habilitation attempt *Potency and Act*, which was, when submitted in Freiburg in November 1931, read by, among others, Martin Heidegger. Also the Thomist Martin Honecker read the manuscript but did not think highly of it (Hugo Ott, "Edith Stein und Freiburg," in *Studien zur Philosophie von Edith Stein* [Freiburg-Munich: Verlag Karl Alber, 1993], 107–45). Heidegger discussed the manuscript of *Potenz und Act* with Stein for two hours (Stein to Ingarden, December 25, 1931, letter 152; and March 9, 1932, letter 153, in *Selbstbildnis in Briefen III: Briefe an Roman Ingarden*, ESGA, vol. 4 (Freiburg: Herder, 2001), 225–26; and in Stein, *Letters to Roman Ingarden*, trans. Hugh Candler Hunt, CWES, vol. 12 (Washington, D.C.: ICS Publications, 2014), 312–15. Heidegger and Honecker both advised Stein that she would be acceptable for habilitation on previous work, but that she should not proceed for political reasons. This attempt was her second, of which we have an extant written work (the first being *Beiträge zur Philosophischen Begründung der Psychologie und der Geisteswissenschaften*, ESGA, vol. 6 [Freiburg: Herder, 2010]). *Einführung in die Philosophie*, ESGA, vol. 8 (Freiburg: Herder, 2015), which Lucy Gelber regarded as a third habilitation attempt for Breslau (Edith Steins Werke [ESW], vol. 13 [Freiburg: Herder, 1991]) is more likely, as claimed by Wulf in her introduction to ESGA, vol. 8, to be the series of lectures held by Stein in Breslau, at which Norbert Elias, among others, assisted (Stein to Fritz Kaufmann, April 30, 1920, letter 31; and May 31, 1920, letter 32, in *Selbstbildnis in Briefen I*, ESGA, vol. 2 (Freiburg: Herder, 2010), 56–59. Although Stein herself talks about a revision, *Finite and Eternal Being* is, in fact, an entirely different work than *Potency and Act. Potency and Act* is a *Formalontologie* in the Husserlian sense and does not yet carry the large-scale *Auseinandersetzung*

(dispute) with Aquinas and Aristotle, which makes up the middle part of *Finite and Eternal Being*.

2. Both of these were left out in the first edition of Stein's works by Herder, Edith Steins Werke (ESW). The new critical edition Edith Stein Gesamtausgabe (ESGA) has amended this, and the English translation is catching up: the Heidegger appendix is due to be included in a new translation of *Finite and Eternal Being* by Walter Redmond to be published in a forthcoming volume in the ICS Publications edition of the Collected Works of Edith Stein.

3. Stein to Hedwig Conrad-Martius, August 20, 1936, letter 473, in *Selbstbildnis in Briefen II*, ESGA, vol. 3 (Freiburg: Herder, 2000), 221; letter 224, in *Self-Portrait in Letters*, trans. Josephine Koeppel, O.C.D., CWES, vol. 5 (Washington, D.C.: ICS Publications, 1993), 233.

4. Other investigations of the relationship between Stein and Heidegger include John Nota, "Edith Stein and Martin Heidegger," in *Edith Stein Symposium: Teresian Culture*, ed. John Sullivan, Carmelite Studies, vol. 4 (Washington, D.C.: ICS Publications, 1987), pp. 50–73 (a German version is found in *Denken in Dialog: zur Philosophie Edith Steins*, ed. Waltraud Herbstrith [Tübingen: Attempto Verlag, 1991], pp. 93–117); Antonio Calcagno, "Die Fülle oder das Nichts? Edith Stein and Martin Heidegger on the Question of Being," in *American Catholic Philosophical Quarterly* 74, no. 2 (revised for Antonio Calcagno, *The Philosophy of Edith Stein* [Pittsburgh: Duquesne University Press, 2007], which is the edition we have used and refer to); Ott, "Edith Stein und Freiburg," in *Studien zur Philosophie von Edith Stein*, 107–45, also gives an account of Stein's and Heidegger's interactions in the early Freiburger years; Lidia Ripamonti, "Being Thrown or Being Held in Existence? The Opposite Approaches to Finitude of Edith Stein and Martin Heidegger," in *Yearbook of the Irish Philosophical Society*, ed. Fiachra Long (Maynooth, Ireland: Department of Philosophy, Maynooth University, 2008), 71–83. Marianne Sawicki's *Body Text and Science* (Dordrecht, The Netherlands: Kluwer, 1997) treats of Heidegger's publication of Husserl's *Time Consciousness* (which Stein edited), but not of Stein's Heidegger critique, which belongs to the writings of the later Stein. Alisdair MacIntyre is right in contrasting Heidegger's attitude to the relevance of philosophy for the living of ordinary life with Stein's (*Edith Stein: A Philosophical Prologue 1913–1922* [Lanham, Md./Oxford: Rowman and Littlefield Publishers, 2006], 5–6).

5. *Life in a Jewish Family* (1891–1916), trans. Josephine Koeppel, O.C.D., CWES, vol. 1 (Washington, D.C.: ICS Publications, 1986, 2016), 409—she was referring in particular to Heidegger's inaugural lecture: *What Is Metaphysics?*

6. Stein to Roman Ingarden, October 15, 1921: "Heidegger enjoys Husserl's absolute trust and uses it in order to lead the students, upon whom he has a greater influence than does Husserl himself, in a direction that is far from Husserl's own position. Everyone knows that except the good Master" (letter 78, in *Letters to Roman Ingarden*, CWES, vol. 12 [Washington, D.C.: ICS Publications, 2014], 193).

7. Stein to Ingarden, October 9, 1926: "However, and this is the real tragedy of the matter, the whole thing [of Husserl's thought] is alive and well in his mind, and in good hours he is able to speak of it, though I doubt that he can put it on paper, never mind bringing it to print; and none of his students are in complete agreement with him. If he becomes professor emeritus, he will probably suggest Heidegger as his successor, and Heidegger is going off on his own way" (letter 100, in Stein, *Letters to Roman Ingarden*, 171–72).

8. Hedwig Conrad-Martius, *Zur ontologie und Erscheinungslehre der realen Aussenwelt. Verbunden mit einer Kritik positivistischer Theorien, Jahrbuch für Philosophie und Phänomenologische Forschung (JPPF)*, vol. 3 (Halle, Germany: Max Niemeyer, 1916): 345–542; *Metaphysische Gespräche* (Halle, Germany: Max Niemeyer, 1921); *Realontologie, JPPF*, vol. 6 (Halle, Germany: Max Niemeyer, 1923): 159–333; Roman Ingarden, *Essentiale Fragen. Ein Beitrag zum Wesensproblem, JPPF, vol. 5* (Halle, Germany: M. Niemeyer, 1925): 125ff. Stein says in a letter to Ingarden, October 2, 1927: "I do not believe that working on the constitution problems (that I do certainly not underestimate) will have to or could lead to idealism. It seems to me that, in general, the question cannot be solved in a philosophical manner but that it is already solved, when one begins to philosophize. And because this involves a really personal attitude, it is also clear why for Husserl this point is not open for discussion" (letter 111, in *Selbstbildnis in Briefen I*, ESGA, vol. 4, 185; *Letters to Roman Ingarden*, 254). *Einführung in die Philosophie* also leaves the question undecided, but does not regard it as impossible for this reason to engage in formal ontology (ESGA, vol. 8 and ESW, vol. 13, sec. 1c).

9. *EES*, HA, "Being and Time," 445.

10. *EES*, HA, "Is the Analysis of *Dasein* Accurate?," 480.

11. Ibid., 465.

12. The quotation on p. 480 continues: "Unredeemed is both its deteriorated everyday being, and that which he holds to be its authentic being. The first is the flight from authentic being, the avoiding of the question: 'being or not being.' The second is the decision for non-being against being, the turning down of true, authentic being." Ibid.

13. Aristotle, *Metaphysics* 5.7; 6.2; 7.1.

14. *EES*, HA, "What Is *Dasein*?" 463.

15. Ibid.

16. "Heidegger justifies his taking his point of departure in the analysis of *Dasein* with the fact that one can only ask a being for the meaning of being, to whose meaning an understanding of being belongs. And as *Dasein* not only has understanding for its own being, but also for other beings, one must start with an analysis of *Dasein*. But does not the opposite follow from this reasoning? Because the human being understands not only its own being but also other beings, it is not referred to its own being as the only possible way to the meaning of being. Certainly the self-understanding of being can be laid bare in its root and critical reservations be encountered from the start. But the possibility of taking a point of departure in either the being of things or primary being always persists" (*EES*, HA, "Is the Analysis of *Dasein* a Sufficient Foundation for Addressing the Question of the Meaning of Being Appropriately?" 481).

17. "Thus transcendence is brought to the centre of the investigation: Because metaphysics—the questioning of being—lies in 'human nature,' the foundation of metaphysics must disclose that in the constitution of [the] being of human beings, which is the reason for their understanding of being. Fundamental ontology is therefore analysis of *Dasein* and especially of its transcendence" (*EES*, HA, *"Kant and the Problem of Metaphysics,"* 485).

18. *Dasein*, hence, "sometimes designates human beings (referred to as 'whom' or 'self'), sometimes the being of human beings (in which case the expression 'the being of *Dasein*' is used)" (*EES*, HA, "What Is *Dasein*?" 465).

19. She quotes Heidegger's *Kant and the Problem of Metaphysics*: "Time is pure intuition only in that it spontaneously performs the aspect of succession and, as an act both receptive and formative, proposes this

aspect as such to itself. This pure intuition solicits itself by that which it intuits (forms). Time is, by nature, pure affection of itself." ". . . Time is not an active affection concerned with the ready-to-hand self; as pure, it forms the essence of all auto-solicitation. Therefore, if the power of being solicited as a self belongs to the essence of the finite subject, time as pure self-affection forms the essential structure of subjectivity . . . as pure self-affection, it originally forms finite selfhood in such a way that the self can become self-consciousness." "Pure self-affection provides the transcendental ground-structure of the finite self as such" (*EES*, HA, "Kant and the Problem of Metaphysics," 486). Note here Heidegger's use of the term "essence," which testifies to the fact that although he attempts to think without the "what" and without essence, he still has to use these ideas to make intelligible what he intends to do.

20. *EES*, HA, "*Dasein* and Temporality," 452.

21. "How should we understand this, if not in the sense of the realization of an essence or a specificity, which is given with being human (i.e., with which one is thrown into *Dasein*), that however, for its development needs free co-operation and hence is entrusted to one?" (*EES*, HA, "Is the Analysis of *Dasein* Accurate?," 477).

22. Ibid.

23. "It is clear, then, that the entire understanding of time given in *Being and Time* needs to be revised. Temporality, with its three "ekstases" and its extension, must have its meaning clarified as the way in which the finite gains participation in the eternal. The significance of the *future*, so strongly emphasised by Heidegger, must be explained in two ways. First as Heidegger does—as the *care* for its preservation stemming from understanding the flux and nothingness of one's own being; secondly as a direction toward a *fulfillment yet to come*, a transition from the dispersion of temporal being to the gathering of authentic, simple, eternity filled being. Moreover, the *present* must be seen as the *way of being of fulfillment*, which—like a flash of eternal light—opens up the understanding to being's fulfillment, as the *past* is the way of being that gives an impression of *durability* in the flux of our being." *EES*, HA, "Is the Analysis of *Dasein* Accurate?," 480.

24. *EES*, HA, "*Kant and the Problem of Metaphysics*," 485–86.

25. According to Heidegger's explanations "what is understood by nothingness is not absolutely nothing. As there is talk of various forms of

nothingness and these are not further explained, it remains unclear what kind of nothingness was meant." *EES,* HA, "*Kant and the Problem of Metaphysics,*" 491.

26. Ibid.

27. Stein's analysis of essence is to be found in Chapter 3 of *Finite and Eternal Being.*

28. Calcagno, *The Philosophy of Edith Stein,* is correct when he writes: "Our being is constituted in such a way that we are fundamentally related because the very fullness of our person implies the fullness of the other—one cannot fully be without the other" (128); however, he is wrong in claiming that Stein affirms that "Each person, besides having his or her own *proprium,* is also a *Mehrheit von Personen*" (ibid.). For Stein, a person is not several—the mistake seems to stem from a mistranslation of a passage concerning *das Man,* which—in contrast with the person—can refer to a multiplicity of persons. The passage is referred to by Calcagno on p. 118, and he refers to it as "MHE 97"—i.e., the old edition of "Martin Heideggers Existentialphilosophie," in *Welt und Person,* Edith Steins Werke (ESW), vol. 6 (Freiburg: Herder, 1962)—in the new edition, which we have used, *EES,* ESGA, vols. 11/12, 469. It reads in our translation: "If it is recognised that the individual needs the community's support—right from becoming awake to his or her own identity 'as such' and 'in a specific sense' (i.e., as a member)—and that to a community belong *leading* spirits, who form and determine its lifeforms, then it is no longer possible to see 'the they' as a form of deterioration of the self and nothing else. It does not designate a person in the strict sense of the word, but a plurality of persons linked in community who fit themselves into it."

11

BEING, AEVUM, AND NOTHINGNESS:
Edith Stein on Death and Dying

ANTONIO CALCAGNO

Edith Stein's philosophy is widely known for focusing on certain traditional themes, including the nature of the human person, empathy, the structures of and relation between the state and the community, the question of being, and philosophical theology. One theme that has not been substantially examined is that of death. Scholars[1] have certainly discussed Stein's treatment of death in relation to her critique of Martin Heidegger's existential philosophy.[2] Stein's own life was touched by death in very significant ways, including the death of her father and her beloved mentor and friend Adolf Reinach. She witnessed firsthand the death and destruction of World War I while she was a nurse serving in a Lazaretto on the Austrian front. She also experienced the death of her beloved mother while enclosed in the cloister, and she experienced many kinds of psychological death, including the death of her desire to secure a university chair through habilitation. She even had intimations of her own

impending death under the Nazis, as testified by her letters and vows to her superiors.[3]

Philosophically, Stein's corpus can be mined in order
to draw a more systematic view of what death and dying
entail. The results of such an excavation are rich when
various philosophical questions concerning our experience of time and existence arise. This will be shown in
the latter part of this essay; however, it is important to
piece together systematically Stein's thought on death
and dying in order to separate and distinguish her from
her fellow phenomenologists, especially Heidegger, and
other thinkers, including Scholastic philosophers like St.
Thomas Aquinas. Why? The legacy of Stein's work has
been plagued by a gross misconception, namely, that her
work is merely a re-elaboration of contemporaries like
Edmund Husserl, Heidegger, and Max Scheler.[4] The
originality of Stein's philosophy has not been able to shine
through because of unhappy historical circumstances, various editing processes of her collected works, and sexism.
With that stipulation, there is no doubt that Stein con-
versed with her contemporaries in phenomenology and
Christian philosophy, including Husserl, Conrad-Martius,
Heidegger, Erich Przywara, and others, but Stein's work
can also stand alone. This essay attempts to show this by
focusing on her views of death and dying.

There are five central philosophical claims. First, death
and dying are two distinct but related moments. Second,
part of the structure of death and dying is a peculiar kind
of questioning that is often ignored but that focuses on
ultimate meaning. Questions like "What comes after?"

present themselves to consciousness as serious questions to be investigated within a phenomenological framework. Stein sees this kind of questioning as conditioning our being in the world and our relation to God. Third, death is not a "for myself," or *jemeinig*, as Heidegger claims, such that it is excluded from a more communal context. In fact, we learn and experience death developmentally and communally through intropathy or empathy [*Einfühlung*] and conscious lived experience. Fourth, death has certain temporal implications that not only translate into an end of time or an end of the possibility of being but also reveal an in-between time, a kind of *aevum*. Finally, a proper metaphysical understanding of death relies on the interplay of fullness/plenitude of being and nothingness.

Given this general schema of Stein's treatment of death and dying, this essay has two objectives. First, it seeks to present for the first time a more systematic account of Stein's views on death and dying by explaining the five above-mentioned constitutive claims. The second task is to make a series of specific critical arguments against Stein's discussion of being, nonbeing, and time. First, I will argue that Stein's deducing fullness from existence vis-à-vis nonexistence is invalid. The opposition between being and nonbeing fails to admit there is a middle point between these two poles, a point where the nonbeing of that which was can continue to signify in the present consciousness of times gone and past.

Further, regarding Stein's discussion of death revealing an *aevum*, I wish to argue that we always bear the mark of our finitude, including our finite temporality, even when

we exist within the eternal mind of God. To claim otherwise is to make identical our eternity with God's eternity,
thereby undermining the traditional Scholastic argument,
which Stein holds, that there is no real relation between
the being (and, therefore, [a]temporality) of God and the
being of human persons. Persons cannot experience eternity as God experiences eternity; death does not imply
an experience of eternity as God experiences it. Second,
I will argue that Stein excludes the category of potentiality from her discussion of death as a relation between
the fullness or actuality of being and nothingness. In fact,
death is more a relation between possibility/potentiality
and nothingness than a relation between actual fullness
and nothingness. What Stein describes as fullness ought
to be read as potential.

Edith Stein's Philosophy of Death and Dying

Stein's philosophical reflections about death can certainly
be traced to her experience of World War I and her existential crisis at that time.[5] Her views mature with her
encounter with and conversion to Christianity. At the
urging of her Carmelite superiors in 1936, Stein began
an extensive reworking and rewriting of her former habilitation thesis (*Potency and Act*).[6] This project sought to
bring together Christian medieval philosophy with modern philosophy, which she understood as phenomenology.
The fruit of this re-elaboration is what many would call
her magnum opus, *Finite and Eternal Being*.[7] Both texts
present an ontology in which the traditional categories of

being, essence, act, and potency occupy a primary place. Stein's mature views on death must be set within this context where she tries to reconcile phenomenology with Christian philosophy. She saw these two schools of philosophy as largely complementary. For Stein, revelation becomes an object of phenomenological analysis, informing the way we perceive, understand, and interpret ourselves, the world, others, and God. Faith and reason are not irreconcilable. In fact, Stein argues that faith not only conditions rational thinking but it also has its own rationality; it is a kind of thinking.[8]

Given this background of Stein's project, let us proceed to unpack the above-mentioned claims regarding Stein's philosophy of death and dying. She notes that phenomenologically there is a difference between dying (*Sterben*) and death (*Tod*).[9] This is the first element of Stein's phenomenology of death and dying. Like Heidegger, Stein believes that one can distinguish death as an end from the lived experience of dying.[10] Death is an end of temporal existence as we experience it here and now, with all of its possibilities, failures, limits, and expectations. Dying, inseparable from death, is a lived experience; it can occur within consciousness and, insofar as it is a conscious lived experience, we can re-present its content in consciousness, delivering a concrete description of its essence, especially as it plays itself out within our human existence.

In a very deep sense, we are dying moment by moment at the same time we are living or existing.[11] It is in this sense that we can experience or are conscious of our death as a dying in existence. Stein says we concretely experience this with the dying of our bodies, especially in the case of terminal disease. Certainly, with death comes angst. Like Heidegger, she maintains that one can have anxiety in the face of one's eventual or anticipated nonpossibility of being. This anxiety is one of the fundamental ways in which dying presents itself in consciousness, but no longer being able to be is not the only source of angst; there is also at the same time an anxiety for that which is going out of the person, namely, the fullness of being that, according to Stein, the human being desires to preserve and not lose.

For Stein, this fullness becomes a central focus, indeed, the ground of being. Being toward death could not exist unless it was preceded by a fullness or positivity that is. It is the relation between living and dying contemporaneously that causes anxiety and not the exclusive existing and being anxious in the face of and for the impending impossibility of one's *Seinkönnen*. Stein describes existence as a positivity, something that is. In dying, the lost being is a nothing because it no longer exists. At the same time, this very experience of loss makes manifest that one is conscious of one's being as a fullness insofar as it is counter-distinguished from nothingness or loss. Existence is full of being as opposed to nothing or a having-been. This fullness becomes manifest in the experience of feeling secure in one's being (*Seinssicherheit*).[12] She describes the experience of being as the security that a child feels as it is being held in its mother's arms.

It should also be remarked that Stein's description of being and nonbeing indicates on one level a very profound lack of agency.[13] We neither generate nor are the source of being and nonbeing; we do not choose to be simultaneously living and dying. We die while we live, and we are not the source of this living and dying, being and nonbeing. Being is given to us as it flees us. The being that is given to us as we continue to live, moment to moment— to use Stein's expression—is experienced as a being held in being, but we do not actively hold ourselves in being. It is this fullness and its concomitant loss, the simultaneous living and dying, that are fundamental for questioning the meaning of being.[14]

The loss of the fullness of being and the concomitant anxiety we feel lead to a deeper sense of existential questioning. This is Stein's second insight concerning death and dying. Drawing from her experience of nursing sick and dying soldiers at the front during World War I, Stein gives a phenomenological description of a person dying. As the person dies, different types of questioning emerge, culminating in many instances, she argues, in a final question. Also, a gravely ill person who confronts death ceases to care about things (*Besorgen*). Stein claims that care for things and what it means to be in the world dissipates. In many instances, the gravely ill person loses all attachment to the world and the importance of worldly objects. At the same time, the sick person feels completely cut off from all other persons who are still occupied with caring for things. Stein even refers to Heidegger's curious footnote about Tolstoy's Ivan Ilych to show how the sick and dying distinguish themselves from the living.[15] Stein notes that another form of care may arise in such circumstances: the explicit preoccupation with one's body. Even with this preoccupation, death might come upon one quite suddenly. Often, after a certain point, the pre-occupation with one's body passes and one is confronted with a fundamental question after one has resigned one-self to dying. Stein identifies this question as: to be or not to be. The being referred to here is not earthly existence.

At this point, one knows that life will terminate. Death is revealed as a termination of this life here and now, but one is still preoccupied about whether there is an afterlife. More concretely, one knows one will die; one might even accept it; but the question of "then what?" surges. What comes after death?[16] The question of the possibility of an afterlife and what it would entail arises. For Stein, this questioning comes poignantly to the fore as one begins to live more imminently one's death. It is also a psychological, existential description that follows closely her observations of those who are in the throes of death. To understand oneself authentically is to include addressing this question, attempting a serious answer.[17] It should be remarked that Stein does not define this kind of questioning as universal; it can occur, and does so.

With this analysis Stein builds upon the foundation of her philosophy of death and dying. Death is an eventual-ity, an object in the phenomenological sense. It is marked by an end of life (not only possibility) and what marks death is not only a detachment from one's preoccupation with the world and with others but also a fundamental questioning of what is to come or what is next. This has an impact on how we live and how we die, depending on how we respond to such questions. For example, we can be hopeful for another life; we can despair; or we can be good stoics and try to dismiss death as something that ought not cause us anxiety. Dying is not merely understood as angst in the face of or for the impossibility of possibility, but as the existing between life and death where one's anxiety is due to an impending end, but also due to the loss of a fullness of life and security that was and can be no longer. This fullness described by Stein as life, always having the Augustinian and Husserlian notions of life before her,[18] is an entry point into all kinds of questions about the sources of such fullness, ultimately culminating in a link between our being full and the fullness of being that is God and the immortality of the soul. It should also be remarked that questioning is an important comportment (*Verhältnis*) of being, but the answers one receives to one's questions also objectively impact the way one exists in the world.

We now move on to the question of the meaning of the death of others. Heidegger argues that it is impossible for us to experience the death of others as it is one's own. Though much can be said about Heidegger's and Stein's views on death, they are not the focus of this paper. Stein argues that death is deeply communal insofar as we learn what it is through living and dwelling in community with others. We develop and learn senses of death from our childhood onward. She argues that the anxiety caused by death and dying is not completely knowable as one's own. Our anxiety is complicated by the fact that others die, and this affects us. Part of death itself is the fact that others die.

When children first experience death they experience it as a no-longer being in the world. They generally do not experience the horror and anxiety of death until they begin to understand more acutely the various values we attribute to death itself, albeit in some cases there is an immediate understanding. Stein agrees with Heidegger's point that we can have an everyday, inauthentic experience of death as unrelated to one's authentic being (*man stirbt*). The child who does not appreciate the existential value of death can be said to dwell in this inauthentic way. As children develop and as children are taught about death, especially within the context of religious education, they begin to appreciate more fully the death of others, not merely as a no-longer being but as a movement from one type of existence to another.

Children and adults participate in the death of others, especially when they participate in various mourning rituals and funeral rites. This ritual and cultural appropriation of death is transmitted through the death of others and informs one's interpretations and values of death. Stein gives the example of Christianity.[19] Children are taught from a very young age, especially when they question and inquire into the nature of death, that in death there is a radical change. Life is not ended; it is transformed. One moves from earthly existence to eternal life. One might not know what eternity is, but within Christianity itself there are cultural, artistic, theological, and philosophical narratives and accounts that can give to believers some kind of intimation of what heaven may be like.

More concretely, the Christian claim that the body is separated from the soul at death is visible, Stein argues, at a wake for a dead friend. The corpse is so remarkably different from the former person that was living with a living/lived-body. The Christian claim, for example, of the immortality of the soul that survives death and burial of the corpse is rooted in communal life. This belief for the Christian will inform his or her life in a significant way, in an existential way. The existential implication is clear: anxiety before death may give way to anticipation of new life, a new or transfigured existence.[20]

The previous argument appeals to culture and history as concrete means whereby one understands death not only as my own, but as something that is profoundly conditioned by the communal undertakings of various cultural, religious, ethnic, and political communities. In her *Philosophy of Psychology and the Humanities*, Stein gives a concrete example of how a troop might communally experience the death of a beloved leader in what she calls a *Gemeinschaftserlebnis*, or a lived-experience of community.[21] The death is experienced individually, but the communal loss is also experienced as a community. The loss to the community affects not only individual members but also the community as a whole. Death can be experienced in consciousness as communal. More will be said about this later.

There is another argument that one could employ to defend the claim that one can know what it means for others to die and how this knowledge can affect an understanding of our own deaths. Turning to Stein's analysis of empathy, she maintains that empathy can bring to presence in more or less a clear fashion the consciousness of the other, but this only happens at a certain point in time and is subject to constant revision and correction.[22] Further, Stein's notion of empathy as reliant upon *Vergegenwärtigungen*, literally the making present of the other's mind in my consciousness, never renders the other's consciousness identical to mine—there is no *Einsfühlung, or identification*. The other is always brought into relief in my consciousness, allowing me to intuit what and who the other is and is not, and who I am and am not. There are always degrees of clarity and obscurity that come with the eidetic reduction that allow us to understand, misunderstand, and not understand the other.

Let us turn to a more specific analysis of *Einfühlung* (identification), or empathy. When I re-present the other to myself in consciousness, various aspects (*Abschattungen*) of the other are revealed to me as they are both analogically similar and different from mine. One can re-present to one's consciousness the anxiety of the other, an anxiety in the face of or for the other's death. One can also understand the other as sad or anxious over the recent death or present dying of a loved one. Stein is aware that love, as an emotion, impacts the way we experience the death of a loved one and how we come to know the pain, suffering, and anxiety of death by understanding the experience of the other through empathy. I learn from my empathic representation that the other suffers and that death and dying cause suffering and loss. In this conscious experience I begin to understand that death entails the dying of a loved one, and I learn what it is for others to die as the dying other also experiences this loss of love. This dying love is experienced intersubjectively and reciprocally.

Uniquely to Stein's philosophy, not only can individuals understand what others think and feel, but Stein also believes that communities can understand and experience things together as communities insofar as they are capable of having a communal understanding (*ineinandergreifen*) or experience. This *Gemeinschaftserlebnis*, or lived experience of community, is a living through together of a conscious experience as a communal experience in solidarity. In the *Gemeinschaftserlebnis*, the intentional rays are shared by members of a community, whereas in empathy the intentional rays are confined to the individual alone who is experiencing the other in his or her consciousness. As mentioned earlier, Stein gives the example of the death of a beloved troop leader causing both individual (unique) anxiety and sadness and communal loss caused by the death of their leader. One feels the loss and concomitant sadness and anxiety of the community as a whole. To borrow from Stein, one lives in and with the experience of the other; there is solidarity about the loss that is death, which is experienced communally in consciousness.[23]

I wish now to discuss the last two key elements of Stein's philosophy of death: temporality and metaphysics. These will serve as the basis for the arguments introduced at the beginning of this essay. Death and dying reveal something about the nature of temporality and our existence. As a Christian philosopher, Stein believes we are created beings, stemming from God; reason and experience, however, tell us that as creatures our being is finite. Finitude marks our being materially, formally or essentially, and temporally. Our material bodies are limited and given definition by their being subject to causality, actualization of potency, generation, and corruption. Unlike the eternal and the divine, who is immaterial, human beings take on a certain material form and earthly existence that is not only limited as to what it can be (for example, a human being is not and cannot be a dog) but also as to how long it can persist in earthly existence. In and of themselves created beings are temporally finite. Revelation and the incarnation and resurrection of Christ, however, render all created beings new. St. Paul reveals that, at the end of time, all things will be taken up again or recapitulated by God, to borrow from Irenaeus of Lyon. The implication is that nothing is lost; all shall be made eternal. In particular, temporally finite human beings are promised the possibility of eternal life with God. We anticipate this eternal end and union with God during life and in our dying and eventual deaths.

Death and dying bring to the fore these two temporal realms and, if anything, show that we are between the two. We are not purely finite temporal beings as the promise of and belief in eternal life changes our constitutive way of being in the world. Also, we are not purely eternal, as we are subject to time; we have a beginning and an end. Stein takes up the Scholastic temporal category of the *aevum*, the in-between time of eternity and finite temporality traditionally reserved for the angels, and applies it to human beings.[24] Death and dying demonstrate the viability of describing our temporal existence not as purely finite but as an *aevum* conditioned by real anticipation. Each moment we live we also die. Though existence is given to us "moment to moment," as Stein describes, we also lose existence and we feel great loss and anxiety over that having-been of this fullness of being that is given to us. A Christian believer also recognizes that death marks a significant transformation in one's life. As one dies, one anticipates or hopes for a new life with God. Death and dying are pivotal in order to understand one's self as existing within a temporal status of the *aevum*.

The final element of Stein's philosophy of death and dying can be understood within ontological and theological contexts. As we die, we move constantly between a feeling of fullness of being and a loss or nothingness of that very same being. The fullness and security of being that we feel is not *causa sui*, as we are not the source of it. We have no control over it. Ontologically, we find ourselves given or thrown, to borrow from Heidegger, in such a way that we are caught between fullness and nothing. We saw how death and dying can represent this constant movement between fullness and nothingness. If we are faithful to Stein's project of questioning the meaning of our being, we, too, have to ask deeper questions about our being thrown, given, or being moved between fullness and nothingness of being. Stein gives two arguments for a source of our being given/thrown in the above-mentioned fashion. First, she recapitulates the classic Scholastic argument concerning cause and effect. Every effect has a cause. We are an effect (*causatum*) insofar as we are created beings. For Stein, this effect points back to an ultimate cause, namely, God. God is identified as the source of our created being. There are always limits to this kind of cosmological argumentation, especially if we think of causality in terms of quantum mechanics and physics.

The Aristotelian science of causes is not very convincing in light of modern physics; moreover, one cannot validly deduce that a first cause is necessarily God. In many ways, Stein recognizes this. In *Finite and Eternal Being*, we are brought to a fundamental perplexity that can be arrived at through philosophical questioning. We can ask why and how is it that we find ourselves given or thrown between fullness and nothingness. Human reason cannot provide any definite answer. Reason has revealed/reached its limit, and this is where the peculiar knowledge that is faith steps in.[25] Scripture tells us that God is the Source, he is Being: "I am who am." God has created all things, giving them being and allowing them to know their end as finite creatures.

The second argument for identifying God as the source of our being is rooted in faith, and it is this argument, in many ways, that is most convincing for Stein. Death and dying permit us to question and answer the question regarding the source of our being: God. They become significant metaphysical/theological apertures that reveal the nature of our existence as flowing between fullness and nothingness but also moving us toward a future, possible fullness in a life with God.[26] For Stein, we can employ our reason enlightened by faith to probe deeper into these mysteries of human existence.

Challenging Two Steinian Claims about Death

Stein's philosophy of death, albeit rich and fruitful, also presents two significant temporal and ontological problems. First, concerning time, death, and dying, these show how we are lodged firmly between finitude and eternity. The latter is contingent upon the divine. Because being is constantly given to us and we are not the source or cause of this constantly regenerating fullness, one must posit the source as other.

> All this signifies a connection of *Dasein* to a being that is not its own. At the same time, it signifies a springing-forth of time: the activity of taking care of oneself does not stop to consider only one thing, but is always projecting itself towards another future; it is not adequate to the "moment." In this, we see how every moment offers a fullness that wishes to be depleted. . . . The "moment" here is not to be understood in terms of a simple point in time, a "cut" between flows of past and future; rather, it defines the contact of a temporal thing with something that is of itself non-temporal. It presents itself within the temporality of the moment.[27]

That which presents itself within that moment as atemporal, that is not subject to created human time, is God. The *aevum*[28] that marks our temporal existence poses a significant problem. From the viewpoint of human existence, that is, *stricto sensu* without any belief in revelation, our existence is experienced in purely finite terms. We are born and we die. We know an end and we experience it unfolding in our living. Stein describes both a fullness and loss that is experienced in our existence as it actualizes itself "moment to moment." Fullness is not a deduction but a value posited in retrospective apprehension when we try to describe the past as an already-having-been. Precisely and concretely, if we accept that existence is a flow of moments and we try to understand the flow or temporal connection between the moments, it is true that moments are given one after the other so long as we continue to live. This is how life can be temporally understood as present: a flow of moments that can be said to exist.

To describe such existing moments as fullness is to attribute a value to such continually presented moments that does not necessarily flow from the moments themselves. In other words, an identification of existing, flowing moments as fullness need not be necessarily true. The descriptor "fullness" describes a positive, effusive, and fulfilling meaning to the actual experience; it suggests a greater quantity or deeper intensity or quality. The descriptor is superimposed post-deduction. That is, as one moment transpires into the next, one can rightly deduce that the moments that are flowing now become moments that once were or already have been. *Tout court* one moment is, it then transpires, and another moment may be given, but to ascribe the value of fullness to such existing moments is a superimposed value stemming more from faith in the security of being held in being than reason. Someone also could impose any other value upon the deduction of moments already having been, including negative ones or no values at all. For example, a moment that is need not be full; one need only reflect on thinkers like Jean-Paul Sartre and Søren Kierkegaard who identify these existing moments as either negations or great moments of self-identification.

If we accept Stein's proposition that we are caught between time and eternity, the *aevum*, certain questions arise. Death and dying, for Stein, open up this new temporal dimension. Why does Stein introduce this philosophical distinction of being between finitude and infinite time or eternity? In Scholastic philosophy, as finite creatures there is no real relation between our being and the being of God. God is wholly other. We analogously bear a trace or *vestigium* of God's being insofar as God imprints himself on our being as our Creator. Part of our finitude is our earthly temporality.

When we are transformed in death and are offered the gift of new life our finite temporality seems to be transformed. We now dwell eternally with or without God, depending on where we ultimately end up. If we dwell with God, the finite limits of our temporality seem to be taken away and we become closer to God's being; we become more like God. This presents a problem: Do God and human beings experience eternity in the same way, and, if so, must there be a real relation between God and human beings as their temporal beings are both similarly eternal? It would seem nonsensical to argue that there are different kinds of eternity, so the possibility of leaving completely behind our temporal finitude seems to be inadmissible, which brings us back to Stein's original claim of our being in the *aevum*.

The *aevum* is an excellent metaphysical category as it makes us capable of living with an eternal God, a God who is not subject to created human time in the same way we are, but it still preserves a temporal difference. The question, though, is this: How do we preserve this category within the realm of the eternal or atemporal afterlife, if one should concede such a possibility? I think one could use the argument from analogy. The analogy of being ensures that we have both similarity and difference with God. Insofar as we are creatures of God we bear the stamp of our efficient cause into being: God. In the afterlife we become eternal, but we never lose our pasts or traces of our already having been. Our past as finite temporal creatures persists along with our new eternal existence with God.

We are different from God because God dwells in the eternal present, whereas we, along with the angels, dwell in the *aevum*, though the *aevum* of the angels would have to be different from our experience of the *aevum*. Insofar as our finite beings are preserved, so is our temporal existence, marked by our births and deaths. We might have existed eternally as ideas in the mind of God, but entering time in and through creation made us profoundly human. We bear the temporal effect of our finite existence, not only as marking us as different from God but also permitting us to preserve what once was as our past temporal earthly existence. Our pasts persist as a finite having-been that is not eliminated but is preserved as a constitutive moment of our eternal life with God. God *a contrario* has no past. Here, the temporality of God is assumed to be the eternal present, following classic Christian medieval philosophy.

Let us now move on to our second claim regarding Stein's ontology. Death and dying show that we move constantly from being (fullness) to nonbeing, nothingness, or loss of that which once was. The claim that we experience loss—this is Stein's language—or nonbeing is troubling. The loss, as we have seen earlier, describes the past that is no longer. The being that is no longer actual might not exist in the same mode as the present or the future, but it still admits a certain kind of being. To admit it as nonbeing or loss is to strip it of its ontological import. The dying person certainly becomes acutely aware of the loss of being, but it is not a nothingness or nonbeing. The fact that it is experienced as a loss suggests that it still has existential import that continues to have consequences, especially *qua* anxiety for and in the face of death, as well as anguish and suffering. One definitely feels the ontological weight and thickness of this loss, which is vivified and re-presented in memory and fantasy.[29]

The past continues to live and has impact on both the present and the future. This, too, suggests that the past has some existential force. Past experiences of others' deaths, our shortcomings, fulfilled and unfulfilled dreams or projects, and things past are constantly being evaluated and reevaluated through our making them living or present once again through our presentifications (*Vergegenwärtigungen*), past memories, fantasies, and imaginations. These will have an impact on our present and anticipated dying and death. Stein notes: "From the point of view of the ego . . . it is also clear why 'what is no longer alive' or 'is past' does not simply sink into nothingness but continues to subsist in a modified form and why it is 'not yet alive' or 'will be in the future' is in a certain manner before it is actually alive."[30] Here, Stein is speaking of the conscious life of the ego and not death. Given this conscious reality, could not death be experienced as subsisting in the past in some mode that is not necessarily described as nothingness or a lack?

Though one may experience loss or absence of being that once was, it does not follow that the being that once was is nonbeing. It still has being, but not in the same way or mode that the present has actual being. To strip away being, reducing it to nonbeing, loss, or absence, is to render the past silent and inefficacious. The past continues to signify and have existential import, sometimes more poignantly than the present or the future as is the case with severe past traumas or memories. Stein is fully aware of the role that memories play in consciousness and in the constitution of the person as evidenced in her early writings on empathy and her *Introduction to Philosophy*. Her description of death as being constituted by a fleeing away or nothingness of death raises a serious question as to the ontological status of memories of the past or of others' dying and deaths that continue to persist and have existential import.

To say that the past has ontological import is to claim that it does so in the present through memories and reliving past moments. Of course, that which is lived in the present as past is never identical to the past that was; rather, the past continues to signify in the present. These memories of the past continue to signify now in consciousness. It is as if there is a trace of the past that lingers in the present, which would account, in part, for the constitution of inner-time consciousness for Edmund Husserl. When we bring to consciousness the passing moments that mark our eventual demise, our dying, these past moments may not exist as they once did, but they continue to signify in the present and may affect our present being and our future projects or anticipations. Given that the past that once was can still live in the present in some form, does the nonbeing of those moments that have passed really admit of absolute nonbeing, especially if these past moments somehow are preserved in one's present consciousness?

Finally, let us examine the ontological significance of fullness itself. If we are constantly in the *aevum* and if we exist between fullness and nonbeing/loss, then do we ever truly experience fullness as it can never fully be actualized because its relation to nonbeing or loss constantly conditions it? Fullness, par excellence, implies that being persists as this is seen as an ontological good. God, who is excellent fullness, persists always in being; God is sempiternal. The fullness we experience can never be full, as it is subject to loss and nonbeing. It is being constantly eaten away and is always potentially subject to loss insofar as we are finite, temporal creatures.

Also, the fullness that we experience as simultaneous living and dying is never fully or purely actual. It can be described as a potentiality that only becomes actualized insofar as it is subject to loss. It is a potential because it stems from a source that gives us the possibility of fullness, but because of our finite ontological and temporal limits we can never fully actualize it in this life. In short, the category of fullness that Stein employs is better described as a potentiality that is somewhat actualized rather than an actuality that is fully so. In death and dying our being emerges as fundamentally potential and not as a simple actual being struggling with nonbeing. It is this potential to be or not to be that emerges as central to the discussion of death.

Conclusion

The potentiality to be or not to be is what makes anxiety and anguish so terrible, because we are not in any fully actualized state. It can be either/or, as Kierkegaard rightly observed, albeit in a different sense. It is also this potentiality that lies at the source of the hope that death and dying lead here and now to another life-giving possibility called communion with God and the saints. We have the potential for an afterlife, and this can serve to condition the way we choose to actualize ourselves in the best way we can with all of our limitations. Perhaps Blaise Pascal's wager comes to take greater significance within this context. Our existence, temporally and ontologically understood, is potential to be or not to be; it is only fully actual in the new creation that is the afterlife. For Stein, as for us all, we can choose life with God or life without God. Freedom is not the source of or foundation of existential analysis as many other existentialists would claim; rather, it is the very givenness of potential to be or not to be that creates an aperture for a decision. Freedom is the motor that pushes or repels one's decision to be or not to be.[31]

Stein's analyses of death and dying bring to the fore interesting metaphysical and phenomenological problems surrounding the nature of time and experience. Her thought presents rich possibilities of philosophical importance. In the end, this essay has tried to show two things. First, it outlines the nature of Stein's claims regarding death and dying. Second, there is a need to wrestle and struggle with such claims as they can assist us in clarifying the very meaning and, to borrow a phenomenological turn of phrase, essence of death and dying.

Notes

1. In particular, see the work of Angela Ales Bello, "*A proposito di isolamento e angoscia. E. Stein interprete di M. Heidegger*," in *Isolamento: depressione e angoscia* (Foggia, Italy: Bastogi Editrice Italiana, 1995), 13–25. See also "*Die Fülle oder das Nichts?* Edith Stein and Martin Heidegger on the Question of Being," *American Catholic Philosophical Quarterly* 74, no. 2 (2000): 269–85.

2. Edith Stein, "Martin Heideggers Existentialphilosophie," in *Welt und Person,* Edith Steins Werke (ESW), vol. 6, ed. Lucy Gelber and Romaeus Leuven (Louvain, Belgium: Nauwelaerts, 1962), 69–135; hereafter referred to as MHE.

3. Sylvie Courtine-Denamy, *Trois femmes dans de sombres temps: Edith Stein, Hannah Arendt, Simone Weil ou amor faiti, amor mundi* (Paris: Albin Michel, 2002), 205.

4. See "Assistant or Collaborator? The Role of Edith Stein in Edmund Husserl's *Ideas II,*" in Contemplating Edith Stein, ed. Joyce A. Berkman

(South Bend, Ind.: University of Notre Dame Press, 2006), 243–70. In particular, see Bello, "*A proposito di isolamento e angoscia,*" 13–25. See also, "*Die Fülle oder das Nichts?*" 269–85. Sylvie Courtine-Denamy, *Three Women in Dark Times* (Ithaca, N.Y.: Cornell University Press, 2006); Marianne Sawicki, *Body, Text and Science: The Literacy of Investigative Practices and the Phenomenology of Edith Stein* (Dordrech, The Netherlands: Kluwer, 1997); Antonio Calcagno, *The Philosophy of Edith Stein* (Pittsburgh, Pa.: Duquesne University Press, 2007), 7–18.

5. Angelika von Renteln, "Moments in Edith Stein's Years of Crisis 1918–1922," in *Contemplating Edith Stein,* ed. Joyce A. Berkman (Notre Dame, Ind.: Notre University Press, 2006), 134–38.

6. Stein, *Potency and Act,* trans. Walter Redmond, CWES, vol. 11 (Washington, D.C.: ICS Publications, 2009).

7. Stein, *Endliches und ewiges Sein,* ESW, vol. 2 (Louvain, Belgium: Editions Nauwelaerts, 1950); hereafter cited as *EES.*

8. See Stein's essay, "Ways to Know God," in *Knowledge and Faith,* trans. Walter Redmond, CWES, vol. 8 (Washington, D.C.: ICS Publlications, 2000), 83–114.

9. MHE, in *Welt und Person,* 102.

10. Ibid., 101.

11. "Denn der unleugbaren Tatsache, daß mein Sein in flüchtiges, von Augenblick zu Augenblick gefristetes und der Möglichkeit des Nichtseins ausgesetztes ist, entspricht die andere ebenso unleugbare Tatsache, daß ich trotz dieser Flüchtigkeit bin und von Augenblick zu Augenblick im Sein erhalten werde und in meinem flüchtigen Sein ein dauerndes umfasse." *EES, 56.*

12. MHE, in *Welt und Person, 104.* See also *EES, 56–57.*

13. On another level, in her analysis of the specifically human, Stein notes that what makes a person uniquely a person is his or her capacity to engage actively in free acts, to enact them, which includes a responsibility for such acts. See Stein, *Der Aufbau der menschlichen Person,* ed. Lucy Gelber and Michael Linssen, O.C.D., ESW, vol. 16 (Freiburg: Herder, 1994), 106.

14. Stein shares the same insight concerning our simultaneous living and dying with thinkers like Simone de Beauvoir, Søren Kierkegaard, Jean-Paul Sartre, Heidegger, Friedrich Nietzsche, Gabriel Marcel, and Simone Weil.

15. Heidegger, *Sein und Zeit* (Tübingen, Germany: Niemeyer, 2001), 254.

16. "und dann steht als Letztes und allein Wichtiges nur noch die Frage: Sein oder Nichtsein? Das Sein, um das es jetzt geht, ist aber ganz gewiß nicht das In-der-Welt-sein. Das ist schon zu Ende, wenn man dem Tod wirklich ins Auge sieht. Er ist das Ende des leiblichen Lebens und alles dessen, was mit dem leiblichen Leben zusammenhängt. Darüber hinaus aber ist er ein großes dunkels Tor: Es muß durchschritten werden aber was dann? Dieses Was dann? ist die eigentliche Frage des Todes, die im Sterben erfahren wird. Gibt es eine Antwort auf die Frage, ehe das Tor durchschritten ist?" MHE, in *Welt und Person,* 104.

17. This question is not an isolated fact. It belongs to a longer line of philosophical speculation that stems from the very origins of Greek philosophy when Socrates gives his proofs for the immortality of the soul prior to his death by poison.

18. See the opening sections of Stein, *Finite and Eternal Being: An Attempt at an Ascent to the Meaning of Being,* trans. Kurt F. Reinhardt, CWES, vol. 9 (Washington, D.C.: ICS Publications, 2002).

19. MHE, in *Welt und Person,* 104–6. Here, one can also include examples of other religions that posit an afterlife, including Islam.

20. "Es gibt aber ein Sterben, bei dem noch anderes geschieht: bei dem schon vor dem Eintreten des leiblichen Todes alle Spuren des Kampfes und Leidens verschwinden, wo der Sterbende, für alle Umstehenden sichtbar, von einem neuen Leben erglüht und verklärt wird, wo seine Augen in ein uns unzugängliches Licht hineinschauen, das seinen Abglanz noch auf dem entseelten Körper zurückläßt. Wer nie etwas von einem höheren Leben gehört oder den Glauben daran von sich geworfen hätte, müßte durch einen solchen Anblick darauf gestoßen werden, daß es so etwas geben müsse. Und es wird sich ihm der Sinn des Todes al seines Durchganges vom Leben in dieser Welt und in diesem Leib zu einem anderen Leben, von einer Seinsweise zu einer anderen Seinsweise erschließen. Dann ist aber auch das Dasein—als Sein zum Tode—nicht Sein zum Ende, sondern zu einem neuen Sein: freilich durch die Bitterkeit des Todes hindurch, durch das gewaltsame Abreißen des natürlichen Daseins hindurch." MHE, in *Welt und Person,* 106–7.

21. "[I]n place of the individual ego we've got a subject in our case that encompasses a plurality of individual egos. Certainly I the individual ego

am filled up with grief. . . . I feel it as our grief. . . . We feel this subject (i.e., unit) affected within ourselves when we have an experience of community. I grieve as a member of the unit, and the unit grieves within me." Stein, *Philosophy of Psychology and the Humanities,* trans. Mary Catharine Baseheart and Marianne Sawicki, CWES, vol. 7 (Washington, D.C.: ICS Publications, 2000), 134.

22. Stein, *On the Problem of Empathy,* trans. Waltraut Stein, CWES, vol. 3 (Washington, D.C.: ICS Publications, 1989).

23. Stein, *Philosophy of Psychology and the Humanities,* 137–39.

24. See both Stein's *Finite and Eternal Being* and *Potency and Act.* See also Sarah Borden's article, "Edith Stein and Thomas Aquinas on Being and Essence," in a special volume on Edith Stein, *American Catholic Philosophical Quarterly* 82, no. 1 (Winter 2008): 87–103; Angela Ales Bello, "The Spiritual Life and Its Degrees According to Edith Stein," *Listening: Journal of Religion and Culture 41, no. 3 (2006): 152–70* [essay two in this volume].

25. See last two sections of Stein's "Ways to Know God," in *Knowledge and Faith.*

26. See discussion of soteriology in Stein, *Potency and Act.*

27. Translation mine. "All das bedeutet Bindung des Daseins an ein Sein, das nicht das seine, sondern für das seine Grund und Ziel ist. Zugleich bedeutet es eine Sprengung der Zeitlichkeit:die besorgende Geschäftigkeit, die bei keiner Sache verweilt, sondern immer schon zu künftigen vorauseilt, wird dem Augenblick nicht gerecht.Darin kommt zum Ausdruck, daß jeder Augenblick eine Fülle bietet, die ausgeschöpft werden will. Vieles ist damit ausgesprochen. Einmal, daß Augenblick hier nicht im Sinne eines bloßen Zeitpunktes zu verstehen ist, eines Schnittes zwischen Strecken der Vergangenheit und Zukunft. Es bezeichnet die Berührung eines Zeitlichen mit etwas, was selbst nicht zeitlich ist, aber in seine Zeitlichkeit hineinreicht." MHE, in *Welt und Person,* 108. One thinks of Søren Kierkegaard's moment as developed in *The Concept of Anxiety.*

28. For medieval Christian philosophy, the *aevum* was the time of the angels, a view that angels were temporally constituted as being in between eternity and finite time. I have appropriated this concept to speak of the time of humans that is between pure finitude and pure eternity.

29. See Stein's *On the Problem of Empathy; and Einführung in die Philosophie* (Introduction to philosophy), ed. Claudia Marièle Wulf and Hanna-Barbara Gerl-Falovitz, ESGA, vol. 8 (Freiburg: Herder, 2010).

30. Stein, *Finite and Eternal Being,* 50.

31. I am very grateful to friends and colleagues who have made very useful comments and suggestions. I would like to thank and acknowledge the help of Amy Phillips, Christina M. Gschwandtner, Joyce Avrech Berkman, Sarah Borden Sharkey, and Patrick J. Mohr, S.J.

12

EMPATHY AND THE FACE:
Edith Stein and Emmanuel Levinas

MICHAEL R. PARADISO-MICHAU

Everything in [Stein's work] is utterly genuine, otherwise I should say that this step [her conversion to Catholicism and decision to join the Carmelite nuns] was romanticism. But— down in Jews there is a radicalism and love faithful unto martyrdom.[1]

I had examined the act of empathy as a particular act of cognition. After that . . . I went on to something which was personally close to my heart and which continually occupied me anew in all later works: the constitution of the human person.[2]

Introduction

The phenomenological movement, inaugurated by Edmund Husserl in the early twentieth century and anticipated by Franz Brentano late in the nineteenth century, continues to have significant influence in contemporary philosophical, religious, and ethical thought, specifically because of the return of an investigation of the lived world (*Lebenswelt*) of human experience and consciousness.

267

Attempts at describing the essential structures of human experience and consciousness in a nonpositivistic (that is, humanistic) fashion are key elements in phenomenological analyses. At root, phenomenology is a humanistic eidetic science; as such it endeavors to uncover essential structures of human intersubjectivity and interhuman relationships. How do humans know and experience themselves and others? How do they ascribe meaning to events and persons? What are the conditions of the possibility for experiencing someone else in the life world? These are some questions that enliven phenomenologists' investigations.

Edith Stein (1891–1942) and Emmanuel Levinas (1905–95) both studied closely with the master of phenomenology, Edmund Husserl. Their dissertations, on empathy and intuition, respectively, expertly discussed major themes in Husserlian and post-Husserlian phenomenology. Throughout their writings, Stein and Levinas embarked upon critical departures from—or one could assert that they critically advanced—Husserl's thought through their insistence on the distinctly and existentially ethical and religious dimensions of phenomenological investigation and description.[3] The significance of, and deep concern for, the singular existing human person in relationship with the Other was paramount in the thought of both Stein and Levinas.

From this initial divergence from their common teacher, the writings of Stein and Levinas intellectually parted ways on the topic of the genesis of a phenomenological account of ethical responsibility. From whence does ethical responsibility generate? Does the self make an empathic movement toward the other individual, thus initiating an ethical relationship? Conversely, is he or she *qua* other revealed to the (responsible) self, exposing the direct and holy command not to kill this unrepeatable human being?

For Levinas, another faces (or regards) me, and in this phenomenon, or revelation of the trace of the infinite, my identity is ruptured and called into question, and I find myself always and already in a relationship of infinite responsibility for each other person. Stein's phenomenology of ethical revelation takes a seemingly different path. For her, an analysis of the concept of *Einfühlung* (in-feeling, empathy) means that I actively go out of myself, my zero point of orientation, and encounter the other person (which is an analogue of the "I" for Levinas). The other who faces the I might even be an anonymous person; nevertheless, the I puts the other that his face reveals before itself. In an empathic act, for Stein, I feel-in with (not instead of or for) the inner life of an other individual. In only a few places does Levinas discuss the concept of empathy, largely due to his legitimate concern that the self attempts to totalize the other through mirroring, or, in Stein's term, "projecting" itself onto that which cannot be contained, the infinity of the other individual.[4] The following schematic should prove useful:

	1		2		3
Stein:	Self	→	Other	⇨	self's responsibility for the Other
Levinas:	Other	→	Self	⇨	self's responsibility for the Other

Here the arrows indicate (1) the initiator of such ethical relationship; (2) the original movement of engagement; and (3) the one-sided direction of ethical responsibility.

This essay continues to explore this notion of "going outward to meet and welcome the Other" in Steinian terms, gesturing toward a critique of Levinasian phenomenology of ethical revelation. This critique will then be mobilized as a bridge to cover the gap left behind Levinas's notion of receptivity of the self for the other's "facing." Stein's theory of empathy, in this argument, does more work by way of a phenomenology of ethical revelation than Levinas's descriptions of the experience of the "face" does. In no way do I mean to suggest that Levinas's phenomenology of the face of the other is in any way deficient. Stein and Levinas can be brought together to constitute a more radical phenomenological ethics of responsibility and love than either one of them is capable of doing individually. As Paul Ricoeur's text indicates, the self is always an other for another individual—we are all others to each other—so Stein and Levinas are not necessarily disagreeing here; they are more or less describing the same phenomenal experience from different perspectives.[5] Some questions that this essay will pose and attempt a response to, are the following:

> Phenomenologically speaking, how does one encounter the other? In other words, how is the other revealed to the self?

> Is it a case of going out to meet the other through acts of empathy, as is the case for Stein?

Is it a case of responding to the other's call, as it is for Levinas?

Are there other options, or is there a felicitous middle ground between Stein's and Levinas's positions?

For Levinas, does Stein's concept of empathy ultimately reduce the other person to the same through the technique of (Husserlian) analogizing or reproducing?

Finally, what can phenomenological analyses do for a description of ethical revelation?

Appropriately, then, what follows will be sectioned off into considerations of and responses to the above questions; however, in order to introduce this paper's interlocutors adequately, I will first offer brief reconstructions of Stein's concept of empathy and Levinas's notion of the face.

Stein and Empathy

The possibility of empathizing with the emotions of another person allows us the means for knowing another and, therefore, of rational sympathy with another. Empathy, according to Stein, is the mode of givenness of foreign subjects. Empathy is a feature of genuine rationality since it provides us with the knowledge of others which is essential both to one's own individuation and one's love for another person.[6]

In his famous fifth *Cartesian Meditation,* Husserl attempted to ground human intersubjectivity phenomenologically so as to describe sociality and community formation and, in so doing, avoid the charge of phenomenology as solipsistic. He investigated how the self experiences and knows other subjects. In her dissertation on empathy, Stein sought to describe more rigorously exactly what it is that goes on in an intersubjective relationship. What are those linkages between two people that form the foundations for ethical intersubjective relationships, families, communities, and nations? The concept and practice of empathy, for her, is the key to discovering and initiating ethically intersubjective relations. Taking a cue from her mentor, Stein notes that the self starts with its own self-consciousness, and that the other person is an alter ego, another I, another zero point of orientation, located over there. How is this achieved? As James Hart observes, "Empathic presencing is an absenting or a de-presencing of my 'here' to a 'there' which too claims to be an original 'here.' It is a making present of what for me is another primordial making present and therefore a making present of what for me remains essentially absent. For this reason empathic perception may be considered a self-displacement."[7] Empathy, then, involves an I's nonprimordial experience of an other's direct experience. The "you" announces and invigorates a primordial experience to the "me" who recognizes feelings that do not originate in its own life. For Stein, the practice of empathy became the foundation for all intersubjective relations.

In phenomenologically describing the human experience of empathy, Stein is keen to observe Husserl's insistence on embodied consciousness and the animate living body (*Leib*). Empathy (like consciousness) must be embodied for it to mean anything to the human individual. The situation of interhuman sociality, not isolated or monadic individuality, is the human condition for Stein. Before there was an individuated self, there was a life-world community of persons. Essentially, for Stein, as well as for Husserl, "you" are another "I" located over there. By analogizing and reproducing what I know of myself and, most important, by being open to you, I am nonprimordially able to feel-with what you are feeling when you describe your joys, fears, and hopes to me. Stein's hallmark example is the emotion of joy. If I see that you are elated over recently hearing good news, I can imagine and intuit how that must feel for you. As I am becoming aware of that feeling within myself, my intentional awareness of that awareness (consciousness of consciousness) makes me happy as well. By drawing on, and displacing, my original self-presence here, I am able to empathize with you.

In Stein's later and more overtly religious writings, the notion of "taking up one's Cross" dovetails neatly with her earlier thoughts on empathy. As she converted from Judaism to Catholicism and became a Carmelite nun, she noted that her vocation was to contemplate and to do penance for the suffering members of the world. She felt that, as a woman, she had a certain predilection toward caregiving and being-for-others—in short, for empathy.

Levinas and the Face

The reduction to an ego, the egological reduction, can be only a first step toward phenomenology. We must also discover "others" and the intersubjective world. A phenomenological intuition of the life of others, a reflection by Einfühlung opens the field of transcendental intersubjectivity and completes the work of philosophical intuition of subjectivity.[8]

access to the face is straightaway ethical. . . . [T]he face signifies the Infinite.[9]

In a trenchant critique of Western philosophical and theological thinking, Levinas argued for the primacy of the human other, or infinity, against the primacy of the same, or totality. That is, he elevated interhuman difference, or alterity, as a functioning philosophical concept over the notion of totality or reducing that which is otherwise into the same. Western philosophy, considered as a tradition of discourse for Levinas, is an egology. He struggled to surpass this definition of limiting and unethical thought. In *Totality and Infinity*, Levinas writes, "The being that expresses itself imposes itself, but does so precisely by appealing to me with its destitution and nudity—its hunger—without my being able to be deaf to that appeal. Thus in expression the being that imposes itself does not limit but promotes my freedom, by arousing my goodness."[10] The relationship with this other is immediately an ethical one, where the other individual commands: "Thou shalt not kill." The face, exposed and vulnerable, expresses both a defenselessness and an injunction against the violent tendencies of the self.

Reminiscent of our discussion of Stein, Levinas claims, "The establishing of the primacy of the ethical, that is, of the relationship of man to man—signification, teaching, and justice—[is] a primacy of an irreducible structure upon which all other structures rest."[11] The self expiates as a hostage to the other individual, welcoming him, responding to him, saying, "Monsieur, après vous." Uncovering and describing essential structures of subjectivity, Levinas writes that "[r]esponsibility prior to any free commitment, the oneself outside of all the tropes of essence, would be responsibility for the freedom of others."[12] It is only when the self defers and declares, "Here I am," before the face of the other that the self truly begins to authentically exist. Levinas contends that "subjectivity as such is initially hostage; it answers to the point of expiating for others."[13]

How Does One Encounter the Other?
Stein and Levinas in Conversation

Three elements of their thought interconnect with one another: First, both Stein and Levinas recognize the primacy of the ethicality of the relationship with the other. They deeply venerate and respect the other person even (at times) ahead of the self. Without the original relationship with the other person, there is neither self nor other. Stein and Levinas are not merely dealing with the epistemological problem of other minds; their projects speak to one another most closely with regard to their insistence on the ethical relationship, through the experience of empathy or the face, that occurs between individuals. For Stein, as well as for Levinas, it is moral conscience that yields consciousness. I would add that, in Levinasian terms, both succeed in arguing that humans are to become non-indifferent to the concerns of others: I am simply not allowed to turn a blind eye to the suffering of the other. Rather, what concerns the other is a matter of concern to me.

Second, concerning responsibility, for Levinas, as the face of another human being regards me, I am immediately placed in a position of infinite responsibility; however, in order to receive the other appropriately, I need to be in a position of response-ability. How this attunement is fleshed out is unclear in Levinas's writings. How do I attend to, or properly anticipate, the face of the other? It is my contention that Stein's concept of empathy could do much to heal this wound in Levinasian thinking. I maintain that Stein's phenomenological description of empathy does the work that Levinas's passivity, which is more passive than the opposite of activity, does not do. In an authentically empathic act, I divest essential characteristics of myself into the life of the other in order to feel with him or her.

Third, the role of woman or the feminine as an ideal type for both otherness and empathy is a notion shared by Levinas and Stein. Kathleen Haney and Johanna Valiquette contend that "Stein's discussion of woman as ethical type must be her major contribution to phenomenological ethics."[14] In her *Essays on Woman*, Stein performs a phenomenological description of the essence and experience of being a woman and contends that the maternal and feminine qualities of personalism, empathy, concern, and cooperation be exalted as proper starting points for any practical (that is, moral) philosophical teaching. Stein proposed an ethics based on the value of the human person. In contrast to Martin Heidegger's notions of anxiety or being-toward-death, Stein prefers openness as the authentic mode of being in an intersubjective life-world. Haney and Valiquette continue, "The significance of feminine singularity is its potential to develop true humanity in the woman herself and in others. Women's fulfillment often includes natural, sympathetic, helpful motherliness, the characteristic value of woman, especially if they do not restrict maternity to blood relations."[15] Stein's feminist ethics closely resembles Carol Gilligan's ethics of care today.

In *Time and the Other*, Levinas declares that the maternal woman served as inspiration for his derivation of the concept "other." It is in this situation that the unborn child as other is vitally dependent on the host, the mother. This is the notion of otherness that galvanizes Levinas's phenomenological concept of alterity. Levinas similarly writes in *Otherwise than Being* that the situation of maternity is the exemplar of having "the other in the same . . . In maternity what signifies is a responsibility for others, to the point of substitution for others. . . . Maternity, which is bearing par excellence, bears even responsibility for the persecuting by the persecutor."[16] For Stein, as well as for Levinas, there is something peculiarly significant about the ethical roles of the feminine and maternal that ethically charges them with longings for empathic otherness.

Is Stein's Concept of Empathy Contra Levinas?

Far from being antithetical to Levinas's notion of the face of the other, I assert that Stein's concept of empathy supports and provides further phenomenological foundation for Levinas's notion of infinite responsibility. Once we look into the ways in which Stein herself embodied the empathic life, we can see strong affinities to Levinas's notion of the face. From the earliest reflections on her childhood, Stein seems to already have exemplified the hallmarks of empathy. She writes in her autobiography that, as early as 1912, she developed a "talent for ready comprehension and . . . [an] extraordinary facility for inserting myself into the other's thought processes . . ."[17] Stein showed the importance not only of understanding but also of experiencing suffering and self-sacrifice and held that they could serve as sources of philosophical insight. Drawing a parallel with Levinas, who claims that the only suffering that can be meaningful is my own, the suffering of another human being is, in a word, useless.[18] For Levinas, I am responsible (1) for the other, (2) for the responsibility of the other, and (3) for the life and death of the other. Taking this into a Christian concept of empathy, Stein would concur, declaring that one must "take up his or her own cross," and atone for the sins committed in this world. For Stein, through contemplative prayer, there can be a becoming one with others that is consistent with others becoming present through oneself.

One pragmatic question that here emerges was brought up by Judy Miles: "What does it really matter whether empathy is described in terms of projection [that is, self-revelation] or reception [that is, revelation]?"[19] In Stein's concept of empathy, as is the case with Levinas's notion of the face, the other person's life is not negatively altered or intruded upon in any fundamental way. The opposite is the case; the other person is brought to life, that is, brought into an intersubjective, ethical relationship with another self. In an ecstatic (*ek-statis*) relationship, the self goes outside of itself and experiences otherness; such is the case with a phenomenological conception of religious-ethical love (*agape*). Stein's concept of empathy and Levinas's theory of the face collaborate to uncover essential structures of love. Empathizing with the face of the other person as an other human individual is the essence of love for Stein and Levinas.

What Work Does Phenomenology Do for the Description of Ethical Revelation?

I . . . believe that the deeper one is drawn into God, the more one must "go out of oneself"; that is, one must go to the world in order to carry the divine life into it.[20]

[T]he social is the very order of the spiritual.[21]

In this concluding section, I am only able to point out a few benefits offered by a phenomenological description of ethical revelation. Phenomenological analyses and descriptions highlight the distinctly human dimension in the co-constitution of the human self and the other. Additionally, phenomenology reveals the structures of everyday, lived experience in the life-world; such structures are always already ethical and social in existence. As Marx and many others have rightly observed, the human is nothing if not a social being. Through the phenomenological method, both Stein and Levinas bracket the ontological commitments to the independence of the world from the knowing subject and reveal the intentional constitution of the subject's ethical consciousness and awareness. Stein's phenomenological account of empathy, when studied alongside Levinas's work on ethical subjectivity, proposes a robust account of the ethical (self-)revelation of one to the other. As Martin Buber aptly opined, "All human life is in the meeting,"[22] the meeting of two subjectivities in the world of human experience and life.

As we have seen, while Stein and Levinas take divergent positions on the phenomenological genesis of ethical responsibility, their thoughts are convergent on philosophy and phenomenology as rigorous ethical sciences. This marks their common point of critical departure from their mentor in common, Husserl. If phenomenological analyses and descriptions disclose and reveal essential structures of human subjectivity, then they ought to see the human in its natural condition of ethical communion with one another.

Haney observes that "phenomenology, for Stein . . . provided an access to religion."[23] For Levinas, ethical responsibility is tantamount to religious obedience and revelation. Haney continues, "For . . . Stein, philosophy and life were one."[24] Living the good life as a philosophical quest was remarkably embodied by the philosophies of both Stein and Levinas. Their common point of departure, phenomenologically discovering the nature and structure of ethical subjectivity, provides a needed corrective to the relative blind spot in Husserl's phenomenological philosophy. The primacy of the human person, both self and other, forms the foundation for Stein's and Levinas's phenomenological ethics of revelation. Such a positioning bears witness to Husserl's observation regarding the "radicalism and love faithful unto martyrdom" of Stein. In the innermost chamber of the individual's soul exists the infinite, God. To empathize with the other's face is to ethically meet soul-to-soul and thus to create a divinely inspired relationship.

Notes

1. Edmund Husserl, quoted in Kathleen Haney, "Edith Stein," in *Encyclopedia of Phenomenology*, ed. Lester Embree et al. (Dordrecht, The Netherlands: Kluwer, 1997), 682.

2. Edith Stein, *Life in a Jewish Family, 1891–1916: An Autobiography*, trans. Josephine Koeppel, O.C.D., CWES, vol. 1 (Washington, D.C.: ICS Publications, 1986), 397.

3. Although Husserl lectured on ethics and value theory (see Ullrich Melle, "Ethics in Husserl," in *Encyclopedia of Phenomenology*, 180–84; and "Edmund Husserl: From Reason to Love," in *Phenomenological Approaches to Moral Philosophy*, ed. J. J. Drummond and L. Embree [Dordrecht, The Netherlands: Kluwer, 2002], 229–48; James G. Hart, *The Person and the Common Life: Studies in a Husserlian Social Ethics* [Dordrecht, The Netherlands: Kluwer, 1992]; and James Mensch, *Ethics and Selfhood: Alterity and the Phenomenology of Obligation* [Albany: State University of New York Press, 2003]); some of these lectures have been collected and published; for the purposes of this paper, I will follow the train of thought that Husserlian phenomenology is primarily (although not solely) an epistemological endeavor. Additionally, Husserl rarely

directly discusses explicitly religious notions in his major published writings, certainly not as explicitly as Stein and Levinas do.

4. See Michael Paradiso-Michau, "Not Only an *Alter Ego*: Rethinking Intersubjectivity with Husserl and Levinas," *Listening: Journal of Religion and Culture* 43, no. 2 (Spring 2008): 71–81.

5. Paul Ricoeur, *Oneself as Another*, trans. Kathleen Blamey (Chicago: University of Chicago Press, 1994).

6. Kathleen Haney, "Edith Stein: Woman and Essence," in *Feminist Phenomenology*, ed. L. Fisher and L. Embree (Dordrecht, The Netherlands: Kluwer, 2000), 231.

7. Hart, *The Person and the Common Life*, 178.

8. *The Theory of Intuition in Husserl's Phenomenology*, 2nd ed., trans. André Orianne (Evanston, Ill.: Northwestern University Press, 1995), 150–51.

9. Emmanuel Levinas, *Ethics and Infinity*, trans. Richard A. Cohen (Pittsburgh, Penn.: Duquesne University Press, 1985), 85, 105.

10. Levinas, *Totality and Infinity: An Essay on Exteriority*, trans. Alphonso Lingis (Pittsburgh, Penn.: Duquesne Univeristy Press, 1969), 200.

11. Ibid., 79.

12. Levinas, *Otherwise Than Being, or Beyond Essence*, trans. Alphonso Lingis (Pittsburgh, Penn.: Duquesne University Press, 1981), 109.

13. Levinas, *Ethics and Infinity*, 100.

14. Haney and Vailquette, "Edith Stein: Woman as Ethical Type," in Drummond and Embree, eds., *Phenomenological Approaches to Moral Philosophy*, 451.

15. Ibid., 456.

16. Levinas, *Otherwise Than Being, or Beyond Essence*, 75.

17. Stein, *Life in a Jewish Family*, 199.

18. See "Useless Suffering," in *Entre Nous: Thinking of the Other*, trans. Michael B. Smith and Barbara Harshav (New York: Columbia University Press, 1998). Compare this notion with Stein's: "when someone desires to suffer, it is not merely a pious reminder of the suffering of the Lord. Voluntary expiatory suffering is what truly and really unites one to the Lord intimately. When it arises, it comes from an already existing relationship with Christ" (Stein, *Life in a Jewish Family*, 92).

19. Judy Miles, "Other Minds and Other Bodies in Edith Stein: Or, How to Talk About Empathy," in *Husserl and Stein*, ed. Richard Feist and William Sweet (Washington, D.C.: The Council for Research in Values and Philosophy, 2003), 123.

20. Stein, *Self-Portrait in Letters, 1916–1942*, trans. Josephine Koeppel, O.C.D., CWES, vol. 5 (Washington, D.C.: ICS Publications, 1993), 54.

21. Levinas, *Ethics and Infinity*, 26.

22. Martin Buber, *I and Thou*, trans. Waler Kaufmann (New York: Simon and Schuster, 1996).

23. Haney, "Edith Stein," 679.

24. Ibid., 683.

13

LIFE AND THE OTHER WORLD:
Edith Stein and Michel Henry

ISOBEL BOWDITCH

How might life live? That was Theodor Adorno's question, which entreats us to find ways of thinking and acting differently so that Auschwitz would not repeat itself; otherwise, he feared that we would be spellbound and compelled to choose between involuntary detachment and the bestiality of involvement.[1] The concept of life has since gained currency in recent philosophy. While its redemption from the nihilistic fate that Adorno predicts is perhaps not (yet) realized, a more affirmative possibility is proposed by two philosophers who share common territory while providing very different accounts of human affective life: Michel Henry and Edith Stein. Although Henry and Stein do not directly address Adorno as such, they do address some possible responses to his question.

Both Henry and Stein, in their own ways, provide insights into how to bridge or surpass the limitations of a purely empirical or materialist philosophy by probing the question of life as embodied, connected, and responsive; both propose a model of thinking that surpasses dualistic notions of self and other, subject and object. That is, they see life not only as a philosophical concept but, crucially, as lived. They also have in common a heritage in phenomenology and share a Christian (Catholic) perspective. Despite this, their approaches differ starkly and represent two almost directly opposing poles of thought.

For Henry, in works such as *I Am the Truth*, it is not whether Christianity is true that is the question for him, but what Christianity might tell us about truth and reality. In Henry's work we find no mysterious external Creator who gives life to humans and determines our very subjecthood, but God as life given to itself in auto-affection. The life of humans, or "livings," cohabits with God in this sphere of absolute affective immanence. Through his exuberant celebration of the self-enjoyment of life that "refuses all lack and ambivalence associated with objectifying thought," Henry proposes an antidote to a nihilistic view of life as anonymous or alien to human consciousness.[2]

Despite the obscure and often quasi-mystical orientation of his writing, Henry has been more readily taken up than Stein by secular thinkers. Gilles Deleuze scholars, for example, find a useful contribution to philosophies of immanence in his radical phenomenology. Some read Henry's version of immanence as theistic and some as an "empirical description of nature rather than divine manifestation."[3]

In contrast to Henry's self-affection, Stein sees the capacity to be affected as an aspect of empathy, which she describes as an "experience of feeling led by an experience that is not one's own." Although, like Henry, she emphasizes the importance of interior subjective life, for her we are irrevocably bound to the other. We inhabit a social and physical world that influences and informs subjective experience at all levels. Stein develops a vocabulary to describe the productive interaction of individual and communal life, bringing together vitalist motifs such as life power with a model of person that details realms of subjective experience, some of which are shareable and some utterly private. We are affected by and through our receptivity to life power, including what she calls an otherworldly (*jenseitige*) power. While Stein advocated that individuals take responsibility for the actions they perform in their name and that of their community, her work builds a case against individualism as such. Her later writing, such as *Finite and Eternal Being*, questions whether a Christian philosophy is possible and concludes that all philosophy must be Christian philosophy, since it is the truth that we seek.[4]

Although Stein's work on empathy has also been influential in the wider sphere of philosophy and psychology of medicine or nursing, for example, she has generally attracted less attention from secular or non-Christian quarters than Henry. This might be in part due to the prominence of the image of Stein as a Carmelite nun and Catholic saint (we have no such images of Michel Henry) and that in her later work, such as *Finite and Eternal Being*, as Sarah Borden Sharkey points out, she was no longer doing phenomenology in the strict sense of "limiting herself to phenomena given to consciousness or that which is necessary to account for what is strictly given," but making an explicit shift toward more metaphysical inquiry that incorporated the idea of Christian revealed truth.[5]

For Henry, invisible and radically subjective life is the locus of a self-generating source of truth or reality, and the outside or appearance is a terrifying neutrality. Stein keeps the distinction between inside and outside open but sees revelation as something that comes from an external source, as though something is done to us, and an action we actively accept or reject. For her, the outside is not neutral or divested of reality but the realm of the other, including the community of human beings and an unconditionally loving God. It is the tension between these two tendencies—immanence or transcendence, subjective agency or radical passivity—that might be most informative for us here. It is present not only between these two philosophers of different genders and generations but also to be found within individual thinkers. This is nowhere more evident than in religious thinkers such as Søren Kierkegaard, the prince of paradox.[6]

Just as the work of both Henry and Stein diverges from a purely phenomenological framework, so their religious perspective may also be relevant to a broader frame of reference. In relation to the theological turn in contemporary continental philosophy, John Caputo recently noted that no one, including the atheists, seems able to stop talking about God. Nevertheless, the rift between religious and secular philosophy, while narrowing, still remains.[7] Stein observes that this gap was not always so wide. For her, "Catholic philosophy (and Catholic scholarship in general) was never quite the same as the philosophy of Catholics," and until the mid-nineteenth century Catholic intellectual life was dependent on a wider, contemporaneous intellectual context that had already more or less disassociated itself from a philosophical tradition concerned with the inquiry into being rather than the problem of knowledge.

Religious scholars (Catholic, Jewish, and Muslim) then returned to an investigation of Greek and medieval thought, which they saw as their intellectual heritage. It was this, Stein says, that allowed modern philosophy to move forward to become an almost entirely godless discipline, seeing itself as autonomous and resistant to the idea of revealed truth. Despite developments in philosophy through the work of Martin Heidegger, for example, at least until the mid-twentieth century, there was a difficulty in finding a common meeting ground between these two strands. One of Stein's concerns was how to bridge this gap and how to reach a mutual understanding about matters that were of concern to both sides.[8]

Finally, before we embark on the discussion, I acknowledge that my choice of Henry and Stein over other candidates is influenced by my personal and philosophical journey. As Richard Kearney suggests, when we choose one philosopher over another, such a choice is never totally impartial, "so much in a philosophical story has to do with history. While history is often aleatory it is never arbitrary. We choose to remake our story according to the history that makes us." The importance of biography is something that this essay will touch on again.[9]

Michel Henry: Life

I first came across Michel Henry a few years ago while working on a project about Kierkegaard and decision in relation to radical subjectivity. Henry's phenomenology of the invisible initially promised to provide a vocabulary to help get behind the subjective movement of faith that Kierkegaard calls inwardness.[10]

Although there is Kierkegaard's inwardness in Henry, Kierkegaard also understood that faith is an individual and ongoing task that requires decisiveness on the part of the subject. In order to activate or engage the reader in the quest, he utilizes various stylistic and polyphonous strategies. Henry does not put his writing to work in this way, but in place of Kierkegaard's trembling, he presents his thesis with mesmerising certainty. Unlike Kierkegaard, Henry describes the realm of truth as though to (re)discover ourselves in our "*pathetik* unimpeachable flesh," requiring nothing of us at all. Not even acceptance of God as life is accessible, Henry reassures us, not through any kind of objective process or reflection but "in life." It is already there as a self-movement that "does not cease to come into itself and thus to enjoyment of itself."[11]

In *I Am the Truth* Henry proposes a compelling and often seductive "what"; however, in any question of conversion (ethical, religious, philosophical, etc.) and, lest we forget, in Adorno's question, it is also the "how" that concerns us. I am not in need of step-by-step instruction, but do I not at least need to know that movement is possible, even if it is a passage from here back to the same spot, so that the position from which I experience the original is transformed, as though I had been looking at life, as it is said, through the wrong end of a telescope?[12]

Henry does not, as far as I know, discuss Stein's work, but he did position himself clearly against other phenomenologists, notably Heidegger. Western philosophy, Henry says, from the Greeks up to and including Heidegger, conceives of a concept of being that excludes the essence of life from it because life cannot be an object of thought: "Life is constituted in its innermost being and in its very essence as a radical interiority."[13]

For Heidegger, human beings have a privileged position among other entities because for *Dasein* existence is a matter of concern. By virtue of the fact that we possess language, we can provide a unique insight into ontological inquiry. Heidegger proposes that the task of philosophy is to think otherwise, that is, through a meditative mode that is responsive and open to what is given in thought, rather than the representational or calculative mode, which tries to regulate and transform the world for our own end. The thinking that we do in our age of technology, as Heidegger sees it, is not thinking in its proper sense, in the Greek sense of *techne*, a kind of "bringing forth of the true."[14]

Despite the shift in emphasis from a thinking that posits, grasps, or explains toward one that receives or listens is called into being and, despite what seems to be a move toward a humility of thought, Heidegger, according to Henry, still misses the point: "language cannot blaze a trail to either reality or truth."[15] Being belongs to what is shown in the world as phenomena, but this is not reality. For Henry, Heidegger is still enmeshed in a representational and dualistic thinking that seeks truth in the realm of thought and language. In the world, according to Henry, things are reduced to representation. Whatever can be shown to be consciousness, as phenomena are cast outside themselves,

> is fractured, broken, cleaved in two, stripped of its own reality—in such a way that, now deprived of that reality that was its own, emptied of its flesh, it is no longer outside itself in the world's image, but just as its own skin, a simple image, in effect, a transparent film, a surface without thickness, a piece of naked externality offered to a gaze that slides over it without being able to penetrate it or reach anything but empty appearance.[16]

Appearance in the world is what Henry calls the process of principled de-realization; in the fact of appearing it is not as though the original state of reality is abolished but from the beginning this thing was passing away.[17]

Being has no relation to life. We cannot say that life is since it is a self-engendering essence, an endlessly occurring self-experiencing that consists in "enjoyment of itself and is exhausted in it."[18] Living is the ability to be affected, in the "*pathetik* phenomenological substance of living," enabling us to experience ourselves in a self-movement "in such a way that . . . nothing is ever detached; nothing slips away from it."[19]

The classical (i.e., Greek) conception of man upon which Heidegger and others draw, Henry says, is that man, endowed with *logos*, is more than "life as such": thus life is less than man. The Christian view is that life is more than man, more than *logos*. For Henry, the condition of being a living subject means that we are in a relationship of "sonship" to absolute Life (God), an immanent affiliation that we may not always remember.

Opposition to a logic of the world is not unusual in Christian thought. There is, after all, what Caputo refers to as "a poetics of the impossible" in the Christian tradition whereby "the way things are counted in the 'kingdom' confounds the calculations of the 'world.'"[20] Henry is not so much investigating a logic or how a state of affairs is accomplished, but is describing or positing a what: reality as life and as the fundamental ground of all manifestation.

Henry's early work, *The Essence of Manifestation*, lays the basis for his phenomenology of the invisible, whereby the invisible itself is the "first and fundamental determination of phenomenality."[21] In this text, after four hundred pages or so of mainly phenomenological explication, Henry turns to Kierkegaard as well as to the thirteenth-century mystic Meister Johannes Eckhart to advance his discussion of the idea of knowledge in relation to faith as an "interior experience of life."[22] Faith, he says, is a kind of nonevidential knowledge available through "the immanence of transcendence," meaning that whatever is revealed in auto-affection (the structure that we can understand as immanence) in "the absence of the world and its light" refuses itself to the phenomenality of the "milieu of representation." Far from being deprived of reality, this darkness is invested with essential truth.[23] There is no opposition between visible and invisible, for any dialectical relation suggests that "each term bears within it the possibility of its passage to the contrary."

The invisible is indifferent to the visible and will never transform itself to its opposite.[24]

For Henry, radical subjectivity in its original self-manifestation is a nonrelational, immediate, nonobjectifying, passive occurrence. The locus and conditions of manifestation occur in self-affection, an atemporal immanence that does not first of all pass through the world in order to appear. As such, Henry's life is like a psychologically and metaphysically subterranean realm.

Henry employs Eckhart to help describe this interior and passive affectivity. Eckhart espoused the idea of self-abandonment, a relinquishing of the will, which, paradoxically, makes me my own creator: "I am unborn. . . . In my unborn manner I have been eternally, and am now, and shall eternally remain."[25] In order for the self to cease its self-willing and to rest in pure Life (God), some kind of decision or action is necessary, and it is about the attainment of this kind of active passivity that Eckhart instructs us.

For Kierkegaard too, it is not evidence but the paradox that compels us through "the tug of decision that changes everything," to abandon ourselves to faith (the absurd).[26] For him, as with Eckhart, the transformative movement of faith occurs through inward obedience to a call.[27] Faith is not inherited nor achieved in one fell swoop, but requires individuals to renew their subjective relationship to the unknown (God) repeatedly and inwardly, a task that must be undertaken by the individual in order for faith to happen.

In Henry's telling, it seems that faith requires no action or effort on the part of the subject, not even the minimal *will not to will* that we find in Eckhart. In Henry's version of life there is no dialectical relation and no possibility of movement from one state of affairs to another.[28] When Henry speaks of action at all, he says, "the relationship between affectivity and action is an internal, immanent relationship, namely, it is the absence of all relationship. . . . Action can no more produce feeling than destroy it."[29]

———

Henry's proposition poses a quandary for us. Life, as truth, seems like an object of faith but if we look to Kierkegaard or Meister Eckhart, as he does, faith cannot be achieved without undergoing some kind of decisive movement. If someone tells me that if I relax, I will be able to let all my worries go, I might well believe that person, but I might not know how to relax. I need some instruction in the method or practice of relaxation, even if ultimately my ability to relax already lies within me.

The notion of ipseity, the original essence which Henry refers to as the identity "between experiencing and what is experienced," illustrates the problem.[30] Ipseity, according to John Taylor, is supposed as an entirely nonrelational experience, but he asks how it can create the *qualia* of experience if it has no content. If it has content, must this not be through some kind of relation to external input? The concept of ipseity suggests that any such relation pollutes the experience itself with external content.[31] Henry's depiction of ipseity as the auto-affection and self-generating movement of life, despite its invisibility and radical immanence, is not, apparently, devoid of content or experience.

The difficulty expressed by Taylor might still apply even in Henry's best efforts to reduce relationality and difference.

Post-Husserlian phenomenology, according to Dan Zahavi, has generally tried to address Edmund Husserl's disregard of exteriority in his account of the relation between immanence and transcendence; however, it is Henry's view that by continually reintroducing a transcendental element into its analysis of immanence, Husserl did not disclose the essential interiority of subjectivity. He reproaches classical phenomenology for overlooking what he sees as this fundamental level of self-manifestation. Henry's solution is apparently to eliminate all exteriority in his analysis of original self-manifestation.[32]

Nick Hanlon suggests that Henry is not speaking of a mere concept of life but of phenomenologically actual life: "the body which is seen, touched, heard . . . presupposes a second body, a transcendental body which feels it, sees, etc." Henry attempts to collapse the difference between these two spheres by turning all materiality inward. Instead of an outwardly motivated intentionality or appearance, this second body is the body made flesh, incarnated existence, an invisible sphere of archi-passivity.[33]

As Zahavi points out, Henry does eventually concede that in every experience something is given to absolute subjectivity, which is different from subjectivity itself (the other or the non-ego). Still, Zahavi asks, are the modifications that he makes to his original thesis enough? How, for Henry, is the subject capable of recognizing other subjects and of being directed toward something different from itself in possession of bodily exteriority, and how can it give rise to the self-division found in reflection? Zahavi argues that Henry's approach is problematic and insufficient because it "conceives of self-manifestation in *abstracto*." In other words, Henry seems to be making the fundamental mistake that phenomenology sought to address, that is, the failure to look at certain concepts as moments of experience, as part of a network of meaning and contexts including intersubjective experience.[34]

In *I Am the Truth*, Henry also admits to self-affection as a dynamic rather than a static notion. The one life (in Christianity) is not an unchanging essence but is active in "deploying itself with an invincible force, a source of the power of engendering that is immanent in anything that lives and unceasingly gives life." This source of power is life, and life is also God. By gesturing toward the inclusion of others (human and divine) in the realm of life, Henry avoids the charge of subjective idealism.

In terms of any intersubjectively constituted meaning or ethical framework, Zahavi is correct in saying that Henry's approach is insufficient, despite the fact that in various publications Henry does indeed demonstrate a concern with ethics, equality, and democracy in human society. The problem of human inequality for Henry emerges from a misunderstanding and misdirected focus. We are already free and equal. It is not a question of proving it or striving for it, but rather, for Henry, as James Williams suggests:

> [E]ven in actual situations where inequality is striven for, underlying the strife there is a pre-condition: life as

auto-affection (for instance in the suffering and predis-
position to affectivity presupposed even by the desire for
the subjection of others). Ethics becomes the struggle to
reveal this precondition and value it against all positions
claiming that any actual situation or goal predicated on
that situation is sufficient for understanding the human
condition. . . . freedom and equality can only be actualized in the reactivation of the internal link that connects every living being to life.[35]

The question of how this internal link is reactivated
remains. Henry proposes a sphere of life as a hermetically
sealed, undivided, almost prenatal state, safe from the
messiness and contingency of existence.

Perhaps Henry is mistaken in opposing himself so
stringently to Heidegger. Seeking to escape duality, they
each opt for either life or world. In life, that is, not a
concept of life but phenomenologically actual life, are
we able to choose one or the other? Is it not the case
that where we find ourselves as existing human beings
we must include both; that the world is a source of our
life and life admits the world without being deceived or
extinguished by it?

The invitation of the other might invite us into conflict, ambiguity, and risk, but equally it might sustain and
guide us. It is both the danger and the refuge of the other
that Stein embraced in her life and work. It is to Stein,
someone whose take on phenomenology also diverges
from Husserl's, but whose emphasis is on the interface
between inner life and external being, that we now turn.

Edith Stein: The Other World

The question is not who, between Henry and Stein, is the better philosopher or who presents the most coherent or convincing philosophical system or model; the question is actually what kind of philosophy allows us to think about how we are altered in life. To become altered, referring to the Latin prefix *al-* (beyond), also means the other (of the two) or in its intransitive form to become otherwise. Kierkegaard adds another layer to the etymology of this word (which suggests that we are changed rather than change ourselves) when, in *The Concept of Anxiety*, he remarks that there is a Danish word, *alteretet* (to become altered), that also means becoming frightened.[36]

How do we understand ourselves as immersed in a life that is open to others, yet is uniquely ours; a life that is nurtured, energized, and uplifted by the fact of being alive but that also threatens us, makes demands on our resources and energy, and which, in times of crisis, obliges us to decide when it seems impossible to do so, when nothing is assured?

In reading Stein, we need not discard Henry's conception of life, but view it, instead, as part of a broader schema of experience that includes an experience of the other (and the Other), an experience that is also immanent to and accessible within an utterly private realm of experience.[37]

Unlike Henry, I did not come across Stein's work through references by other philosophers. Instead, I encountered her quite by accident when, while browsing the shelves of a bookshop, Alasdair MacIntyre's biography of Stein drew my attention.[38] My encounter with Stein is probably typical. Her biography presents itself first and then, in approaching her philosophical work, we may have to work through a deluge of imagery and anecdotes about her personal life. Perhaps it is to urge us beyond the stories of sainthood and martyrdom that Marianne Sawicki suggests that if we want to get to grips with the validity of Stein's thinking, then her biography is irrelevant. Sawicki's concern is understandable; although Stein was a contemporary of Heidegger and others, her unique contribution to philosophy has been largely eclipsed by the details of her extraordinary life. Even so, it seems to me that the relation between her life and work is significant, if not inextricably intertwined, and it is in this relation that one of the key differences between her and Henry's approach can be located.[39]

Stein was born in Breslau, Poland, in 1891 into a devout German-Jewish family, becoming an atheist as an adolescent and later converting to Catholicism before entering the Carmelite Order in 1934. In 1917, at the age of twenty-five, Stein published her PhD thesis, *On the Problem of Empathy*, which she completed under the supervision of Husserl, for whom she was also working as an assistant. She sought to understand empathy within the framework of phenomenology that Husserl was establishing as a new direction for philosophical inquiry. She had an outstanding capacity for self-giving, evident, for example, in her service as a Red Cross volunteer nurse in World War I, and also in her role as Husserl's dedicated assistant. Stein also drew on her life experience to inform her philosophy. Her work as a nurse had a profound impact on her work on empathy and allowed her to make a significant breakthrough and contribution to Husserl's project.

Indeed, as MacIntyre comments, it is likely that her conversion to Catholicism and eventual decision to enter the Carmelite Order was informed by her "empathetic perception and understanding to which she had earlier devoted so much philosophical attention." Stein was a critic of the Nazi regime, and, in 1942, along with her sister Rosa, she was killed in Auschwitz. In 1998 Edith Stein/Sister Teresa Benedicta of the Cross was canonized.[40]

Stein's philosophical reputation was already endangered in her lifetime by her unconventional approach. When she began to argue that an experience of faith affords a kind of indubitable knowledge unattainable by other means and can be brought to bear on philosophical questions, some, such as her friend and colleague Roman Ingarden, felt that she had ceased to be a philosopher (since faith had no role to play in philosophy). Adolf Reinach, a friend and teacher of Stein, converted to Christianity just as Stein did; however, while he set about writing a strictly phenomenological account of his experience and remained accepted within the philosophical community, Stein took a more interdisciplinary and personal approach to her subject matter. If a detailed account of Stein's life is not feasible here, the few bare facts that I have recounted already indicate what was at stake for Stein in pursuing her path. Her philosophical work was both influenced and impeded by life's events and perhaps, as MacIntyre suggests, the events of her life were at least in part influenced by her thinking. [41]

Stein's earlier work in *Philosophy of Psychology and the Humanities*, in particular the "First Treatise: Sentient Causality," was written before she departed from Husserlian phenomenology and before she began to explicitly incorporate Christian revelation into her philosophy. In this work, she brings together psychology and philosophy in order to investigate human life as a holistic and interconnected system. Her style is less literary and more sober than Henry's and often seems to present a more technical mode of reflection, possibly informed by her work with Husserl; her measured approach allows us to work through her thinking discursively.

Stein suggests that while there are levels of external causality or determination against which we are utterly helpless, at the same time we also hold within us the possibility of acting with or against such forces. In Stein's view, we human persons are both private and public, determined and determining, and crucially embedded in and intimately involved with the others.

Philosophy of Psychology and the Humanities is preceded by *On the Problem of Empathy*, which paved the way for what would in essence become Stein's lifelong project in the practice of, and investigation into, the concept of empathy. Empathy, at that time, was a new concept for philosophy, which Theodor Lipps in his *Ästhetik* (1906) defined as a form of responsive action. It was this notion of Lipps that Husserl suggested to Stein as a starting point for her thesis. Husserl was interested in empathy but, as Sawicki points out, saw it as a form of egoistic accomplishment or constituted sense. At this stage Husserl thought of empathy as a way of knowing the other, which assumed that the other was already there for us from the start and did not take into account the possibility of inter-subjectivity in such constitution. If, for example, a community shares certain values and thus constitutes them, then the question, as Sawicki puts it, is whether the "we" of the community is jointly or individually constituted? If it is the former, then the "'we' doing the constituting must also have been constituted somehow." Stein detected this flaw in Husserl's theory of constitution, and her thesis shows how empathy is not a constituted sense but rather the "prior condition of the possibility of any constitution at all."[42]

Stein's theory of empathy asks how we understand one another not just through transfer of information but by grasping the fundamental processes by which we produce meaning, as well as the networks of meaning into which such processes are embedded (that, by necessity, have an intersubjective component). Intersubjectivity became crucial for Stein's theory of empathy as an "experience of feeling led by an experience that is not one's own, that is, the source of an experience of the 'foreign.'"[43] Empathy may not be primordial in content but it is primordial in present experience. For example, I might feel grief when someone is bereaved and, although this feeling has its distinctive sense content that can be shared between subjects, including me, it doesn't originate in me. What we experience is a manner of appearing of experience, that is, someone else's experience. Through empathy, within egoistic experience, we primordially experience a grieving person and may even experience some form of grief ourselves, but we do not directly participate in another's grief as it is lived through by that person.[44]

Philosophy of Psychology and the Humanities, published in 1922, continues the investigation into empathy in relation to intersubjectivity. In the "First Treatise: Sentient Causality," Stein analyzes the interplay between causal constraints and motivated choices originating in the natural and social world and looks at how these impact on human action and creativity. The model of intersubjectivity that she proposes is experienced subjectively at both conscious and unconscious levels. Stein takes up Husserl's metaphor of the current or stream of lived experience and likens it to the flow of electricity, or what she calls life power. She questions whether intentionality as a constitutive performance, that is, a process allowing for manifestation and signification, happens as the result of an individual or a shared activity. Sometimes other egos are not apparent to us as discrete entities, and it is possible that there are egoistic experiences that, as Sawicki says, "are not personalized or owned by me." Even some intimate or unshareable experience of myself may include also an experience of another.[45]

Stein distinguishes between a realm of conscious pure experiencing of a life feeling that is associated with the pure ego "experienced as a point of radiation of pure experiences" and the psyche, which she calls simply the ego. The latter, what she calls the real ego, is in possession of an enduring real property or life power. The real ego is sentient and "grasped only as a bearer of its properties, as a transcendent reality that comes to givenness by manifestation in immanent data but never becomes immanent itself."[46] Life power is used up and replenished through sentient experience. Life feeling at the level of pure ego exists in pure passivity and is never awakened from its slumbers to act in the world and neither expends nor produces power; however, Stein holds that constitution of experience itself cannot be obtained through such passivity. In the current of experience, "no moment is standing still," it is "uninterrupted occurring and uninterrupted effecting." In a consciousness without life power no sentient individual would itself be constituted.[47]

Within the stream of experience, the I can trace both causal and motivated sequences, thus detecting relations or networks of meaning between ourselves and others. Causal connections belong to physical reality and are defined by causal necessity. We can only know these from the outside. Motivated sequences, however, appear to the I as having originated in another's choice rather than through material necessity, and this fact allows the I to relive them and to understand them empathically. What Stein calls motivation is a particular configuration of a phenomenological act, a "connection that acts get into with one another—an emerging of one act in the other, a self-fulfilling or being fulfilled of one on the basis of the other for the sake of the other."[48] For example, consciousness directs itself toward (intends) an object, whether of a determinate or incomplete sense content that can be judged as valuable, desirable, and so on (or not). Let's say something strikes you as beautiful, Stein says; then it is recognized as valuable and, at the same time, "confronts you as something that ought to be." Stipulating that, she says, a norm is inferred that "whoever brings value to givenness . . . should set himself the goal of its realization."[49]

Although the pivot of motivation is the ego (real ego), the motivator is not the execution of the initial act but rather the sense content of that act. In experiencing an image as beautiful, I partake in a shared sense content. I cannot share the experience that prompted the artist to engage in creative activity, but, through my experience of the image, I share something of the artist's motivation, no matter how mediated or imagined my experience might be. I can also experience firsthand a sense content of beauty, even if I cannot say that this is exactly the same as that experienced by others. For Stein, whether we are moved by what is given to us, whether we have any kind of experience at all is determined not necessarily by the quality of the object in front of us but by our receptivity and by the level of our life power:

> Whether I'm capable of receiving sensory data and with what intensity the data impose themselves on me, depends upon the level of my life power at the moment. But which data presents themselves whether sounds or colors and which colors in particular—that's independent of my life power.[50]

Causality is correlated to physical nature, whereas motivations are correlated to values, sense content, choice, receptivity, and so on. In reality, causes and motivations are intricately intertwined so that even when the I feels in a motivated sequence, it eventually comes up against two kinds of impasse that block the possibility of empathic experience. The first is physical causality. For example, if someone is depressed and the illness is partially due to a chemical imbalance in the body, I can empathize with the feelings of despondency, but the chemical imbalances that cause depression are not available to me as experience. Since I know that some of that person's behavior is due to physical causes, I can attempt to distinguish which parts of their action are voluntary and either respond to those in an appropriate manner or simply replay the feelings if the causes are not available.[51]

The other frontier that the I eventually encounters when tracing motivational sequences is the uniquely personal input driven by internal connections that are not intelligible to me, perhaps not even to the individual person. The realm of personal decision in creative choices, choices of relationships, and so on, can be just as impenetrable to our understanding as the realm of matter. For Stein, there are realms of experience that we can share with each other and those that are impenetrable. In order to understand this further, she sets out an account of person. "Person" in Stein's terminology does not mean human being, but instead refers to layers of phenomenality or realms of appearance. These aren't spatial, but in order to talk about them, a spatial model such as Marianne Sawicki's is of great value. Sawicki has drawn the image of an H turned on its side, like a capital I with serifs, which I have adapted and copied here.[52]

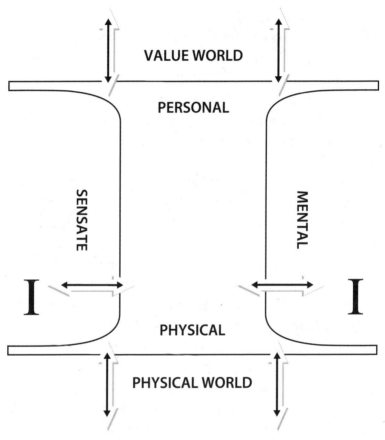

Figure 1: Reworked version of Marianne Sawicki's diagram of Edith Stein's model of person.

---

52. I am very grateful to Marianne Sawicki for granting me permission to make use of her diagram in this way and for making her expertise so available to those such as myself, who need help working through Stein's often dense and difficult text. Her guidance in the introduction to *Philosophy of Psychology and the Humanities* has also been invaluable in this discussion.

The top and bottom layers (the serifs of the I) are shown as private and unshareable realms of experience. The top layer, the personal or individual, is the surface through which we are plugged into the realm of value and through which we both create and receive meaning. The bottom layer represents the physical in which matter, physical organs, and the physiological processes of the body interface with the physical world. When we act upon the world or it acts upon us, chains of cause and effect come into play across this surface.

The two levels of person at the side, the mental or intellectual and the sensory or sentient, can be shared or experienced by someone else; that is, through this interface, someone else can detect my motivations and be influenced by them as well as indirectly detect what is happening in the other two realms that are off-limits to direct experience, that is, physical causes and personal meanings. These two levels let influences pass up and down between the physical and the personal and are open to each other as well.

The I with these four functional layers of person not only follows motivational traces or tracks but also receives, and is what Sawicki calls a transistor for the modulation of power, an image that aptly describes the role of these layers as active rather than passive conduits. The sentient and mental layers pass influences into and from the material world, as well as between the material and the personal, and provide access to someone else's thoughts, feelings, and motivations. Crucially, the private levels also have to have a level of permeability to allow the sentient and mental levels of experience to influence them.

Stein draws on another principle from physics: that energy is neither created nor destroyed, and all living processes consume energy, to show how these four levels are effectively and mutually permeable. Similarly, life power is not an infinite source but maintains itself in a balance of influxes and outflows. Life processes at the sentient and intellectual levels use up more power than they could gain from physical sources (nutrition and rest). We cannot measure life power exactly, but, according to Stein, "more" and "less" are qualitative terms, and by comparing two cases we can tell when something is more or less than something else. We can in effect observe variations in, if not actual measurements of, life power.[53]

If the intensity and range of data increases then there is a change in the life sphere. A decrease in life power manifests itself to me when I feel the exertion of a transition from vigor to weariness, for example: "Life power converts itself into enhanced receptivity that manifests itself in the broadening of the experiential range or in the greater intensity of the experiential content." If no variation of the life sphere were noticeable in connection with a variation in the range of experiential content, then receptivity wouldn't come to givenness at all as a sensate status. Receptivity to data and intensity of receptivity are dependent on the level of my life power, but which data present themselves (for example, whether sounds or colors and which colors in particular) is independent of my amount of energy. Although sensate experience is causally conditioned and the level of life force can't determine the kind of data that comes in, motivation can mobilize life power so that such data are converted into meaning and content.[54]

There is also a range of data that our consciousness is capable of spanning with no drain on life power, where the ego can drift along on the current of data without really looking at it; nevertheless, Stein says, a minimal form of intentionality is already present in the having of immanent data. The ego deploys its mental gaze and points itself at something either as a review of experience or in reflection and may even alight upon something transcendent. The *intentio* that arises on the basis of immanent data indicates a new class of experiences, apprehensions, or acts. These acts of intentionality and the performance of constitution require life power, so that the mental world provides meaning for us (mental living is the life of culture, value, sentiment, spirit—as *Die Geisttige Welt*—the world of meaning).

For Stein the mind, body, and soul are distinct. The body for her is essential to an experience of empathy, to sensate causality, to the wholeness of the person, and to community with others. Her model of person shows how these levels of personal and interpersonal experience are all interrelated and mutually affecting.[55]

For Stein, motivation involves two things: decision and levels of available life power. In following a motivational sequence, a choice is made to pay attention, to notice, or to follow. At the same time, by following we come to understand the information we receive as not always necessary but perhaps also chosen by another person. We know this because we, too, are motivated and we, too, make decisions according to what is presented to us in experience. Motivation can be logical, practical, or emotional but in itself it is not enough to induce me to take the step forward toward experience: "It takes a certain aliveness to accept any kind of content at all and to be able to experience it." Motivation involves a variety of experiences such as attitude, inclinations, or impulses that in themselves require a level of aliveness in order to become fulfilled or to translate into action of any kind: "a lifeless and powerless inclination is not capable of converting itself into a doing. . . . only a powerless silhouette turns up."[56]

Forming attitudes, like absorbing information, Stein says, is something that befalls me. They seize possession of me. I cannot make an attitude befall me (for example, she notes that I can yearn for religious faith and fret about it, yet it doesn't happen for me). If an attitude does befall me, I can take a stance. Just as I can accept it and plant my feet upon it, declare my allegiance to it, I can also refuse it. Stein uses the example of a convinced atheist who is drawn into a religious experience of God's existence; he can't escape nor deny the experience but he can act as though it were not there, make it inoperative in himself, and stick to his scientific worldview. By refusing whatever befalls me, I do not eliminate it but simply comport myself in a kind of intentional neutralizing.[57]

Impulses, another level of experience, also come and go, depending on the state of one's body and energy levels. Stein likens inclining to a kind of conversion of the impulse, a goal consciousness that directs a "previously aimless impulse" toward a particular representation that promises satisfaction: "When a feeling is not 'living,' when no life-contributing power develops within me, then no living inclination arises from the feeling either."[58]

––––––––

In the first treatise of *Philosophy of Psychology and the Humanities*, Stein's discussion of life power, motivation, attitude, inclination, and impulse all occur in the realm of individual experience. In the second treatise, "Individual and Community," she recognizes the person as a psycho-physical being in the context of community and as essentially social and political. Stein traces the sources of the influxes of life power that keep the individual psyche in operation through an investigation into the network of the mental world. She starts with a distinction between community and association (similar to that of Ferdinand Tonnies):

> [W]here a subject accepts the other as a subject and does not confront him but rather lives with him and is determined by the stirrings of his life, they are forming a community with one another. In the association, everyone is absolutely alone, a "windowless monad." In the community, solidarity prevails.[59]

For Stein, although community as such has no subjectivity, it nonetheless is constituted as a higher level subject. There is no super-individual communal consciousness, yet private experience still might constitute a super-individual experiencing. The life of social groups has its source in the individual egos that belong to the community, and community only becomes conscious of itself in us. What she calls the "experiential current of the community" is not an original constitutive flow but the experiences of the community combined into a unity. She discusses the experience of grief over the death of an army leader. The members of the unit will experience grief in their individual way but at the same time there will be a shared sense that both imposes an expectation onto the individual of a particular conditioned expression of that grief and, in turn, affects the individual and private experience of loss. In this instance, an experience that might be thought of as utterly private becomes, at least partially, constituted by the community (and by the individuals belonging to that community). The life of the community and of those individuals within it becomes in certain instances supra-individual.

As Borden Sharkey succinctly summarizes, for Stein the central layer of human being is the personal realm. This core is both common to other humans and distinctive to our individual structure: "In each of us the 'world strikes a chord' in a special way. We are each susceptible to different kinds of values and we see what kind of person someone is when we see which world of values she lives in."[60]

We can see even in this provisional account that Stein's philosophy of person addresses some of the limitations of Henry's philosophy of life. Her model of person allows us to consider that, even in our utterly private and inward realm of subjective life, the world of others has an inescapable influence that enriches rather than annihilates but which, at the same time, exposes us to demands.

Henry's vision of life, free from ambivalence, lack, or despair, might be seductive, but how do we discover such a realm? If we do not need an injunction to lead us there, do we not at least need to be directed or to direct ourselves toward it, in other words to decide for or against what he is proposing as truth? In Henry we are presented with the destination as though the reason for going there and the problem of arriving have already been dealt with.

Stein, on the other hand, allows us to understand ourselves as intersubjective persons whose encounter with the outside involves body, mind, and soul, which influences and affects us whether we are aware of it or not. It is this vulnerability to and responsibility toward the other that underpins her theory of empathy. Unlike Henry, Stein also provides an account of how we can decide for or against whatever it is that befalls or affects us.

Henry and Stein: Life and/or the Other World

Adorno's question, the one that we started with (How might life live?), was an urgent call for reorientation of thought and action in the wake of the Second World War, a time of political and ethical crisis and of profound disillusion in the traditions and history that preceded it. Adorno's plea continues to resonate today, inviting us to ask how the external factors in our life, the ethical and social dimension, that often present us with unexpected events, might affect and change us from the inside out, from the very core of our being.

By looking at two philosophers who present an affirmative notion of life, Michel Henry and Edith Stein, I hoped to discern not the "what" of such a radical transformation but something of the "how." Do we become altered by resting in pure affective passivity, through the hearing and responding to a call or demand of the other? Is it through our own efforts or through being acted upon? Adorno warned that the kind of alteration he had in mind was one that required careful negotiation between immersion in the crowd or retreat into individual subjectivity, either of which would diminish the possibility of thinking and acting differently. Is it a turning around, a conversion, a decision made by or for us (who knows) or the event whereby something disturbs, unsettles, blows through us like "the wind of thought" or where, in crisis, the situation we find ourselves in becomes untenable?[61]

I indicated from the start that with Henry and Stein we are dealing with two different thinkers; however, both of these thinkers approached their discipline freely in order to have fidelity to their vision, and it is in this spirit that I have put them together in this discussion. Through them we can see that different perspectives coexist even in thinkers so closely aligned in professional philosophical interest and in personal religious faith.

We know few details of Henry's biography, except that his involvement in clandestine activities for the French Resistance in 1943 (using the code name Kant) had a profound impact on his philosophy, and that he wrote fiction as well as philosophy. As it is, the availability of Stein's biography suggests a genuine and profound relationship between thought and lived experience.[62]

When we respond to a solicitation that befalls us but that, at the same time, we choose to follow, the transformation might not occur in one fell swoop; it might not be dramatic or particularly remarkable; it might, in fact, quietly and gently set us on another course of action. In Stein's *Philosophy of Psychology and the Humanities* there is a short passage that describes a state of utter passive relaxation that Stein calls "resting in God." This is very different from the cessation of activeness from lack of life power that is a form of dead silence but is instead

> the feeling of being safe, being exempted from all anxiety, responsibility, duty to act. As I surrender myself to this feeling, new life begins to fill me up, little by little, and impels me towards new activation. . . . This reviving infusion appears as an emanation of a functionality and a power which is not my emanation and which becomes operative within me without my asking for it. The sole prerequisite . . . seems to be a certain receptivity.[63]

This short passage echoes Henry's conception of life as an immanent and original power of revelation that "constitutes not the content of experience but the form of all possible experience in general,"[64] and where, as Stein says, there is no "anxiety, responsibility or duty to act." This state that is so very much like Henry's notion of self-affection is not already given in Stein; it has to be prepared for and sought. There is a prerequisite of receptivity that requires the individual to mobilize energy in mind, body, and soul in order to receive and to respond to whatever occurs.

In later works, Stein uses the phrase "resting in God" in relation to prayer. Once again, what she says recalls Henry's descriptions of immanence but, as in Jean-Luc Marion, reminds us that this is a state from which we can be summoned, subject to the call of the Other: "Anyone who feels inspired . . . to search for God will . . . retreat from the realm of the senses," and in "the barren solitude of the inner self" find with God "who is present although concealed" a place of profound peace. That is, "until the Lord decides to transform his faith into vision."[65] Even in this interiority, protected and hidden from the world, there is a risk, to use Jacques Derrida's term, of the "in-coming," the visitation of something "wholly other," that might blow us to "kingdom come."[66]

Henry's exuberant celebration of life as auto-affection eliminates the need for reflection, doubt, or action. His truth might be ultimately *the* truth (who knows?), and Stein might well not have argued with him on that; however the truth, any truth (even if one holds that the truth is that there is no such thing) strikes us perhaps only when we have been bereft of it. We might feel compelled to search for it, be called out of ourselves by the bolt from the blue that shakes the foundations of our lives, or by small niggling doubts, a gradually accumulating awareness, a word in our ear, a book we have read that lingers.

Henry, unlike Stein, does not address the permeability of life, the ebb and flow, the contingency and vulnerability of human living in all its social, psychological, bodily, and spiritual aspects. What he offers seems like an affirmative antidote to Heidegger's anxiety-laden thrown-ness, but in the end it is more the flip side of, rather than an unflinching look at, lived experience. Henry's realm of affectivity, by admitting no outside, denies itself the possibility of being altered. While it is possible to make a correspondence between Henry's notion of radical subjectivity and the private unshareable realms in Stein's model of person, where Henry proposes "invisible interiority as the first and fundamental determination of phenomenality," Stein sees empathy as the fundamental condition of possibility of any constitution in which even the most private layers of personal experience are permeable to others. Our innermost experience, for Stein, is not immune from ambivalence or from the influence of the outside.

In her life, Stein heard and responded to solicitation in the form of an ethical demand of concrete life as well as the inward spiritual realm. Such things befell her, and she accepted and responded in ways that required a fundamental change in both her external status and her internal state of being. Her very existence became one of contradiction: Stein, the Carmelite nun and saint, and Stein, the philosopher. She writes that "even in the contemplative life one may not sever the connection with the world." Even as one is being drawn more deeply into God, "one must go to the world in order to carry the divine life into it."[67]

With Stein we enter the very realm of ambivalence that Henry wants to resolve. What Stein's legacy offers is a document about how living and thinking are inextricably intertwined. In many ways her philosophical work cannot be detached from her life (as a woman, as a Jew and Catholic convert, as one called by God, as one whose fate was both chosen but also politically and religiously determined) and exemplifies how the interaction between lived experience and theoretical reflection opens onto an unavoidable ambivalence, which itself becomes operative at the very boundary between the two and which, in the end, might be essential for any discussion of ethics and ethical decision.[68]

The hope is that, in this brief discussion, we might also start to see how the work of Stein, who did not survive Auschwitz, was so prescient in relation to Adorno's plea. Henry's philosophy gives us a gloriously unproblematic and singular version of life where neither stranger nor neighbor may be found, so that the question that we began with returns. Stein's philosophy draws us into both a philosophy and a practice of empathy. If we really want to respond to the question of how a philosophy of life may help us think differently, and if we were in any doubt about the relevance of Stein's insistence on intersubjective empathy to this question, we could do worse than to take heed when she says:

> [For the Christian] there is no such thing as the "stranger." There is only the neighbor—the person who happens to be next to us, the person in most need of our help. Whether he is related to us or not, whether we "like" him or not, doesn't make any difference.[69]

Notes

1. Theodor W. Adorno, *Negative Dialectics* (London: Continuum, 1983), 364. Adorno began his work, *Minima Moralia: Reflections from Damaged Life*, written while he was in exile from fascism during World War II, with the epigram "Life does not live." Later, the question arises again in *Negative Dialectics*.

2. Michel Henry, *I Am the Truth: Towards a Philosophy of Christianity* (Stanford, Calif.: Stanford University Press, 2003), sleeve notes.

3. James Williams, "Gilles Deleuze and Michel Henry: Critical Contrasts in the Deduction of Life as Transcendental," *Sophia* 47, no. 3 (November 2008): 268. As he notes, John Mullarkey sees Deleuze and Henry as closer than Williams himself does. Henry's emphasis on suffering is part of his phenomenological empiricism that makes it less Christian. For Mullarkey, Henry's use of suffering can be understood as test, ordeal—*experimentation* in the French (experiment or experience) or *épreuve* (test or ordeal), on a par with life as experiment in Deleuze.

4. Edith Stein, *On the Problem of Empathy*, trans. Waltraut Stein, CWES, vol. 3 (Washington, D.C.: ICS Publications, 1989); and section 4 of Stein, *Finite and Eternal Being: An Attempt at an Ascent to the Meaning of Being*, trans. Kurt F. Reinhardt, CWES, vol. 9 (Washington, D.C.: ICS Publications, 2002).

5. Sarah Borden Sharkey, *Thine Own Self: Individuality in Edith Stein's Later Writings* (Washington, D.C.: The Catholic University of America Press, 2009), 9.

6. I felt an unease at putting these two thinkers together but, at the same time, found their difference compelling. I would like to thank John Caruana, Ryerson University, for helping me to clarify my thoughts on this.

7. John Caputo, *On Religion* (*Thinking in Action*) (London: Routledge, 2001), 2.

8. Stein, *Finite and Eternal Being*, 1–8. Caputo echoes Stein when he says that the philosophers' God is a "scholastic, modernist and Enlightenment mode of thinking that deserves nothing better than a decent burial" (Caputo, *On Religion*, 3).

9. Richard Kearney, *Anatheism: Returning to God After God* (New York: Columbia University Press, 2009), xviii. My interest in these two

thinkers, the reasons I encountered them in the first place, and the way that they subsequently affected me are to do with personal history.

10. Søren Kierkegaard, of course, was not interested in explaining the mechanics of faith but in alerting us to its paradoxical nature. Even if he proposes various states such as anxiety, repetition, and so forth, it is not an analysis as such. Kierkegaard, *Concluding Unscientific Postscript to Philosophical Fragments* (Trenton, N.J.: Princeton University Press, 1974), 387–88.

11. Henry, *I Am the Truth*, 198–99; 54–56. I first heard Henry's work referred to by the philosopher Peter Hallward, who—as far as I know—has no personal religious conviction. At the time, I saw myself as someone with merely intellectual interest in religious writings; however, through Stein, as we will see, the intellectual cannot be treated as a discrete way of understanding. It is also an opening up, an affective relation, if you like, and it is here that Stein's model of the human as a holistic entity seems so pertinent. Stein, like Kierkegaard, was always conscious of her reader.

12. I am drawing on Kierkegaard here, who also notes that any new understanding might be through the subtraction rather than the addition of knowledge, a qualitative rather than quantitative alteration. Kierkegaard, *Concluding Unscientific Postscript*, 275–76n.

13. "What Is Meant by the Word 'Life,'" *Philosophique* 5 (1979): 134; trans. Michael Tweed in 2005, available online: *www.pensum.ca/Texts /Henry-Life.pdf* [last accessed August 2009]. Henry discusses his position in relation to Heidegger on many occasions, for example, in *I Am the Truth*; and in "Material Phenomenology and Language (or Pathos and Language)," *Continental Philosophy Review* 32, no. 3 (1999): 343–65.

14. Martin Heidegger, "The Question Concerning Technology," in *Basic Writings* (London: Routledge, 1993), 379. Heidegger says that the question "What is called thinking?" calls upon our very being: "We ourselves are the text and the texture of the question," he says, in "What Is Called Thinking," also found in *Basic Writings*, 362.

15. Henry, *I Am the Truth*, 18.

16. Ibid., 10.

17. Ibid., 20.

18. Ibid., 55.

19. Ibid.

20. Caputo follows Derrida, Kierkegaard, St. Paul, etc. Caputo, *The Weakness of God: A Theology of the Event* (Bloomington: Indiana University Press, 2006), 106.

21. Henry, *The Essence of Manifestation* (The Hague: Nijhoff, 1973), 438.

22. Ibid., 406.

23. Ibid., 438.

24. Ibid., 415; 443–44.

25. Bernard McGinn, *Meister Eckhart, The Essential Sermons, Commentaries, Treatises, and Defense* (London: Paulist Press, 1981), 203.

26. Kierkegaard, *Concluding Unscientific Postscript to Philosophical Fragments*, 387–88.

27. I use this term in the sense that Étienne Balibar does when he talks of subjective obedience as *subditi*, where subjects will their obedience to divine authority rather than the subject as *servus*, who are, by contrast, forced to obey, as in the relation of slave to master. Étienne Balibar, "Citizen Subject," in *Who Comes After the Subject?* ed. E. Cadava, P. Connor, and J. L. Nancy (London: Routledge, 1991), 41.

28. I do not know whether Henry talks about death as such an alteration. Death, in Henry, might be when this reality no longer experiences itself.

29. Henry, *The Essence of Manifestation*, 646.

30. Henry, *I Am the Truth*, 57.

31. John G. Taylor, "Paying Attention to Consciousness," *TRENDS in Cognitive Sciences* 6, no. 5 (2002): 208.

32. Dan Zahavi, "Subjectivity and Immanence in Michel Henry," in *Subjectivity and Transcendence,* ed. A. Gron, I. Damgaard, S. Overgaard (Tübingen, Germany: Mohr Siebeck, 2007), 133–47. As Zahavi points out, Heidegger discusses the hidden or unconcealed; Jean-Paul Sartre, the lived body invisibly present in every action; and Maurice Merleau-Ponty, the visible and the invisible.

33. Henry, "Phenomenology of Life," *Angelaki: Journal of Theoretical Humanities* 8, no. 2 (2003): 104 ; introduction by Nick Hanlon. This article summarizes much of Henry's thinking.

34. Henry, *The Essence of Manifestation*, 646; Zahavi, "Subjectivity and Immanence."

35. Henry, quoted in James Williams, "Gilles Deleuze and Michel Henry: Critical Contrasts in the Deduction of Life as Transcendental," 274.

36. Søren Kierkegaard, *The Concept of Anxiety: A Simple Psychologically Orienting Deliberation on the Dogmatic Issue of Hereditary Sin*, Kierkegaard's Writings, vol. 8 (Princeton, N.J.: Princeton University Press, 1981), 274n59.

37. She would eventually call this private realm prayer.

38. Alasdair MacIntyre, *Edith Stein; A Philosophical Prologue* (London: Continuum, 2006). I was drawn to read it initially simply because I realized that unless I made a concerted effort, I was not going to read many (or any) women philosophers. I was vaguely aware of Stein and her interests, and at that moment they coincided with mine. I was struck by MacIntyre's admission that he was writing the book not as a scholarly work but for the educated common reader (see introduction). Now, I imagine that for him, an analytical philosopher, as for some of Stein's colleagues, her admission of faith and her biography makes it difficult for him to treat her as a serious philosopher. I was grateful to start with this biography, as her writing, I would discover, is challenging for the educated common reader.

39. For a fuller account, the biography of Stein's good friend, Waltraud Herbstrith, is highly recommended. Waltraud Herbstrith, *The Untold Story of the Philosopher and Mystic Who Lost Her Life in the Death Camps of Auschwitz* (San Francisco: Ignatius Press, 1992).

40. MacIntyre, *Edith Stein*, 2006. Stein's nursing experience also gave her insights into the nature of death, which later allowed her to argue against Heidegger that it is not, as he proposed, our own death that defines our lives but experiencing the death of others. Death always happens in communities. See Antonio Calcagno, "Being, *Aevum*, and Nothingness: Edith Stein on Death and Dying," included as chapter 11 in this volume.

41. MacIntyre, *Edith Stein*, 172 and 180. Herbstrith also notes that Stein "was painfully aware of the restrictions her lack of theological training imposed on her work." There were few women working in philosophy at the time, and Stein was subject to prejudice because of her status as a woman and a Jew. This undoubtedly played a part in her being sidelined by the philosophical community, although her unconventional approach would also have contributed to her marginalization.

42. Marianne Sawicki, "Personal Connections: The Phenomenology of Edith Stein." These remarks are abridged from lectures delivered at St. John's University in New York on October 15, 1998; and at the Carmelite Monastery in Baltimore on November 13, 1998. They are available at *http://www.library.nd.edu/colldev/subject_home_pages/catholic/personal_connections.shtml* (last accessed August 2009).

43. Stein, *On the Problem of Empathy*. For Sawicki: *Einfühlung*. The German equivalent for the English term "empathy," meaning in-feeling, that is, both feeling-into and feeling-within, she says, is thus an ambiguous term.

44. Husserl does appear to address this in *Cartesian Meditations*, published in 1931. I would need to do more work to establish the influences.

45. Sawicki, "Personal Connections."

46. Stein, *Philosophy of Psychology and the Humanitites*, trans. Mary Catharine Baseheart and Marianne Sawicki, CWES, vol. 7 (Washington, D.C.: ICS Publications, 2000), 23–24.

47. Ibid., 29.

48. Ibid., 41.

49. Ibid., 43.

50. Ibid., 33. Terminology such as "life power" or "sentient causality," as Sawicki warns, must be distinguished from the vocabulary of psychoanalytic and Marxist theories: libido, the unconscious, false consciousness, and so on. These, she says, do not make the crucial distinction that Stein insists upon: the distinction between causality and motivation.

51. Ibid., 4.

52. I am very grateful to Marianne Sawicki for granting me permission to make use of her diagram in this way and for making her expertise so available to those such as myself who need help working through Stein's often dense and difficult text. Her guidance in the introduction to *Philosophy of Psychology and the Humanities* has also been invaluable in this discussion.

53. Stein, *Philosophy of Psychology*, 68.

54. Ibid., 30–33.

55. Stein noted that a key difference between herself and Husserl, at least in 1917, was that she claimed that the existence of the body is necessary for an experience of empathy.

56. Stein, *Philosophy of Psychology*, 80.

57. Ibid., 48.

58. Ibid., 80.

59. Ibid., 130. In a footnote Sawicki writes that the idea of the monad comes from Gottfried Leibniz. As a simple substance, it has no parts, hence "no windows" through which it could receive or send messages to and from other monads. "On a more subtle level," she says, "this means that we can communicate only that which we already have available within our own beings, for each human monad already has all others internal to itself. Stein's theory of empathy is consistent with this more subtle understanding."

60. Sharkey, *Thine Own Self*, 11.

61. For the metaphor of the wind of thought see Hannah Arendt, *Life of the Mind* (London: Harcourt, 1977), 174. I also borrowed from John Caputo's notion of God as restlessness.

62. See *http://www.michelhenry.com/biographie.htm*; last accessed August 9, 2012.

63. Ibid., 84.

64. Henry, *The Essence of Manifestation*, 533.

65. Quotation from *Finite and Eternal Being*, cited in Herbstrith, *The Untold Story*, 157.

66. Jacques Derrida from Caputo, *The Weakness of God*, 108.

67. Stein to Sister Callista Kopf, February 12, 1928, letter 45, in *Self-Portrait in Letters, 1916–1942*, trans. Josephine Koeppel, O.C.D., CWES, vol. 5 (Washington, D.C.: ICS Publications, 1993), 54.

68. We must be careful when using the term "ethics" in relation to Christianity. While the term "ethics" belongs to philosophy and to the "logic of the world," here we will be mindful of "the more ethical than ethical" of Kierkegaard (*Fear and Trembling*), of Emmanuel Levinas's notion of alterity or difference, and of Derrida's notion of responsibility, all of which reframe what the ethical might mean in this context. In Caputo's words this might be more adequately described as an-ethics or para-ethics, an "eccentric ethics, where the trace of God is inscribed in the other one, the neighbor or the stranger or the outsider" (Caputo, *The Weakness of God*, 136).

69. Quotation from *Finite and Eternal Being*, cited in Herbstrith, *The Untold Story*, 153.

14

EDITH STEIN: BETWEEN HUSSERL AND THOMAS AQUINAS:
Phenomenology and Christian Philosophy

ANGELA ALES BELLO

If we ask about the reasons that Edith Stein was cited in Pope John Paul II's encyclical *Fides et Ratio* (on the Relationship Between Faith and Reason)—and she is the sole woman philosopher mentioned—I would put forward two possible responses. The first concerns her thought in reference to the content of the papal document; the other relates to the attention that John Paul II pays to women and the condition of women.

The encyclical originates, in my view, in the pontiff's concern for the intellectual formation of those who wish to follow the path of priestly ministry, in particular, and of all the faithful within our Western culture, but not excluding those from different cultures. One notes, in fact, that the philosophical *humus* in which the message of the Gospels has been sown has not been revealed merely as an accessory; rather, it is foundational, because it has made possible an awareness of problems, the acuity of analyses, and the organization of knowing. Today, following that moment of rare equilibrium represented by the philosophical-theological elaboration of the Middle Ages, achieved through great difficulties and controversies, there exists a fracturing of two cultural processes that appears to be becoming always more acute. The prevailing tendency, albeit not exclusively so, has been to separate secular culture from religious culture. Often secular culture excludes the theological dimension as well as the ever-rarer parallel discussions of religious experience, understood as a subject in itself or in reference to Christianity.

Such a situation, which stems from the cultural milieu of the last two centuries, was received with wonder, even stupefaction, by the young Edith Stein. After her conversion to Roman Catholicism, which formally occurred at the beginning of 1922, Stein became aware of the existence of a line of thought whose philosophical and theological foundations lie, in large part, in the great texts and lessons of the Middle Ages. This line of thinking was passed down through Benedictine Abbot Raphael Walzer and Jesuit Father Erich Przywara, the great supporters of her conversion, who were formed in seminaries that followed the tradition of Catholic thought closely linked, even in modern and contemporary ages, to the intimate relationship between philosophy and theology.

This fact appeared as absolutely novel for Stein, given that she was used to finding herself in environments deeply influenced by either Judaism or Lutheran Christianity, and that were marked by, more often than not, an attitude of open hostility to the mixing of religious experience and intellectual pursuits or that wished to separate religious experience from intellectual life. On the one hand, faith was considered a private and personal affair. If one thinks, for example, of Edmund Husserl, who, though profoundly religious and who converted from Judaism to Lutheran Christianity, one is struck by the fact that he never publicly took a religious position, thereby separating his philosophical investigations from his religion. On the other hand, one can also think of faith as marking the belonging of various members to a group. One thinks here, for example, of the Jewish community. In both cases, we are dealing with environments in which the Catholic philosophical and theological traditions were largely ignored.

Stein set for herself the task of grasping the mutual understanding of two great lines of thinking: she defines them as Catholic philosophy, which proceeds from the Scholastics, above all from St. Thomas Aquinas; and modern philosophy, which starts with the Renaissance and culminates in Immanuel Kant. It would be fair to say that the modern legacy lives on today in and through a series of interpretations and consequences of Kant's philosophical view. These two areas of philosophy, until recently, were primarily uninterested in one another. The non-Catholic would not have been interested in studying Scholastic philosophy, and the average Catholic student would not have studied Kant. It is only in the last few years that the reciprocal knowledge of both philosophers has made some headway; this mutual knowledge of both traditions had a double bookkeeping (*doppelete Buchführung*) and was not really considered a legitimate part of the questions of philosophy.[1]

The path was opened up in an unforeseen way by Stein's teacher, Husserl, who never really "distinguished himself as exclusively belonging to one camp or another" because of the influence of his teacher, Franz Brentano— an ex-Catholic priest who knew the Scholastic tradition very well. Husserl absorbed the spirit of philosophizing from Brentano's tradition, even though he might not have absorbed explicitly its teachings. Stein recognizes that "in non-Catholic environments no one contributed better than Husserl in preparing the ground for this knowledge, even if he did not have such a goal in mind."[2] In what follows, we will see what content Stein draws upon in this context. For now, it is important to note that if one of the objectives of *Fides et Ratio* is to draw closer to a so-called secular philosophy, this goal was already realized by the young Stein, who will use this as one of the methods of her philosophical investigations.

St. Thomas Aquinas and Edmund Husserl: The Encounter and Difference between the Middle Ages and Contemporary Times

Phenomenology opens up this third way, which is meaningful for philosophy itself but decisive for a renewed encounter with theology, in a manner that is fundamental for the very elaboration of theology itself. Stein demonstrates how this is done by her particular engagement with Husserl and her new teacher, Aquinas. From 1924, the year in which Stein writes "What Is Phenomenology?" from which the preceding observations are drawn, to 1929, the year in which "The Phenomenology of Husserl and the Philosophy of St. Thomas Aquinas: An Attempt at a Comparison"[3] appeared, many things happened from the vantage point of Stein's intellectual formation. The first important thing to note is her translation of Aquinas's *Quaestiones disputatae de veritate*. This translation allowed her to enter into the thought of the great philosopher, which she encountered in the encyclical *Aeterni patris* (1879) of Pope Leo XIII on the restoration of Christian philosophy, in which the study of Thomas Aquinas's thought was strongly recommended.

Stein's essay of 1929 attempts to gather the principal lines of thought that she feels are present in Aquinas's position as well as those she inherited from Husserl. The article also represents for her a crucial moment for her philosophical choice, a moment that could have presented a crossroads and an alternative. Her choice was in one direction, and the crisis was overcome by a new attitude that would become constant, namely, "placing in harmony."

Stein does not compromise here, and neither does she proceed by making arbitrary syntheses; rather, on the contrary, given that Stein is clear about the role that philosophical research must play, according to the teachings of Husserl, it is possible to find all of this in Aquinas. Even Husserl, without knowing it, as we have noted previously, inherited directly from Aquinas the view of philosophy as a rigorous science through his teacher Brentano. Stein writes: "Brentano had been brought up in the austere school of traditional Catholic philosophy and its manner of thinking had shaped his mind. And in Husserl we find something like it in the precision of his thought and in the economy of his language."[4]

In order to avoid being accused of arbitrarily combining the two thinkers, she remarks, "Of course we ought not to think this means he passed on specific ideas. When people talk as they do about a *philosophia perennis* (perennial philosophy) they usually have a ready-made doctrinal system in mind, and this is already quite opposed to the phenomenological way of doing philosophy."[5] That which draws the two thinkers together is their belonging to *philosophia perennis*, which is understood not as a closed doctrinaire system, but as "the spirit of genuine philosophy alive in every true philosopher, in anyone who cannot resist an inner need to search out the *logos* of this word, its *ratio* (as Aquinas translated the word)."[6]

The rigor consists in the fact that, in the case of philosophy, we are dealing with neither an ambitious dream nor a personal view, but serious and impartial rational research. This is the guiding thread that will always accompany Stein's philosophical project, from her analyses that are properly phenomenological to her reflections on mysticism.[7]

Her ordered words communicate the intellectual honesty that ought to inspire every authentic philosopher, but even with this there is no guarantee that anyone would be able to grasp all that is comprehensible by the human mind. This is why the work of research is a communal undertaking that transcends time and space. If there are limits to the process of discovering the *lógos*, this is brought about by the limited nature of the human intellect, and the validity of that which we seek is confirmed by the evidence of the thing itself, the ideal cognition toward which we must tend.

The rigor of philosophical research is not in itself a guarantee for the encounter between philosophy and theology; rather, it only represents a serious and honest effort toward the achievement of truth, which is the great theme that inspires Stein. Philosophy represents an important way, even though it is not without risk: it is not absolute or absolutizable. From this vantage point, Stein's judgment on the global relevance of phenomenology in the essay in which she compares Husserl and Aquinas is rather severe. She writes:

> Phenomenology proceeds as though our reason had no limits in principle. Certainly, it grants that its task is endless and knowledge is an unending process. But it heads straight for its goal: that is, the full truth, which as a regulative idea sets the course it is to take. From the perspective of this philosophy there is no other way to the goal.[8]

This is natural reason, according to Aquinas, and here Husserl reaches a limit, whereas Aquinas proceeds with the line of thinking that employs supernatural reason. Here, there are two ways to reach the truth. Husserl never denied the importance of faith in order to establish the possibility of profound contact with God. Having examined this theme numerous times,[9] I maintain that what his students knew of Husserl was only an external, formal aspect, while we have the possibility of accessing his private papers, perhaps those that he never wished to be made public. In these papers, his position concerning the relationship between philosophy and religion, and even philosophy and theology,[10] becomes clearer.

It is true that Husserl did not in every case explicitly discuss a multiplicity of ways for achieving truth; he did keep private about his adherence to his own faith, which was a very common attitude in the Protestant world. While teaching at a state-run university, he did not wish to expose himself as operating within a religious framework, even though he held a seminar on the philosophy of religion in which Martin Heidegger also participated. It is for this series of motives that he certainly could not take account of the truths of faith, according to Stein.

We might observe that the "material and form dependence" of philosophy upon faith, theorized by Stein in the above-mentioned text on Aquinas, is perhaps the fruit of the strong impression made upon her by the discovery of the world of medieval thought. She seized, at one time, this very aspect, which was present in the ground of faith, a ground that moved such thought. Certainly her deepening appreciation of Aquinas's works did not lead her to the idea expressed by Husserl, that ideas and thoughts in the Middle Ages were only of a theological character and not of a philosophical one.[11] Unlike Husserl, she asserts the presence of the philosophical in that age, even before her encounter with Jacques Maritain, who was very helpful for Stein in understanding the idea of a Christian philosophy. One could suppose that the opening of a horizon, so important for Stein from a spiritual point of view, struck her forcefully and even dazzled her. Further, there emerges from the very text we are examining an interesting oscillation between a rapprochement and an opposition between the two positions: that of Husserl and that of Aquinas. We can read this oscillation as the guiding thread of truth and as the way to reach it. In Stein's view, Husserl's philosophy emerges as egocentric because it separates itself from the question concerning the first truth: "For Thomas, the first axiom of philosophy—if we wish to use the word—is that God himself is the first Truth, the principle and criterion of all truth. From God proceeds any truth we can grasp."[12] This is why philosophy must first move from God in order to elucidate the idea of God. All the other philosophical questions must be inserted within this basic insight. In this sense, Aquinas's philosophy is theocentric.

These two basic contrasts notwithstanding, the two positions are close to one another on many points that concern philosophy. Stein maintains that both Aquinas and Husserl made important contributions to philosophical research. It is interesting to note that she considers both philosophers as pure theoreticians who are also deeply engaged in the investigation of ethics and practice, a relationship that will draw the two thinkers closer. To this end, it was necessary to employ a knowing based on essences, and this is a shared motivation in both thinkers.

Whereas Husserl, in order to uphold such a demand, brackets facticity—I would add that this was done against positivism, naturalism, and relativism—while moving on the plane of possibility, Aquinas wished to determine an essence of this world, and, by extension, the position of factual existence was always valid for him. One could underline here that the philosophical context in which both thinkers found themselves was different and pushed them to take positions on certain aspects. Husserl had to combat the absolutization of scientific knowledge and the weaknesses of historicism. He had to indicate forcefully the very plane that he sees as belonging to essences, that is, ideal possibilities. In fact, Stein recognizes that the adversaries of phenomenology accused Husserl of returning to medieval Scholasticism in his *Logical Investigations*.

Aquinas, too, admits the validity of the eidetic sphere, which Husserl considers the object of his new ontology. This ontology does not refer to existence but to the essence that characterizes every particular territory/region, ultimately rendering it unified: pure mathematics, pure logic, the pure sciences of nature. Here we are dealing with the delineation of regional ontologies that can be distinguished into material and formal ontologies. According to Stein, if one were to ask oneself the question in such terms, "It would then emerge how far there is an agreement."[13] Certainly the term "ontology," for Aquinas, refers to existence. As *De ente et essentia* demonstrates, Aquinas also emphasized essential truths and, from this point of view, the two positions can be seen to converge.

Following this direction, Stein underlines two key points of agreement between the two thinkers vis-à-vis knowledge. First, all knowledge begins with the senses. Second, all new knowledge is obtained through the intellectual elaboration of sense material. It would seem that an obstacle to drawing both thinkers closer could be presented by the role of intuition, but only because Stein considers the *Evidenz* of such a cognitive instrument to be a strong point of phenomenology—a strong point that she will never abandon. She attempts to draw closer together the epistemology of Aquinas with that of Husserl. She interprets the abstraction that Aquinas discusses as an *intus legere*—reading inside things. Both the phenomenologist and the Thomist must "penetrate into the object and into the connections of the objects . . . When Thomas described the proper task of the intellect as *intus legere*, the phenomenologist can accept the words as an apt paraphrase of what he himself means by intuition."[14]

Aquinas spoke of the primacy of intuitive knowledge with respect to the two fundamental domains: that of logical principles and that of universal knowledge of the good. We are dealing here with extending the potential of this instrument and must ask ourselves whether it is present in his speculation and even beyond in later interpretations.

The comparison of Husserl and Aquinas is seen by Stein as demanding because it draws her in both interiorly and speculatively. With her characteristic intellectual honesty, she seeks to establish objectively the limits and connections between the two positions and, in the end, her conviction that the ways of seeking truth are more than one is confirmed. The plurality of ways to seek the truth falls not only to philosophy but also to faith and, I would add, to mysticism. In this sense, she maintains that she has overcome the phenomenological imprint of her formation, but she never abandons the phenomenological approach that is important for dealing with certain philosophical themes. The complexity of her position is delineated in her last works, which offer a rigorous comparison of the two philosophers regarding the theme of philosophical anthropology. One readily finds this in the *Der Aufbau der menschlichen Person* (*Structure of the human person*)[15] and in *Potency and Act.*[16]

I have decided to focus on the comparison of Husserl and Aquinas because I wish to highlight the importance of Stein's philosophical turn after her conversion to Catholicism, a turn that would lead her to develop, in her own way, a Christian philosophy.

The Meaning of Christian Philosophy

As mentioned previously, to understand Stein's position in relation to Christian philosophy we must trace her speculative path back to her philosophical formation under Husserl.

As she has subsequently maintained, and taking into account her position and the various stops along the way, Stein finds it important that she encountered Husserl's phenomenology in the varied philosophical panorama of the first half of the twentieth century. Against positivism, historicism, psychologism, and against every position that terminates with factual experimentation or epistemological relativism, Husserl posited the human need to investigate the essence of that moment of recognition of the meaning or sense of things, which is graspable by every human being open to investigating with correct intention and which allows one to obtain objective knowledge.

Stein accepts her teacher Husserl's proposition and with this interpretative key in hand she first explores human interiority and the opening of the intersubjective dimension through her investigation of empathy.[17] She then studies the meaning of various human associative relationships and, among these, she maintains a central place for community.[18]

While she is carrying out such essential analyses, as indicated above, an eruption of religious experience occurs that configures itself in a particular way as the acceptance of faith in Christ and animates her conversion to Roman Catholicism. She feels it is her duty to open herself up to the cultural traditions of Christian philosophy and, in doing so, retrace the central figures of medieval thought, starting with Aquinas. It is necessary to point out that he was the first medieval thinker whom Stein encountered, but she does not stop with him, as we will discuss later.

The theme of essence, already indicated by Husserl within the framework of knowledge, takes on for Stein a metaphysical meaning, especially in her engagement with ancient thought—Plato and Aristotle—and medieval philosophy. In her most important work, *Finite and Eternal Being* (1936), reality is examined under the profile of essentialities present in the divine mind, the structure that created things. Within this framework, the human being is seen to have a particular dignity. An original synthesis between certain elements of contemporary thought and the great metaphysical tradition is achieved. She does this by examining the contribution of each thinker that aims at the clarification of an aspect of reality.

We are not dealing here so much with an adherence to a certain stream of thought or a given interpretative framework, but with the acceptance of suggestions of various thinkers that can better illuminate human knowledge, the surrounding world, and God. According to the sage counsel of St. Paul, we must examine everything but only hold on to that which is valid: the criteria of our choice must be reality itself as it gives itself. We can see here a solution being offered to the great problem of truth, understood in a philosophical sense. The theme of truth does not exhaust itself in the aforementioned proposal; it is necessary to take stock of the truth that is revealed. One must wonder about the relation between philosophy and revelation, between religion and faith.

While reflecting on these arguments, Stein came to understand what certain French thinkers were developing: through the works of Etienne Gilson and Jacques Maritain she commenced her reflections on the possibility of a Christian philosophy.

In the 1930s, she took a firm and original position on this argument, accepting the ideas of the French philosophers in which Christian revelation had already illuminated the mind of those who investigate reality, including within the field of philosophy. This inquiry allows us to observe certain aspects of reality that human limitations do not allow us to see spontaneously or often with great fatigue and effort; hence, the necessity for the Christian philosopher to open him- or herself to the content of faith without becoming a theologian, but by employing the same truths of faith as illuminating, complementing, or as an object of philosophical reflection. For example, on this score one can certainly read as interesting Stein's treatment of the angels.[19]

Philosophy, on the one hand, maintains its autonomy, delineating itself as a particular field of research in which human reason can obtain valid results, even if limited. On the other hand, philosophy can allow itself to be illumined by faith in order to proceed further. Philosophy has, above all, the great task of achieving harmony among the diverse sources of truth represented by reason and faith, and this through a philosophically elaborated awareness. This is properly achieved through human reflection. The full achievement of truth is not obtained while we are on the way, but only when we are at home, that is, when we take part in the beatific vision. This very same mystical knowledge, which seems to anticipate a direct vision of God, is intermittent and granted to few.[20]

A Theology *Sui Generis*

After indicating with large brushstrokes Stein's path of inquiry, one rightfully could ask about the reasons that motivated John Paul II to insert her into *Fides et Ratio*. Stein's observations concerning Christian philosophy could serve as a convincing response to the aforementioned question. I believe that we need to consider some other elements in order to understand the development of her foundational work, *Finite and Eternal Being*, vis-à-vis the question of the relationship between faith and reason.

The work presents itself as a sort of *Summa*, like the medieval *Summae*, that moves within the terrain that borders the disciplines of both philosophy and theology. The former gives not only a conceptual structure but also a solution to numerous questions of an epistemological, anthropological, ethical, and metaphysical nature that can be focused through a rational lens: it is the exercise of that which Stein would call pure philosophy. Because she wishes to develop a kind of analysis that operates within the framework of Christian philosophy, her investigation must lose its character of purity and must reckon with the other source of truth, revelation. The latter illumines the analytical path already taken, yielding further instruments useful for the investigation, and confirming and amplifying that which philosophical investigation has already delineated. The key to such an amplification is given by the theme of the Trinity, which is deeply inspired by Augustine's *De Trinitate*, and which Stein develops in her study of the Middle Ages.

The first part of Stein's treatment follows the path of phenomenological investigation. Husserl achieved, through an analysis that moves from the terrain of interiority to the discovery of lived experiences by the acts we carry out that characterize us in an essential way, the confirmation of a tripartite interpretation of the human being as body, psyche, and spirit. One could ask whether Husserl would have known, with his conversion to Christianity, the text of St. Paul in which he speaks of the flesh, the soul, and the spirit. One could only suppose such a link. In any case, the justification of a tripartite vision moves on a plane of pure immanence and is probably motivated more by the fact that the then-nascent psychology was delineating the dimensions of the psyche without taking account of other important operations that could have been justified only by spiritual activity.[21]

After maintaining that the human being is a living body, animated and spiritual, Stein finds the deep reason for such a division in the image of God. This becomes the guiding thread for a new anthropological foundation based on a truth of faith but justified with rational proofs that corroborate revelation. Such proofs are analytical in nature and are rooted in her use of applied phenomenology. In this case, she applies phenomenology to the interior process that concomitantly involves the human being and the divine Trinity.

The human being is the source of proof. Examining the Thomistic interpretation regarding the relation between the intellect and the will and the Augustinian triad of memory-reason-will, Stein develops that which she considers to be the deepest inspiration of the two thinkers, which consists in retaining love as the ultimate and definitive term: "If St. Augustine in his tripartite division (memory-intellect-will) no longer refers specifically to love, this omission can be justified in view of the fact that love must be regarded as the origin and end of his threefold spiritual activity."[22] The same human reflection on love opens up for us the vision of the Trinity, even if, without revelation, we do not become aware of it. Following Augustine once more, Stein argues that the essence of love unveils a trinitarian movement: "If love in its highest fulfillment is mutual self-giving and a union of persons, then a plurality of persons is required."[23] It is for this reason that divine life is the reciprocal gift of the Divine Persons to one another.

All of this is grasped in one's interiority, where one finds the dwelling place of God. A crucial question arises here for understanding the human being–God relationship and for understanding where the human being moves from in order to speak about God: "If it is true that they can attain even to the knowledge and truly fulfilled love of other human beings only if the lovers lovingly reveal themselves . . . how can human beings attain to the love of God, whom they do not see, unless God loves them first?"[24] The power of attraction that the divine life exerts on the soul reveals the trinitarian structure:

> [F]or it is the triune God to whom the soul gives its own self. It surrenders its self to the will of the Father, who generates in the soul anew, as it were, the Son. The soul unites itself with the Son. It desires to disappear in him, so that the Father may see in the soul nothing but the Son. And the life of the soul unites itself with the Holy Spirit and thus becomes an outpouring of divine love.[25]

The term "image" is not exact, Stein observes. Here, divine filiation realizes itself. The soul becomes the *vas spirituale* (spiritual vessel), as the Marian Litany of Loreto describes it. This soul as *vas spirituale* is prototypical for every human soul.

We see here not only theological reflection, because there is a presupposition of the truths of faith, but also a confirmation of them through a demonstration of their reasonableness. Even if we eliminate the great abyss that exists between the human being and God, a great knowledge is still brought to clarity, always ably utilizing, of course, the tool of analogy.

The presence of God in the soul is confirmed by mystical experience. For this reason, Stein maintains that the analysis of the interior castle, as developed by St. Teresa of Ávila, is truly fitting because it follows the same path in interiority that was followed from a philosophical point of view. The life of the mystic, understood in its essence, allows us to confirm the other two: the philosophical and theological paths. Mysticism draws close to these other two paths with the great advantage of seizing, through direct contact, the divine life, which ultimately prefigures the beatific vision.

Notes

1. Edith Stein, *Che cosa è la fenomenologia? La ricerca della verità—dalla fenomenologia alla filosofia Cristiana* (What is phenomenology? The search for truth—from phenomenology to Christian philosophy), ed. Angela Ales Bello, 2nd ed. (Rome: Città Nuova, 1997), 56. Original in German in *Theologie und Philosophie* 66 (1991): 570–73.

2. Ibid., 56 (570).

3. Now translated as "Husserl and Aquinas: A Comparison," in Stein, *Knowledge and Faith*, trans. Walter Redmond, CWES, vol. 8 (Washington, D.C.: ICS Publications, 2000).

4. Ibid., 7.

5. Ibid., 56 (570).

6. Ibid.

7. Angela Ales Bello, *Edith Stein—La passione per la verità* (The passion for the truth) (Padova, Italy: Ed. del Messaggero di Padova, 2003).

8. Stein, "Husserl and Aquinas," 11.

9. Bello, *Husserl sul problema di Dio* (Husserl on the problem of God) (Rome: Studium, 1985); "Dio nella prospetiva fenomenologica" (God in phenomenological perspective), in *Dio e il senso delll'esistenza umana* (God and the sense of human existence) (Rome: Armando, 1999), 101–34; "Il teismo nella fenomenologia: Edmund Husserl e Edith Stein a confronto" (Theism in phenomenology: A comparison between Edmund Husserl and Edith Stein), in *Pensare Dio a Gerusalemme* (Thinking of God in Jerusalem), ed. Angela Ales Bello (Milano: P.U.L.-Mursia, 2000), 279–98; *The Divine in Husserl and Other Explorations*, in Analecta Husserliana, vol. 98 (Dordrecht, The Netherlands: Springer, 2009).

10. Bello, "La teologia in un inedito husserliano" (Theology in an unpublished Husserlian manuscript), *Aquinas* 25, no. 2 (1982): 349–56.

11. Bello, "Modernità e crisi (*La lettura husserliana della nostra epoca*)" (Modernity and crisis [Husserlian interpretation of our age]), *Per la filosofia 7, no. 18 (1990): 43–53.*

12. Stein, "Husserl and Aquinas," 29.

13. Ibid., 38.

14. Ibid., 44–45.

15. *Stein, Der Aufbau der menschlichen Person*, ed. Beate Beckmann-Zöller, Edith Stein Gesamtausgabe (ESGA), vol. 14 (Freiburg: Herder, 2004).

16. Stein, *Potency and Act: Studies Toward a Philosophy of Being*, trans. Walter Redmond, CWES, vol. 11 (Washington, D.C.: ICS Publications, 2009).

17. Stein, *On the Problem of Empathy*, trans. Waltraut Stein, CWES, vol. 3 (Washington, D.C.: ICS Publications, 1989).

18. Stein, *Philosophy of Psychology and the Humanities*, trans. Mary Catharine Baseheart and Marianne Sawicki, CWES, vol. 7 (Washington, D.C.: ICS Publications, 2000).

19. Stein, *Finite and Eternal Being: An Attempt at an Ascent to the Meaning of Being*, trans. Kurt Reinhardt, CWES, vol. 9 (Washington, D.C.: ICS Publications, 2002), chap. 7, sec. 5.

20. Ibid., sec. 4.

21. Bello, "Riflessioni sull'antropolgia (Reflections on anthropology), *Per la filosofia* 17, no. 49 (2000).

22. Stein, *Finite and Eternal Being*, 454.

23. Ibid., 457.

24. Ibid., 457–58.

25. Ibid., 458.

15

GENESIS AND BEYOND:
Phenomenological Feminism
in St. John Paul II and St. Edith Stein

KATHLEEN HANEY

Sister Teresa Benedicta of the Cross was canonized by Pope John Paul II in 1998. While she was still a recent convert (at the age of thirty-one) and before she entered the Carmelites (at the age of forty-three), Edith Stein was the most important Catholic feminist writer and speaker in the intrabellum German-speaking world. She has had little influence on European and American feminists until recently. Lately, third- and fourth-wave feminism has made many of Stein's discoveries, without often discovering her. Her writings on woman are a basic text for New Feminism.

Less well-known still is St. John Paul II's feminism, also fundamental for New Feminism. Although his stance on the question of the ordination of women leads many to imagine that they are familiar with his teachings, his doctrines display much more complexity. Unlike most feminist writers, the pope had the good fortune to have access to Edith Stein's work, as well as that of her contemporaries,

Max Scheler and Roman Ingarden, among others. For all his reputed conservativism, John Paul II's work reveals him as a feminist in the mode of his fellow phenomenological philosopher St. Teresa Benedicta of the Cross. I shall maintain that their feminism values woman not so much for a potential equality with man, but for the specific differences that women embody, as well.

Philosophical personalism plays a significant role in their advocacy of the cause of women. Edith Stein and Karol Wojtyla share an essentialist view of woman, yet both hold that personhood trumps gender. They promote women by valorizing difference: women are worthy not only if they are equals with men, but also if they are different from men in ways that the prevailing "culture of death" would do well to incorporate for the good of humankind.

Before the Fourth World Conference on Women, held in Beijing in September 1995, John Paul II wrote a letter addressed to women.[1] He had earlier discussed the topic of the dignity of women in the apostolic letter *Mulieris Dignitatem* (August 15, 1988),[2] and he discusses women in the work collected as *The Theology of the Body*, as well as in his encyclical on the Mother of God[3] and elsewhere.[4] I propose to consider themes that his feminist thought shares with Stein's talks and essays, which have been collected in a volume titled *Essays on Woman*.[5] These will be my main texts, though I shall refer to Wojtyla's *The Acting Person* and *Love and Responsibility* and to Stein's *On the Problem of Empathy* as well. Since my topic concerns the coalescence of their thought on feminist topics, I shall include material that they do not share. For instance, John Paul II writes at length about biblical women in their roles as exemplars and their functions in salvation history. Also, and appropriately, the pope makes more of the defects of men, while Stein emphasizes women's deficiencies. Both find the Blessed Virgin Mary, the new Eve, to be the perfection of humankind.

Method

On this occasion, little needs to be said about John Paul II as phenomenologist. The consensus should be established that *The Acting Person*[6] employs the method of transcendental phenomenology insofar as it asks about the necessary conditions for the possibility of action, an analysis that uncovers intentional meanings bestowed by the human person. Stein's career and phenomenological credentials include studying under the master, the father of twentieth-century phenomenology, Edmund Husserl, and writing her dissertation, *On the Problem of Empathy*, to fill in a significant lacuna in his first introduction to phenomenology in *Ideas I*. She became his first assistant and edited the manuscripts that were published as *Ideas II* and *The Phenomenology of Internal Time Consciousness*. Another of her early works, translated as *Philosophy of Psychology and the Humanities*,[7] adheres to phenomenological method and considers phenomenological topics such as consciousness, motivation, and the relationship of the individual to the community, which was also Husserl's concern in his K manuscripts. As illustrious a Thomist as Alasdair MacIntyre finds Stein's work of interest in its remarkable consistency and in its effect in her life. He writes, "The direction of Stein's life beyond a certain point becomes intelligible only in the light of her philosophy, and even before this her philosophical stances are in significant ways informed by her life experiences."[8]

For our purposes, suffice it to say that classical phenomenology encourages the participation of all who think about its discoveries since its touchstone is always the reader's or thinker's own experience. Husserl makes the claim that our authors share: intuitive grasp, insight, is the mark of philosophical truth. Stein understood the attitude that Wojtyla expressed in an early writing:

> This work is open to every echo of experience, from whatever quarter it comes, and it is at the same time a standing appeal to all to let experience, their own experience, make itself heard, to its full extent: in all its breadth, and all its depth. . . . *Love and Responsibility*, with this sort of methodological basis, fears nothing and need fear nothing which can be legitimized by experience. Experience does not have to be afraid of experience. Truth can only gain from such a confrontation.[9]

Philosophy, as phenomenology, is not opposed to lived experience; rather it requires it for its validation. Our thinkers hold that our experience of woman and our attempts to make sense of that experience ground their work, since intuition provides verification.

Both Stein and Wojtyla trained in phenomenological philosophy and enrich their considerations of gender with the creation stories in Genesis, that is, with revelation. We see here the curious marriage of their theology with their phenomenology, since they consider these stories to be essential in understanding man and woman in their creation as Adam and Eve. After all, according to Husserl, we can analyze the abnormal well only if we consider it as deviation from the normal.[10]

Pre-Fall humankind embodies the nature of the human and represents the norm with which an analysis of sex and gender must begin. The descendants of the first parents suffer the effects of sin, including the distortions to their preternatural beginnings that accompanied their sin. We are all familiar with the catastrophe that the first parents wrought in the garden by their disobedience. For our purposes, we consider the pre-Fall couple as Wojtyla and Stein do.

We know the story: Adam was lonely, so God created Eve out of his side while he slept. Let us pause here. God created man after the cosmos, after the planet, after the animals, yet none of Adam's potential or actual pets provided him with the companionship that he desired. Genesis tells us that Adam wanted a helpmate. A helpmate is neither slave nor lackey. A helpmate, especially when there are only two persons, must provide intellectual companionship as well as physical supplementation. Stein states, "It is not a question here of a *sovereignty* of man over woman. She is named as *companion* and *helpmate*, and it is said of man that he will cling to her and both are to become one flesh."[11]

Both Wojtyla and Stein are taken by the magnitude of male and female participating in the one flesh. Eve was created separate but equal to be united with Adam in a bond that made them one, obviating differences through their mutual fulfillment of each other. Any third person that their love generated came from this union of flesh. Commenting on Genesis 1:27, St. John Paul II wrote that "both man and woman are human beings to an equal degree, both are created in God's image."[12] John Paul reminds us of feminine images of God, particularly in the Old Testament as well as devotions to what we may sum up as Christ as mother.

Both Edith Stein and Pope John Paul II find an original complementarity of the sexes in the creation of woman as a helpmate to man as he was to her. "Woman complements man, just as man complements woman. . . . Womanhood expresses the 'human' as much as manhood does, but in a different and complementary way."[13] Let us pause here. Women and men complete each other; both are vital to the new unity that comes about through their reciprocal union. Domination by man, according to John Paul II, or the patriarchy, as Stein puts it, results from Adam's and Eve's sin. Stein is very clear that patriarchy is as much punishment for sin as is painful childbirth, exhausting work, and banishment from the garden.

Mankind, as the human species, is composed of men and women, different, co-essential, and mutually implicated as images of the triune God.

The calamity of the Fall changed all that. Sin destroyed the original nature of the species. As her punishment, woman became subjugated to man. God cursed Eve, by placing her under the domination of the man who would exploit her and belittle her genuine gifts. Woman's penalty for the first sin rests in fulfilling the painful demands of motherhood under the unjust rule of her fallen husband. Though God ordained that man should rule over woman, as Christ is head of the church, Stein reminds us with her characteristic gentle humor that, as many wives recognize, "[t]he husband is not Christ. . . . And since he himself is not perfect like Christ . . . his highest wisdom may be to permit the gifts of other members to compensate for his defects, just as it could be the highest political wisdom of the sovereign to allow a judicious minister to rule."[14] For Stein then, woman's vocation may still involve being a helpmate to man, according to her feminine differences, already established before the Fall and accentuated thereafter. Each woman has her unique talents as well. Woman is created as a helpmate; she is not a servant, not a tool, but a partner. She provides "a help which is not one-sided but *mutual.*"[15]

Men and women are co-essential members of the one species, the human species; they differ from all the rest of God's creation because, as male and female together, the species images God and co-creates with him. Again, quoting from Stein, "man needs woman to fulfill the meaning of his being, she was created for his sake. It does not seem to me that this means that woman was created only for the sake of man; for every creature has its own meaning, and that is its particular way of being an image of the divine being."[16] Instead, men, fallen children of God, must sustain their existence through the sweat of their brow and attempt to dominate and exploit their wives, on the personal level perhaps, but certainly on the level of cultural structures even in societies today.

Power substitutes poorly for love. Domination is sin as well as punishment for the first sin. Love requires that we condemn relations of exploitation, domination, and slavery. None of these have to do with human persons living lives of peace that help them to become clearer images of their Creator. Both Stein and John Paul II remind us of the famous passage from Galatians 3:24: "There is neither Jew nor Greek, nor slave nor free, there is neither male nor female. For you are all one in Christ Jesus." According to Stein, the new kingdom of God will bring a new order of relationship between the sexes, one which would restore the original order when Love reigned.[17]

Stein does not decry the leadership of the man, but she does deny that his leadership makes a woman subservient to all of his whims and desires. The pope, perhaps because he is a man, is more adamant still about condemning man's lust and exploitation of women. In what appears to be an extreme position, John Paul holds that sexual intercourse between spouses may be rape. He says, "Man can commit this adultery in the heart also with regard to his own wife, if he treats her only as an object to satisfy instinct."[18] The philosophy of personalism guides his thinking about Matthew 5:28. Persons are not things; persons are not objects to be used for convenience. Each person is a trust to be cherished so that each one is protected, nourished, and sustained until returning to the Love that is his or her origin and end.

When Christ spoke of a man who looks lustfully, he indicated not only the dimension of intentionality in looking, thus indicating lustful knowledge, the psychological dimension, but also the dimension of the intentionality of man's very existence. In the situation Christ described, that dimension passes unilaterally from the man, who is the subject, to the woman, who has become the object.[19]

He adds, "A certain woman begins to exist for a certain man not as a subject of call and personal attraction or as a subject of communion, but exclusively as an object for the potential satisfaction of the sexual need."[20] Relations with things are meant to be one-sided, while relationships between persons reciprocally unite them.

Essential Differences

We turn now to consider the essences of masculinity and femininity and their differences, though we do so with some apprehension, since feminism is a historical movement that has been guided by various notions about women. Also, difference and essence are not without their controversies that will need adjudication. First things first, though: it seems to me that the debate about difference has often been more intense than it needed to be, not only in matters of sex and gender but also of race and culture. Those who stress equality too often obviate obvious differences. For instance, feminists depreciated, rejected differences between men and women, even when doing so required ignoring scientific data and personal experiences.

Facing the cry that "woman's place is in the home" and
taking individualism as their goal, Edith Stein observed
in 1928, early feminists "in the heat of battle . . . went
so far as to *deny* completely the feminine *singularity*—that
women were any different from men. Consequently, one
could not speak of an intrinsic *feminine value*. (As a matter of fact, their only goal was to insist that women were
equal to men in all fields.)"[21]

Both Stein and John Paul II believe that the sex of the
body matters, though the significance of the body on personality depends upon factors including talents, society,
vocation, choices, and circumstances too. Here I insert a
word of caution. Neither Stein nor the pope endorses the
position that "biology is destiny" and the abuses that have
followed from it; rather, their phenomenological formation
encourages them to take the body as a serious, though not
determinant, factor in the lived life of any particular individual. The human being is not a consciousness inserted into a
body, but a soul that lives in a body that is sexed as well as
gendered. John Paul believed that "the body expresses the
personal human 'self,' which derives its exterior perception
from within."[22] He writes, "In its masculinity and femininity, the body is called 'from the beginning' to become the
manifestation of the spirit."[23] The body matters, but it is
not all that matters to human personality.[24] After all, the
personal and maternal aspects of any particular woman
draw from a body that features brains as well as breasts.

The constitution of the woman is different, as compared
with the man. We know today that it is different even in

the deepest bio-physiological determinants. It is manifested externally only to a certain extent, in the construction and form of her body. Maternity manifests this constitution internally, as the particular potentiality of the female organism. With creative peculiarity it serves for the conception and begetting of the human being, with the help of man.[25]

Still, just as fatherhood does not subsume a man's professional life, neither does motherhood necessarily sum up a woman's life.

Saints John Paul II and Edith Stein share the view that woman is of inestimable value not only in familial life but also in the life of the workplace, in the church, and in the public arena as well. Despite her unusual academic success as a student, Stein was prevented early on from holding a university post because she was a woman. Her work at a girls' teaching college led her to reflect on women's education. She came to believe that woman's soul should be encouraged to become expansive since her natural, physiological inclination was to embrace and nurture living beings. Woman's desire to give herself completely makes it easier for her to give herself to God and to others than it is for man. In Stein's time, as in ours, most women make their own livings. She writes: "The singular mission of the working woman is to fuse her feminine calling with her vocational calling and, by means of that fusion, to give a feminine quality to her vocational calling."[26] In his letter to women, John Paul offers a predictable word of thanks to women who are wives and mothers but also to *"women who work!* You are present and active in every area of life—social, economic, cultural, artistic and political. In this way you make an indispensable contribution to the growth of a culture which unites reason and feeling, to a model of life ever open to the sense of 'mystery,' to the establishment of economic and political structures ever more worthy of humanity" (italics in the original).[27] Already we see that although woman's nature suits her for familiar life, nothing intrinsic about her determines that she is designed to contribute exclusively to the home, though at times women's possibilities have been so limited by their societies and cultures.

Stein writes that:

> there is no profession which cannot be practiced by a woman. A self-sacrificing woman can accomplish astounding achievements when it is a question of replacing the breadwinner of fatherless children [Stein's own father died when she was two years old, leaving her mother to manage a lumber business to support the family], of supporting abandoned children or aged parents. But, also, individual gifts and tendencies can lead to the most diversified activities. Indeed, no woman is only woman; like a man, each has her individual specialty and talent, and this talent gives her the capability of doing professional work, be it artistic, scientific, technical, etc. Essentially, the individual talent can enable her to embark on any discipline, even those remote from the usual feminine vocations.[28]

Even so, there are professions that seem to suit most women better, the traditional ones of nursing, teaching, caregiving, and so forth; yet the individual woman, just as the individual man, must discover and develop herself. To be clear here: the concept of woman is essentially different from the concept of man, but how the essential difference plays out depends upon the individual person, in the process of his or her self-realization in the unique circumstances of a particular life situation. Self-realization is not straightforward or simple. Part of becoming ourselves involves seeking others' self-fulfillment too; for many women this means nurturing their children or those of others physically, educating them intellectually, sharing their emotional needs, and teaching them to love by showing love for them. Many men care for others and mature themselves in these ways too. Both men and women are to become the persons whom God created them to be; to do the work that he has prepared for them. After all, both share the human vocation.

> God has given each human being a threefold destiny: to grow into the likeness of God through the development of his faculties, to procreate descendants, and to hold dominion over the earth. In addition, it is promised that a life of faith and personal union with the Redeemer will be rewarded by eternal contemplation of God. These destinies, natural and supernatural, are identical for both man and woman.[29]

Keeping in mind that each woman is a particular person and only an imperfect embodiment of the ideal woman, we turn to the *essence* of femininity. According to Stein, "Woman naturally seeks to embrace that which is living, personal and whole. To cherish, guard, protect, nourish and advance growth is her natural, maternal yearning." Stein continues that unlike men, "Lifeless matter, the fact, can hold primary interest for her [woman] only insofar as it serves the living and the personal, not ordinarily for its own sake."[30] Though not all women are called to be wives and mothers, woman's nature is determined by her original vocation. The female body is fashioned to "'be one flesh' with another and to nurse new human life in itself . . . at the same time, it is a source of power and a habitat for the mind. . . . Both spiritual companionship and spiritual motherliness are not limited to the physical spouse and mother relationships, but they extend to all people with whom woman comes into contact."[31]

Though women are often criticized for being too emotional, Stein stresses that woman's emotional life is to be revalued since she believes that the emotions are means for an immediate grasp of values. After all, all values derive their merit from their use to persons. Women live in their feelings and are attuned to other persons' feelings. Although philosophers such as Aristotle held that women's emotions deprive them of rationality, for Stein feelings are sensitivities that can point to realities beneath the surface. Many women are more likely than their male counterparts to realize that there may be unplumbed depths to a child's report that school is fine. To guide young people rationally and usefully, a concerned adult must be aware of how the child feels about a distressing concrete situation in order to educate the child's feelings and help her formulate rational reflection about what to do about the difficulty. Woman can infuse her culture and the life of her nation with her acknowledgment of and concern for the person. John Paul and Stein agree that many women seem especially suited to the tasks that encourage spiritual maturity in themselves and others. According to the pope, "Perhaps more than men, women acknowledge the person, because they see persons with their hearts. They see them independently of various ideological or political systems. They see others in their greatness and limitations; they try to go out to them and help them."[32]

Stein and John Paul agree that (in Stein's words): "The specific degeneracy of man is seen in his brutal despotism over creatures—especially over woman, and in his enslavement to his work up to the point of atrophy of his humanity." Stein describes how man, left to his own devices, is too inclined to be all-absorbed by his work to the detriment of his family and other relationships. Women, by and large, participate in another temptation. Women are more likely to be so enmeshed in their relationships that their work is displaced by misplaced concern for others. Stein writes that a woman will be better as a helpmate if "she does not lose herself in association with her husband, but on the contrary, cultivates her own gifts and powers."[33] Woman's emotions can be a source of strength, but they can also dominate her one-sidedly. Likewise, her involvement with her husband and children can trap her into thinking that their appearance and performance sum up her own value so that she becomes excessively dependent on them and thus a burden to them.

> Her own husband must be recognized as the very best husband, her own children must be known as the most beautiful, clever, and gifted. This is blind feminine love which dulls realistic judgment, renders her completely unsuitable for the designated feminine vocation. Along with this excessive vindication of her own person goes an excessive interest in others, a perverse desire to penetrate into personal lives, a passion of wanting to confiscate people.[34]

All women should have their own objective work and creative outlets, though these might be centered in the home or the office. A clean floor is an objective accomplishment, albeit fleeting, and can carry with it the satisfaction that derives from a job well done. Stein asks how it is possible to release "valuable feminine character from the raw material of feminine singularity with all its faults and weakness," which all the daughters of Eve inherit.

> [A] good natural method for this is *thoroughly objective work*. Every such work, no matter of what kind, whether housework, a trade, science or anything else, necessitates submitting to the laws of the matter concerned; the whole person, thoughts just as all moods and dispositions, must be made subordinate to the work. And whoever has learned this, has become objective, has lost something of the *hyper-individuality* and has attained a definite freedom of self; at the same time she has attained an inner depth—she has attained a basis of self-control.[35]

Self-abnegating service to others can consume a woman and leave her devoid of inner life. In these opposite deficient tendencies, men and women can help each other, as when he takes the children to the park so that she can have some time to herself, or she reminds him of his mother's birthday or his son's game, as in increasingly more millennial families, the woman is the primary bread-winner and her spouse takes on major responsibilities for the home. The children's needs for emotional nurturance remain and often the professional mother supplies them.

Since the idea of essence is a complicated one with a contentious history, let me suggest instead that, for our purposes, we employ the notion of type when referring to any particular person. Types are exemplifications of material universals that we constantly see when we perceive, thematically or marginally, anything at all.[36] Women are a type of human being, the species then comprises two types. John Paul writes: "*both man and woman are human beings to an equal degree*, both are created *in God's image*" (italics in the original).[37] Again, from John Paul we read: "Womanhood and manhood are complementary not only from the physical and psychological points of view, but also from the ontological. It is only through the duality of the 'masculine' and the 'feminine' that the 'human' finds full realization."[38]

Stein puts it this way: "I am convinced that the species *humanity* embraces the double species *man* and *woman*; that the essence of the complete human being is characterized by this duality; and that the entire structure of the essence demonstrates the specific character."[39] The essence of humankind instantiates itself in two types: the feminine and the masculine. The essence of a particular human being, however, cannot be summed up in body type, cultural type, or any type insofar as the individual is unique, unrepeatable. Its material essence has to do with its bodily form, its historical moment, its geographical location, its mother tongue, its native gifts, its experiences, and on and on, but most of all with a *Kern*, the soul of the soul of a person, unique in each of us. The material essences of masculinity and femininity in persons are notions that derive from their sex organs with gender specific functions (i.e., breasts for nursing), even though not all persons exercise their reproductivite capacities. Nevertheless, being-in-a-body sexed and gendered in particular ways must affect persons so constituted, but to what effect can only be answered through knowing this or that person. We all have experiences of all types of persons in their memberships in various groupings. Only for the purposes of this paper is the type woman of more interest than the type American or middle-class or used-car salesperson.

Both John Paul II and Edith Stein consider the Virgin Mary as more than the instantiation of a material essence. She serves as exemplar of woman in her maternity and in virginity, but most of all in her complete self-fulfillment through her self-giving. Mary embodies the universal essence of humankind, in its female aspect. Some contemporary feminists, notably Luce Irigaray, as well as John Paul II and Stein, recognize the validity of both motherhood and virginity for women. The mother must turn inward sometimes to the private cell in her heart for perspective, peace, and prayer, although the inner life cannot be the whole of life. Stein sees the duality of Mary, the Virgin Mother of God, in each particular woman. Indeed, she encourages each woman in her work as well as in the tasks of nurturing either her own children or those whom she teaches or nurses, etc.

> The wife and mother must also have this *virginity* of soul: indeed, only from that does she get the power to fulfill her vocation; from this source alone flows the ministering love which is neither servile subjugation nor imperious self-assertion and imposed self-will. The ministering love is not only the essence of maternity; in the love of Christ, it must needs devote itself to all creatures coming into its ken. It is for this reason that the woman who is not wife and mother must also be true in thought and deed to this spiritual maternity.[40]

John Paul takes a less integral approach. He believes that either physical motherhood or the virginity of the celibate life may provide the individual woman the means to fulfill herself through giving herself to others. Self-giving may be to God, to colleagues, to students, to patients, and so forth. The important aspect is dying to self by freely giving of the self to others. He avows the position that both physical and spiritual motherhood evidence a spiritual dimension. According to essentialist views, a woman's suitability for motherhood (of both physical and spiritual varieties) shows itself in her body, which manifests her feminine spirit.

Stein, writing and speaking out against the Nazi vision of woman's value as contributor to the number of new members of the Aryan master race, and Pope John Paul, speaking and writing to the late twentieth-century world that too often still saw women as chattel, possessions of their fathers, husbands, or brothers, share the view that a woman as well as a man is of inestimable value not only in personal life but also in the life of the workplace, in the church, and in the public arena.

Conclusion

In conclusion, I return to St. John Paul II as phenomenologist. To observe that woman, the concept, refers to an essence is as well within the purview of Husserlian phenomenology, given that neither John Paul nor Stein dwells exhaustively on that which determines the event of an actual woman, nor hold that woman is materially different from man. Because of this, they remain on the margins of phenomenological critique, and this is not incidental. Both John Paul II and Stein recognize that woman is a material essence, instantiated in this or that particular person as an integral outgrowth of her *Kern*, her particular essence. Stein is quick to follow along the Aristotelian line that the female body expresses or manifests a female soul. More importantly, though, each soul is an individual soul and each person realizes her native potentialities within the confines of her given existential circumstances, including her historical epoch, her culture, her religion, her lived body, and so forth. Much of the early critiques of the so-called realistic phenomenologists on the topic of women seem dated now that thinkers within the feminist movement are eager to grasp what Stein refers to as the "value of woman's singularity." After all, woman's singularity presents an opportunity to challenge the present culture by valuing persons over things and life over death.

Stein and John Paul II share an essentialist view of woman insofar as woman is a meaningful concept that points to an essence that an individual woman exemplifies, yet both hold that personhood is more important than either gender or sex. Men and women share a common purpose and a reciprocal need for each other. Both Stein and the pope teach us that the proper equality between men and women is not in women behaving as men, which John Paul II warns can deform their nature in some cases. The gifts and strengths of men and women can provide a partnership so that together they combine strengths and compensate for their natural deficiencies. The unity of male and female can make them a useful pair, but not a pair on the order of a pair of socks. Together they can be more like the blades of a pair of scissors, and who can say that one blade is more important?

Notes

1. Pope John Paul II, *Letter to Women*, June 29, 1995.

2. Pope John Paul II, *Mulieris Dignitatem*, Apostolic Letter on the Dignity and Vocation of Women, August 15, 1988.

3. Pope John Paul II, *Redemptoris Mater* (Mother of the Redeemer), encyclical, March 25, 1987; *The Theology of the Body* (Boston: Pauline Books & Media, 1997).

4. Although not directly cited, Brooke Williams Deely has recently edited a collection of all of St. John Paul's writings on the subject of women: *Pope John Paul II Speaks on Women* (Washington, D.C.: Catholic University Press of America, 2014).

5. Stein, *Essays on Woman,* trans. Freda Mary Oben, CWES, vol. 2 (Washington, D.C.: ICS Publications, 1996).

6. Cardinal Karol Wojtyla, *The Acting Person,* trans. Andrzej Potocki, Analecta Husserliana, vol. 10 (Dordrecht, The Netherlands: D. Reidel Publishing Company, 1979).

7. Stein, *Philosophy of Psychology and the Humanities,* trans. Mary Catharine Baseheart and Marianne Sawicki, CWES, vol. 7 (Washington, D.C.: ICS Publications, 2000).

8. Alasdair MacIntyre, *Edith Stein: A Philosophical Prologue, 1913–1922* (Lanham, Md./Oxford: Roman and Littlefield Publishers, 2006), 6.

9. Karol Wojtyla, *Love and Responsibility,* trans. H. T. Willetts (New York: Farrar, Straus and Giroux, 1981), 9.

10. Edmund Husserl, *The Cartesian Meditations,* trans. Dorian Cairns (Dordrecht, The Netherlands: Martinus Nijhoff, 1960), 125.

11. Stein, *Essays on Woman,* 60.

12. John Paul II, *Mulieris Dignitatem.*

13. John Paul II, *Letter to Women,* 17.

14. Stein, *Essays on Woman,* 68.

15. John Paul II, *Letter to Women,* 7.

16. Stein, *Essays on Woman,* 196.

17. Ibid., 69.

18. Pope John Paul II, *The Theology of the Body,* 157.

19. Ibid., 150.

20. Ibid., 151.

21. Stein, *Essays on Woman,* 254.

22. John Paul II, *Theology of the Body,* 56.

23. Ibid., 163.

24. Since John Paul II provides no discussion of a substance or nature within, I plausibly regard the above quotations as references to experiences

of inner perceptions, introjections, inner-time consciousness, interior and/or spiritual life, and so forth.

25. John Paul II, *Letter to Women*, 23.

26. Stein, *Essays on Woman*, 254.

27. John Paul II, *Letter to Women*, 10–11.

28. Stein, *Essays on Woman*, 49.

29. Ibid., 100.

30. Ibid., 45.

31. Ibid., 133.

32. John Paul II, *Letter to Women*, 23.

33. Stein, *Essays on Woman*, 109.

34. Ibid., 256.

35. Ibid., 257.

36. Much of the discussion that follows on the topic of types and essences owes a significant debt to Professor Lester Embree, in particular his work on "The Continuous Awareness of Universals," in *Husserl's Ideen*, ed. Lester Embree and Thomas Nenon (Dordrecht, The Netherlands: Springer, 2012), 225–39.

37. John Paul II, *Mulieris Dignitatem*.

38. John Paul II, *Letter to Women*, 17.

39. Stein, *Essays on Woman*, 187.

40. Ibid., 203.

Contributors

Prudence Allen, R.S.M.

Sister Prudence Allen, R.S.M., PhD, is a member of the Religious Sisters of Mercy of Alma, Michigan. She held the Charles J. Chaput, OFM Cap Endowed Chair in Philosophy Professor at St. John Theological Seminary, Denver, Colorado, until her retirement. She is Distinguished Professor Emeritus, Concordia University, Montreal. She completed her BA at the University of Rochester and her PhD in philosophy at Claremont Graduate University. The last volume of her prodigious three-volume history of *The Concept of Woman* in Western philosophy from 750 BC to AD 2015, *The Search for Communion*, was published by Eerdmans in 2017. She has lectured widely in Canada and the United States, and published in such journals as *Communio, Thought, New Blackfriars, American Catholic Philosophical Quarterly, Homelitic and Pastoral Review, Seminary Journal, International Philosophical Quarterly*, and *Maritain Studies*. Pope Francis appointed her for five years to the International Theology Commission, 2014–2019.

Michael F. Andrews

Michael F. Andrews, PhD, is the director of the John Felice Rome Center, an international academic campus of Loyola University of Chicago, located in Rome, Italy. He is the former dean of the College of Arts and Sciences at the University of Portland, where he also served as the director of the Catholic Studies Program and the McNerney-Hanson University Endowed Chair in Ethics. He earned his BA in systematic theology from Georgetown University; his MA in philosophical theology from Yale University; his PhL/M Phil in Greek and medieval metaphysics from the Pontifical Gregorian University in Rome; and his PhD in philosophy from Villanova University. He has published widely and lectures extensively on the philosophy of Edith Stein and in the areas of phenomenology, ethics and discernment, biomedical ethics, and Catholic intellectual thought. He is presently working on a manuscript relating empathy and imagination.

Ann W. Astell

Ann W. Astell is Professor of Theology at the University of Notre Dame. She was Professor of English and Medieval Studies at Purdue University from 1988 until 2007. Past president of the Society for the Study of Christian Spirituality (SSCS) and of the Colloquium on Violence and Religion (COV&R), she holds her PhD from the University of Wisconsin-Madison and her MA from Marquette University. She is a member of the Schoenstatt Sisters of Mary, an international secular institute. The author of six books, including, most recently, *Eating Beauty: The Eucharist and the Spiritual Arts of the Middle Ages* (2006). She has also edited or co-edited six collections of essays, including *Lay Sanctity, Medieval and Modern: The Search for Models* (2000); *Joan of Arc and*

Spirituality (2003); and *Sacrifice, Scripture, and Substitution: Readings in Ancient Judaism and Christianity* (2011). While much of her scholarship has concerned medieval and early modern saints and their spiritual writings, she has also published on nineteenth- and twentieth-century figures: Dietrich Bonhoeffer, Gertraud von Bullion, Dorothy Day, René Girard, Joseph Kentenich, Emmanuel Levinas, Chiara Lubich, Thérèse of Lisieux, Edith Stein, and Simone Weil. Her articles have appeared in such journals as *Contagion, Listening, Spiritus, Studies in Spirituality, Franciscan Studies,* and *Christianity and Literature.*

Angela Ales Bello

Angela Ales Bello is Professor Emeritus of History of Contemporary Philosophy at Lateran University in Rome and past Dean of the Faculty of Philosophy. She is the president of the Italian Center of Phenomenological Researches (Rome) affiliated to the World Phenomenological Institute, Hanover, N.H.; president of the International Society of Phenomenology of Religion, Rome, Italy; and director of the International Research Area dedicated to Edith Stein and Contemporary Philosophy at the Lateran University. She is Visiting Professor in the Faculty of Psychology of the State University in São Paulo, Brazil. Her research is directed toward German Phenomenology in relationship to other contemporary philosophical currents according to a historical and theoretical approach. Her last books are *Introdução a Fenomenologia* (*Introduction to Phenomenology*) (Brazil, 2006) *L'universo nella coscienza. Introduzione alla fenomenologia di Edmund Husserl, Edith Stein, Hedwig Conrad-Martius (The Universe in the Consciousness. Introduction to the Phenomenology of Edmund Husserl, Edith Stein, Hedwig Conrad-Martius)* (2007); *The Divine in Husserl and other Explorations,* (Springer, 2009); *Edith Stein—Sull'armonia (Edith Stein—On Harmony)* (2010). *Io Coscienza Mondo. La fenomenologia di Edmund Husserl* in . . . *e la Coscienza? Fenomenologia, Psicopatologia, Neuroscienze,* a cura di Angela Ales Bello e Patrizia Manganaro (*I, Consciousness, World. Husserl's Phenomenology* in . . . *and Consciousness? Phenomenology Psychopathology Neurosciences,* edited by A. Ales Bello and P. Manganaro) (2012); *Il senso delle cose. Per un realismo fenomenologico,* (2013); *The Sense of Things. Towards a phenomenological Realism,* (Springer, 2015) and *Il senso del sacro. Dall'arcaicità alla desacralizzazione.* (2014). (*The Sense of the Sacred. From the Antiquity to the Contemporary Age*). Her last book is *Il senso dell'umano tra Fenomenologia, Psicologia e Psicopatologia* (2016). She is the co-editor of the Italian translation of Edith Stein's works (OCD-Città Nuova Publishers, Rome).

Isobel Bowditch

Isobel Bowditch works as an Academic Developer in The Teaching & Learning Innovation Centre at Goldsmiths, University of London. Between 1995 and 2009, she worked as a lecturer and research fellow in Fine Arts (theory and practice) at the University of the Arts, London. She completed her BA degree at Goldsmiths College, University of London, and earned her MA and PhD degrees from Chelsea College of Art and Design, University of the Arts, London. Her interests are in the intersection of continental philosophy, particularly phenomenology, aesthetics, and philosophy of religion with the arts especially film and literature. She has written on Søren Kierkegaard and Michel Henry. She has published in *PhaenEx: Journal of Existential and Phenomenological Theory and Culture;* she has staged *Onlookers*, in a Performative Interventions Series at the University of the Arts, London and in a Contemporary Thought series at Goldsmiths College, University of London. Her DVD/book *Reading Michel Henry* presents a diary of the experience of reading *The Essence of Manifestation.* Her longstanding interest in writing, thinking, and practice currently centers on writing poetry.

Antonio Calcagno

Antonio Calcagno is Professor of Philosophy at King's University College at Western University in London, Canada. He earned his BA from the University of Toronto, a MPhil from University of Louvain and a PhD from the University of Guelph. He specializes in twentieth- and twenty-first-century continental European thought as well as medieval and Renaissance thought. He works on questions of community and intersubjectivity, statehood, interiority, consciousness, humanism and post-humanism. His publications include: *Giordano Bruno and the Logic of Coincidence* (Peter Lang), *The Philosophy of Edith Stein* (Duquesne University Press), *Badiou and Derrida: Politics, Events and their Time* (Continuum), and the *Lived Experience from the Inside Out: Social and Political Philosophy in Edith Stein* (Duquesne University Press), which received the Edward Goodwin Ballard Book Prize in Phenomenology from the Center for Advanced Research in Phenomenology in 2015. He is also the editor of the collected volume, *Edith Stein— Women, Social-Political Philosophy, Metaphysics, Theology and Public History: New Approaches and Applications* (Springer). He has a special interest in Edith Stein's thought and has written numerous articles on various aspects of it, especially her social and political theory.

Kathleen M. Haney

Kathleen Haney is adjunct Professor of Philosophy at the University of St. Thomas, Houston, Texas, and former director of the university's Women Culture, and Society program. She formerly served as Professor of Philosophy and chair of the Social Science Department at the University of Houston–Downtown. She was educated at Northwestern University (BA) and Tulane University (MA, PhD) She has written on the fifth of Husserl's *Cartesian Meditations* in a monograph, *Intersubjectivity Revisited* (Ohio University Press). She has published several chapters on Edith Stein in *Feminist Phenomenology, Phenomenological Approaches to Moral Philosophy*, and *Ideen* (all Kluwer). Her articles on Edith Stein and empathy have appeared in *The Journal of the Southwestern Society for Philosophy*, *Listening*, and Analecta Husserliana. Recently, she has been writing, lecturing, and publishing on a phenomenology of autism, inspired by what she calls the Husserl/Stein Theory of Intersubjectivity. She collected and edited this volume of essays.

Mette Lebech

Mette Lebech has been a Lecturer in Philosophy at the University of Maynooth, Ireland, since 1998. She holds degrees in philosophy from the University of Copenhagen, the Catholic University of Louvain-la-Neuve, and the Catholic University of Leuven. She has lectured and published widely on human dignity, friendship, various topics in bioethics, and the philosophy of Edith Stein. Her publications include *On the Problem of Human Dignity. A Hermeneutical and Phenomenological Investigation* (Köningshausen und Neumann, 2009); *The Philosophy of Edith Stein. From Phenomenology to Metaphysics* (Peter Lang, 2015); and, as co-editor with Haydn Gurmin, *Intersubjectivity, Humanity, Being. Edith Stein's Phenomenology and Christian Philosophy* (Peter Lang, 2015). She is a past founding president of the International Association for the Study of the Philosophy of Edith Stein (IASPES). Her current research interest is in phenomenological value theory.

Michael R. Paradiso-Michau

Michael Paradiso-Michau (PhD Purdue University) is Lecturer in the Department of Liberal Arts at the School of the Art Institute of Chicago. Co-founder of the North American Levinas Society, he has published articles and reviews in *Continental Philosophy Review*, *Ethics*, *Journal of Scriptural Reasoning*, *Radical Philosophy Review*, *Listening: Journal of Religion and Culture*, *Atlantic Journal of Communication*, *Minerva*, and *Shofar*. He has contributed book chapters to *Reflections on the Religious, the Ethical, and the*

Political (Lexington Books, 2012), *Neither Victim Nor Survivor* (Lexington Books, 2009), and *Shifting the Geography of Reason: Gender, Science, and Religion* (Cambridge Scholars Press, 2006).

Walter Redmond

Walter Redmond, now retired, continues to teach courses and lecture in the United States, Europe, and Latin America. Formerly chair of the Department of Philosophy and Religion, Huston-Tillotson College in Austin, Texas, he has held teaching positions in the Instituto de Investigaciones Filosóficas of the National University of Mexico, the Institut für Philosophie of the University of Erlangen (the Catholic University of Eichstaet-Ingolstadt Germany), and the philosophy departments of the University of the Americas (La Universidad de las Americas Puebla, Mexico), the University of Puebla (La Benemerica Universidad Autonoma de Puebla, Mexico), and the Catholic and National Universities of Peru (La Pontificia Universidad Catolica del Peru and La Universidad Nacional Mayor de San Marcos). He earned his BA from the Aquinas Institute of Philosophy. He holds three masters degrees, from University of Texas at Austin, the Aquinas Institute of Philosophy, and the Aquinas Institute of Theology. He earned his PhD from the National University of Peru (La Universidad Nacional Mayor de San Marcos). His special interests are philosophical theology, logic and the history of logic, and the philosophy of Edith Stein. He has written many books and articles on these and other topics in English, Spanish, German, and Latin. He has published translations of Stein's *Knowledge and Faith* and *Potency and Act*, and is currently preparing a new translation of her *Finite and Eternal Being*.

Sarah Borden Sharkey

Sarah Borden Sharkey is a Professor of Philosophy and chair of the department at Wheaton College in Illinois, her undergraduate alma mater. She earned her PhD from Fordham University. Her thesis focused on the intersection of phenomenology and medieval philosophy. She has published two books on Edith Stein: *Edith Stein* in the *Outstanding Christian Thinkers* series (Continuum, 2003); and *Thine Own Self: Individuality in Edith Stein's Later Writings* (Catholic University of America Press, 2009). In addition, she maintains a bibliography of secondary sources on Stein (available on the Baltimore Carmel website) and has published articles on various topics in Stein's thought, including her account of being and essence, women, suffering, political philosophy, and her relation to Thomas Aquinas and John Duns Scotus.

John Sullivan, O.C.D.

John Sullivan is a priest of the Discalced Carmelite Order and currently chairman of the Institute of Carmelite Studies of its Washington Province. He completed graduate studies in both Rome and Paris with a doctorate in Sacred Theology *magna cum laude*. He served as editor of the ICS

Publications series The Collected Works of Edith Stein. In 1995 the Edith Stein Guild conferred on him its Edith Stein Award. He edited an anthology of spiritual writings by Edith Stein in 2002 that was issued in Spanish by Sal Terrae publishers (Santander). He is a member of the international Edith Stein Circle (IASPES). On sabbatical from September 2014 to November 2015 he gave presentations at Stein symposia held in Germany and Austria.

Johanna Valiquette

Johanna Valiquette is a nurse practitioner with a Master's degree in Philosophy. She is currently working at Mount Sinai Medical Center in New York City. She holds a B.S. degree from St. Louis University, a Masters' degree in philosophy from University of St. Thomas Houston, Texas, and a Master's of Science degree from Columbia University in New York. She has co-authored an article with Kathleen Haney on Edith Stein's ethics, *Phenomenological Approaches to Moral Philosophy*; "Edith's Stein's Ethics: Woman as Ethical Type" (2002) and published in bioethics: *Medicina e Morale*, vol. 58, no. 3; "Surgically placed Feeding Tubes in End-Stage Dementia" (2008) and *Incapacity and Care*; "PEG tubes in End-stage Dementia: Benefits and Burdens" (2010). She serves on the hospital bioethics committees of two hospitals in Manhattan.

Published Works of Edith Stein

Edith Stein's works were first published in German, and have subsequently appeared in two series in German, published by Herder/Germany. Twelve volumes of her work have been published in English translation in the Collected Works of Edith Stein series, published by ICS Publications.

English Translations in the Collected Works of Edith Stein (CWES) Series

Life in a Jewish Family: An Autobiography, 1891–1916. Translated by Josephine Koeppel, O.C.D. CWES, vol. 1. Washington, D.C.: ICS Publications, 2016. First published in 1986.

Essays on Woman. Translated by Freda M. Oben. CWES, vol. 2. 2nd rev. ed. Washington, D.C.: ICS Publications, 1996. First published in 1987.

On the Problem of Empathy. Translated by Waltraut Stein. CWES, vol. 3. Washington, D.C.: ICS Publications, 1989.

The Hidden Life: Essays, Meditations, Spiritual Texts. Translated by Waltraut Stein. CWES, vol. 4. Washington, D.C.: ICS Publications, 2014. First published in 1992.

Self-Portrait in Letters, 1916–1942. Translated by Josephine Koeppel, O.C.D. CWES, vol. 5. Washington, D.C.: ICS Publications, 1993.

The Science of the Cross. Translated by Josephine Koeppel, O.C.D. CWES, vol. 6. Washington, D.C.: ICS Publications, 2002.

Philosophy of Psychology and the Humanities. Translated by Mary Catharine Baseheart and Marianne Sawicki. CWES, vol. 7. Washington, D.C.: ICS Publications, 2000.

Knowledge and Faith. Translated by Walter Redmond. CWES, vol. 8. Washington, D.C.: ICS Publications, 2000.

Finite and Eternal Being: An Attempt at an Ascent to the Meaning of Being. Translated by Kurt F. Reinhardt. CWES, vol. 9. Washington, D.C.: ICS Publications, 2002.

An Investigation Concerning the State. Translated by Marianne Sawicki. CWES, vol. 10. Washington, D.C.: ICS Publications, 2006.

Potency and Act: Studies Toward a Philosophy of Being. Translated by Walter Redmond. CWES, vol. 11. Washington, D.C.: ICS Publications, 2009.

Edith Stein: Letters to Roman Ingarden. Translated by Hugh Candler Hunt. CWES, vol. 12. Washington, D.C.: ICS Publications, 2014.

German Editions of Edith Stein's Works

Volumes of the work of Edith Stein have been published in two series starting in 1950 by Herder under the series titles Edith Steins Werke (ESW) and Edith Stein Gesamtausgabe (ESGA). According to the publisher, the Edith Steins Werke editions were selections. Since that time Herder has undertaken a comprehensive program to publish all of Stein's work in critical editions under the series title Edith Stein Gesamtausgabe (ESGA); there are now twenty-seven volumes of her work in publication in German in that series. According to the International Association for the Study of the Philosophy of Edith Stein, the Edith Stein Gesamtausgabe series has replaced the Edith Steins Werke as the standard critical edition of Stein's work.

Edith Steins Werke (ESW)

This first set of volumes published in the Edith Steins Werke series is billed as "a first attempt at a complete edition of Edith Stein's work." The volumes were edited by Lucy Gelber and Romaeus Leuven, O.C.D., and Michael Linssen, O.C.D.

Kreuzeswissenschaft. Studie über *Johannes a cruce.* ESW, vol. 1. Freiburg: Herder, 1950.

Endliches und ewiges Sein. Versuch eines Aufstiegs zum Sinn des Seins. ESW, vol. 2. Freiburg: Herder, 1950.

Des hl. Thomas von Aquinos Untersuchungen über die Wahrheit I (Übers.). ESW, vol. 3. Freiburg: Herder, 1952.

Des hl. Thomas von Aquinos Untersuchungen über die Wahrheit II (Übers.). ESW, vol. 4. Freiburg: Herder, 1955.

Die Frau. Ihre Aufgabe nach Natur und Gnade. ESW, vol. 5. Freiburg: Herder, 1959.

Welt und Person. Beitrag zum christlichen Wahrheitsstreben. ESW, vol. 6. Freiburg: Herder, 1962.

Aus dem Leben einer jüdischen Familie. ESW, vol. 7. 2nd ed. Freiburg: Herder, 1985. First published in 1962.

Selbstbildnis in Briefen I. ESW, vol. 8. Freiburg: Herder, 1976.

Selbstbildnis in Briefen II. ESW, vol. 9. Freiburg: Herder, 1977.

Heil im Unheil. Das Leben Edith Steins: Reife und Vollendung. ESW, vol. 10. Freiburg: Herder, 1983. Romaeus Leuven wrote this biography of Edith Stein.

Verborgenes Leben: Essays, Meditationen, geistliche Texte. ESW, vol. 11. Freiburg: Herder, 1987.

Ganzheitliches Leben: Schriften zur religiösen Bildung. ESW, vol. 12. Freiburg: Herder, 1990.

Einführung in die Philosophie. ESW, vol. 13. Freiburg: Herder, 1991.

Briefe an Roman Ingarden. ESW, vol. 14. Freiburg: Herder, 1991.

Erkenntnis und Glaube. ESW, vol. 15. Freiburg: Herder, 1993.

Der Aufbau der menschlichen Person. ESW, vol. 16. Freiburg: Herder, 1994.

Was ist der Mensch? ESW, vol. 17. Freiburg: Herder, 1994.

Potenz und Akt. ESW, vol. 18. Freiburg: Herder, 1998.

Edith Stein Gesamtausgabe (ESGA)

This series of volumes, published from 2000 onward, is billed as a "new critical edition" and is edited by the Carmelite Monastery of Mary of Peace in Cologne, Germany, which has all the texts and rights to the works of Edith Stein; this work is done in collaboration with Professor Hanna-Barbara Gerl-Falkovitz and numerous scholars.

A. Biographical Writings

Aus dem Leben einer jüdischen Familie und weitere autobiographische Beiträge. ESGA vol. 1.
Freiburg: Herder, 2002 [and 3.Aufl. 2010].

Selbstbildnis in Briefen I: 1916–1933. ESGA vol. 2. Freiburg: Herder, 2000 [3.Aufl. 2010].

Selbstbildnis in Briefen II: 1933–1942. ESGA vol. 3. Freiburg: Herder, 2000 [2.Aufl. 2006].

Selbstbildnis in Briefen III: Briefe an Roman Ingarden. ESGA vol. 4. Freiburg: Herder, 2001 [2.Aufl. 2004].

B. Philosophical Writings

1. Early Phenomenology

Zum Problem der Einfühlung. ESGA vol. 5. Freiburg: Herder, 2008 [2.Aufl. 2010].

Beiträge zur philosophischen Begründung der Psychologie und der Geisteswissenschaften. ESGA vol. 6. Freiburg: Herder, 2010.

Eine Untersuchung über den Staat. ESGA vol. 7. Freiburg: Herder, 2006.

Einführung in die Philosophie. ESGA vol. 8. Freiburg: Herder, 2004 [2.Aufl. 2010].

2. Phenomenology and Ontology

"Freiheit und Gnade" und weitere Beiträge zu Phänomenologie und Ontologie. ESGA vol. 9. Freiburg: Herder, 1917–1937 [2014].

Potenz und Akt: Studien zu einer Philosophie des Seins. ESGA vol. 10. Freiburg: Herder, 2005.

Endliches und ewiges Sein: Versuch eines Aufstiegs zum Sinn des Seins. ESGA vols. 11 and 12. Freiburg: Herder, 2006 [2.Aufl. 2013].

C. Writings on Anthropology and Pedagogy

Die Frau: Fragestellungen und Refflexionen. ESGA vol. 13. Freiburg: Herder, 2000 [4.Aufl. 2010].

Der Aufbau der menschlichen Person: Vorlesungen zur philosophischen Anthropologie. ESGA vol. 14. Freiburg: Herder, 2004 [2.Aufl. 2010].

Was ist der Mensch? Theologische Anthropologie. ESGA vol. 15. Freiburg: Herder, 2005.

Bildung und Entfaltung der Individualität: Beiträge zum christlichen Erziehungsauftrag. ESGA vol. 16. Freiburg: Herder, 2001 [2.Aufl. 2004].

D. Writings on Mysticism and Spirituality

1. Phenomenology and Mysticism

Wege der Gotteserkenntnis: Studie zu Dionysius Areopagita und Übersetzung seiner Werke. ESGA vol. 17. Freiburg: Herder, 2003 [3.Aufl. 2013].

Kreuzeswissenschaft: Studie über Johannes vom Kreuz. ESGA vol. 18. Freiburg: Herder, 2003 [4.Aufl. 2013].

2. Spirituality and Meditation

Geistliche Texte I. ESGA vol. 19. Freiburg: Herder, 2009 [2.Aufl. 2014].

Geistliche Texte II. ESGA vol. 20. Freiburg: Herder, 2007. E. Translations

Übersetzungen I: *John Henry Newman: Die Idee der Universität.* ESGA vol. 21. Freiburg: Herder, 2004 [2.Aufl. 2010].

Übersetzungen II: John Henry Newman*: Briefe und Texte zur ersten Lebenshälfte (1801–1846).* ESGA vol. 22. Freiburg: Herder, 2002 [2.Aufl. 2009].

Übersetzungen III: Thomas von Aquin*: Über die Wahrheit I.* ESGA vol. 23. Freiburg: Herder, 2008.

Übersetzungen IV: Thomas von Aquin*: Über die Wahrheit II.* ESGA vol. 24. Freiburg: Herder, 2008.

Übersetzungen V: *Alexandre Koyré: Descartes und die Scholastik.* ESGA vol. 25. Freiburg: Herder, 2005.

Übersetzungen VI: Thomas von Aquin*: Über das Seiende und das Wesen.* ESGA vol. 26. Freiburg: Herder, 2010.

Miscellanea thomistica, Übersetzungen—Abbreviationes—Exzerpte aus Werken des Thomas v.

Aquin u. der Forschungsliteratur. ESGA vol. 27. Freiburg: Herder, 2013.

Index

Page numbers followed by the letter "n" indicate notes.

About Us

ICS Publications, based in Washington, D.C., is the publishing house of the Institute of Carmelite Studies (ICS) and a ministry of the Discalced Carmelite Friars of the Washington Province (U.S.A.). The Institute of Carmelite Studies promotes research and publication in the field of Carmelite spirituality, especially about Carmelite saints and related topics. Its members are friars of the Washington Province.

The Discalced Carmelites are a worldwide Roman Catholic religious order comprised of friars, nuns, and laity—men and women who are heirs to the teaching and way of life of Teresa of Avila and John of the Cross, dedicated to contemplation and to ministry in the church and the world.

Information about their way of life is available through local diocesan vocation offices, or from the Discalced Carmelite Friars vocation directors at the following addresses:

Washington Province:
1525 Carmel Road, Hubertus, WI 53033

California-Arizona Province:
P.O. Box 3420, San Jose, CA 95156

Oklahoma Province:
5151 Marylake Drive, Little Rock, AR 72206

Visit our websites at:

www.icspublications.org   and   *http://ocdfriarsvocation.org*